PARADISE PRESERVED

A history of

forestry on Fraser Island

ROBERT ONFRAY

Published in 2025 by Connor Court Publishing Pty Ltd.

Copyright © Robert Onfray

ALL RIGHTS RESERVED. This book contains material protected under International and Federal Copyright Laws and Treaties. Any unauthorised reprint or use of this material is prohibited. No part of this book may be reproduced or transmitted in any form or by any means, electronic or mechanical, including photocopying, recording, or by any information storage and retrieval system without express written permission from the publisher.

Connor Court Publishing Pty Ltd.
PO Box 7257
Redland Bay QLD 4165
sales@connorcourt.com
www.connorcourt.com

ISBN: 9781923568051

JGD the front cover design.

Top cover photo: Sandy Luck standing on a load of logs on an International truck, c1965. Photo Robert Postan.

Bottom cover photo: Andy Postan sitting on logs at the Poyungan Creek log dump in the late 1930s. Photo Postan family collection.

Printed in Australia.

CONTENTS

Acknowledgements	ix
Conversion	xii
Glossary	xiii
Names	xv
Important statistics and facts	xviii
Acronyms	xxii
Botanical names of trees and plants mentioned in the book	xxiii
Significant timeline on Fraser Island	xxvii
Foreword	xxxii
Introduction	xxxvi

Part 1 – The beginning

1. A land shaped by sand and time	1
2. A world-class natural wonder	9
Coastal vegetation: nature's first line of defence	10
The forested heart	10
Specialised plant communities	13
The wild residents	14
The jewels of the island	16
The veins of life	19
3. The original guardians	23
Early encounters with Europeans	25
The alleged massacre	27
The Europeans arrive	31
The missions	32
A tragic legacy	37

4. The Eliza Fraser saga — 39
   The wreck of the *Stirling Castle* — 41
   Survival at sea — 43
   Landing on Fraser Island — 44
   Captivity and harsh treatment — 45
   The rescue — 48
   Impact and legacy — 51

5. The new arrivals — 53
   Early European observations — 53
   The Petrie expedition — 55
   Settlement and the quarantine facility — 59
   Overcoming the navigational challenges — 60
   Early agricultural ventures and the brumby legacy — 64

Part 2 – Utilising the timber

6. Early timber exploitation — 71
   The first timber getters — 71
   The next wave of timber utilisation — 75

7. Chasing forest conservancy — 83

8. Some action taken: greater control of forestry operations — 91
   The challenge of sand and distance — 91
   Battles over timber rights — 92
   Southern exploiters and local defenders — 95
   Continued exploitation — 98

9. McKenzie's Fraser Island gamble: timber, triumph and turmoil — 107
   Fraser Island ambitions — 108
   Building a settlement at North White Cliffs — 110
   Financial struggles and union pressures — 117

10. Tramlines of Fraser Island: a legacy on rails — 121
   Pettigrew and Sim's wooden tramway — 121
   The Woongoolbver skipway — 122
   Pioneers of Fraser Island rail — 122
   McKenzie's ambitious venture — 125

CONTENTS

11.	**Satinay: from misconception to majesty**	**129**
	Discovering the redeeming features of satinay	134
	The utilisation of satinay	137
12.	**The journey to the sawmills**	**141**
	The log dumps	141
	Transport across the Great Sandy Strait	145
	Forestry transport	149

Part 3 – Making and managing new forests

13.	**Roots of Queensland's forestry: early silviculture and reforestation**	**155**
	Challenges of kauri reforestation	155
	The genesis of Queensland's hoop pine plantations	159
	Experimental plantings and early forestry failures	160
	Emerging silvicultural practices in the 1920s	163
14.	**The blackbutt story: a legacy of innovation and sustainability**	**169**
	The rise of blackbutt on Fraser Island	169
	Swain's vision	170
	From degradation to productivity	170
	Flowering and fruiting patterns of blackbutt	173
	The challenges of regeneration burning	174
	Season of regeneration burning	176
	Tending blackbutt regeneration	177
	The evolution of thinning practices	179
	Enrichment planting	179
	Measuring the forests and sustained yield	180
15.	**Fire management: a legacy of mismanagement and lessons unlearned**	**185**
	The early fire exclusion policies	186
	Hard lessons learned and forgotten	187
	A shift towards broad-scale prescribed burning	190
	The struggles continued	192

16. People and settlements — 195

- Aboriginal contributions to the island's early forestry history — 195
- Forestry settlements — 198
- Forestry camps — 206
- Logging contractors — 209
- The dangers of tree felling — 217

Part 4 – From prosperity to controversy

17. Sand mining and the beginning of the end for logging on the island — 223

- The Cooloola back down: a prelude to a larger battle — 223
- A defiant new voice — 226
- Sand mining meets the courts — 226
- Whitlam's vision — 227
- Federal intervention, the inquiry and science versus sovereignty — 230
- Used as political pawns — 231
- Political fallout: jobs, compensation and community anger — 232

18. The pied piper of environmental deceit — 235

- Fraser Island's false saviour — 235
- A campaign of half-truths and misinformation — 236
- Contradictions exposed in his war on sand mining and forestry — 237
- Tourism hypocrisy: from advocate to opponent — 240
- Arrogance and different rules for himself — 242
- Legal battles and a tarnished legacy — 244
- Vilification or just consequences? — 247

19. From forests to footsteps: managing land use change on Fraser Island — 251

- Tourism beckons: early efforts to regulate — 252
- The fragmentation of Fraser Island through freehold tenures — 255
- A patchwork of governance — 256
- Tourism's tipping point: the rise of vehicular access — 258

20. Tourism reshapes the island — 261
- Fishing pioneers and early tourism — 261
- Early development — 262
- Ad hoc tourism — 263
- Tour operators organise regular tours — 265
- Improved access and booming tourism — 269
- The environmental and social impacts of tourism — 272
- The barge war — 273

Part 5 – The end of an era

21. When protests override promises: Fraser Island's forest conflict — 279
- Building momentum against forestry — 280
- Changing political fortunes and their implications — 280
- The drawn-out forest blockade — 281
- Escalation and countermeasures — 284
- The broader implications — 288

22. The inquiry and end of logging — 289
- The genesis of the inquiry — 289
- Cooperation and conflict — 290
- Findings and recommendations — 292
- World Heritage Listing — 293
- The sad end: from logging to tourism — 294
- Reflections on the legacy — 296

23. The uncertain future of Fraser Island — 297
- The tourism paradox: loving the island to death — 297
- The myth of passive preservation — 299
- The consequences of fire mismanagement — 302
- A manufactured problem: the dingo dilemma — 303
- A new approach to preservation — 304
- Concluding remarks: rethinking Fraser Island's future — 305

Bibliography — 307

Index — 313

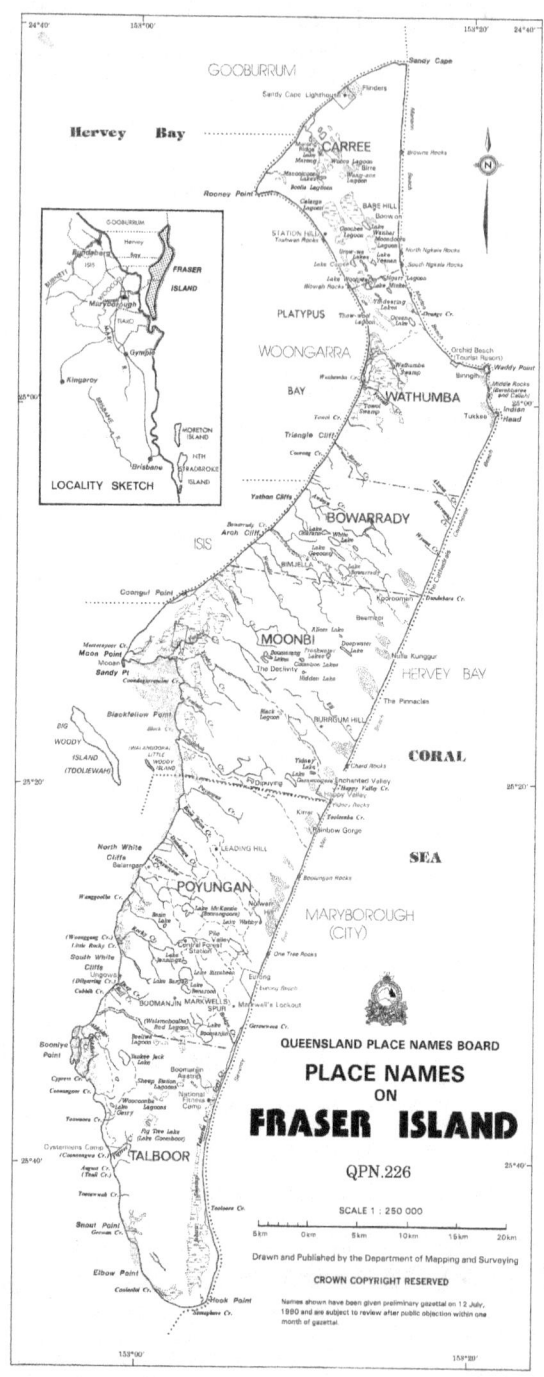

Fraser Island 1980 (Queensland Place Names Board)

Acknowledgements

Writing this book has been a journey of rediscovery, made possible by the generosity of those who shared their knowledge, stories, and time. This book is as much yours as it is mine.

I owe a great deal of gratitude to Queensland's premier forest historian, John Huth. Not only did he offer professional editing advice on my earlier drafts, but he also shared photos, stories, and valuable information. He was always prompt in assisting with my numerous enquiries.

Retired Queensland foresters Gary Bacon, Dr Ian Bevege, and Dick Pegg provided invaluable feedback on each chapter, as did Peter Lear for some of the later ones. Mike Anderson generously shared his unpublished paper on blackbutt silviculture from Fraser Island, which formed the basis for Chapter 14. Andrew Dunn, the last forester on the island, contributed valuable insights from his diaries during the forest blockades.

I have interviewed several foresters and rangers associated with the island since 1958. I would like to thank George Luke, Dick Pegg, Peter Kanowski Snr, Norm Clough, Brian McCormack, Warren Edwards, and Cliff Raddatz for their insights.

Brian McCormack kindly loaned me a working map of the island. Grahame Applegate generously shared maps and was an excellent host during a tour of the island in 2023. Julie Tadman provided insights from her late husband, John, a forester who compiled the forestry department's response to the 1990-91 Fraser Island inquiry. Gary Hopewell identified the species of wood samples taken from the McKenzie jetty piles.

Beyond the Forestry employees, many individuals with direct experience in the island's timber industry offered invaluable insights. Special thanks to logging contractors and their families for sharing their fascinating stories – David and Helen Postan, Doreen and Tom Cunningham, Janette Butcher, Peter and Colin Wilson,

Julie Burnett, and Rafe Cornwall. Valery Weaver also contributed helpful information about Vic Hope.

Local historians and community members also played a crucial role in reconstructing the island's past. Geoffrey McWilliam and Bronco Jensen contributed to its tourism history. John and Sue Erbacher shared their research and personal stories about Fraser Island. John Andersen from the Hervey Bay Village and Pioneer Museum was invaluable, as was Hervey Bay historian Delma Taylor, who generously provided information and images. Thanks also to Shane Bradbury for supplying drone footage from our trip to the island.

Karel McLaverty offered background information about Hepburn McKenzie. I am thankful to her mother, Ruth Jones, for permitting me to use the brilliant photos taken by Charles McKenzie during McKenzie's operations from 1918 to 1926. I appreciate Tony Clift, Roy Smalley, Ian Scougall, and Jackie Templeton from the Maryborough Wide Bay and Burnett Historical Society for providing high-quality copies of the McKenzie photos and many others. Tess Patterson generously granted access to Edward "Ned" Armitage's family photos, while Cameron Coward contributed high-quality photographs from the Department of Forestry collection.

Archaeologist Karen Townrow provided valuable insights from her studies of Postan's logging camp and the North White Cliffs and McKenzie settlement. Queensland historian Thom Blake contributed invaluable feedback to Chapters 3 and 4.

I am grateful to the staff at the Queensland State Library and the Queensland State Archives for their assistance in locating historical material. Additionally, I would like to express my gratitude to Helen Best, a volunteer researcher from the Royal Historical Society of Queensland, for sending extracts from William Pettigrew's diary.

I want to thank Allan Jamieson, a colleague and fellow writer from Tasmania, for generously sharing his indexing program with me. I'm also grateful to Brad Colin for his meticulous work in preparing the index.

ACKNOWLEDGEMENTS

A special thank you to illustrator Ana Rubino for her beautifully rendered coloured maps of the tramlines, grazing runs, and log dumps.

Kudos to Michael Gilchrist for his patience and attention to detail in producing a high-quality layout, and to my publisher, Anthony Cappello, for his belief in the project and willingness to bring this book to publication.

I want to extend heartfelt thanks to Tim Macartney-Snape, a long-time supporter of my blogs and a passionate advocate for the sustainable use of natural resources. I'm deeply honoured that he kindly agreed to write the Foreword for this book.

As a world-renowned mountaineer, explorer, international speaker, author, and entrepreneur, Tim's contribution brings a depth and distinction to this work that I greatly value. His legendary achievements – being one of the first Australians to summit Mount Everest in 1984, and the only person to have climbed it from sea level to summit in 1990 – exemplify his determination and pioneering spirit. His solo ascent, immortalised in the film *Everest: Sea to Summit*, remains a landmark in mountaineering history.

Tim's dedication to adventure and environmental awareness has earned him numerous accolades, including the OAM, AM, and the Australian Sports Medal. He serves on the board of the World Expeditions Foundation and is a patron of The World Transformation Movement.

What truly connects us, though, is his deep appreciation for professional forestry management. With a background in forestry studies at ANU, his insights have been invaluable. It was Tim who recommended including the final chapter as a commentary on the challenges that followed the end of forestry management on Fraser Island.

Finally, a big thank you to my wife for her patience and support.

To everyone else who contributed in ways big and small – thank you.

Conversion

Even though I wrote this book in the era of decimal currency and metric measurements, I've chosen to stick with imperial conversions to align with the figures provided during the imperial period. The transition from imperial weights and measures began in 1974 and was finalised by 1982. Decimal currency was introduced earlier, in 1966.

Here are the relevant conversions to help people understand the relativity of the figures I provide. Bear in mind, when it comes to currency, converting, say £1, isn't straightforward, as it is difficult to compare the purchasing values of £1 in the early 1900s to $1 in today's economy.

12 pence = 1 shilling
20 shillings = one pound (£1)
1 super feet = 0.00236 cubic metres
332.8 super feet hoppus = 1 cubic metre true
1 mile = 1.609 kilometres
1 chain = 20.11 metres
1 acre = 0.4046 hectares
1 tree per acre = 2.47105 trees per hectare
1 inch = 2.54 centimetres
1 US gallon = 3.78541 litres
1 ton = 1,016 kilograms
1 foot = 0.3048 metres

Glossary

Barge: A flat-bottomed vessel designed to transport logs or processed timber, typically on rivers, lakes, or coastal waters, often to sawmills or export docks.

Bobtail: A type of arch or device used in logging to lift the front end of a log off the ground during snigging. This reduces friction, making it easier to move logs while minimising soil disturbance and damage to the logs.

Brushing: Removing unwanted saplings, shrubs, or undergrowth to reduce competition for resources, improve timber growth, or lower fire risk. It is often done manually with brush hooks or can also be carried out mechanically with mulchers.

Cant hook: A traditional logging tool consisting of a long wooden lever handle with a movable metal hook at the other end used to grasp, turn or roll logs.

Jinker: A trailer designed to transport logs. It is mounted to a prime mover.

Parbuckle system: A simple and efficient method for rolling heavy cylindrical objects, such as logs or barrels, onto a platform, wagon, or vessel using ropes or wires.

pH: A scale that measures how acidic or alkaline a substance is. It ranges from 0 to 14, with 7 being neutral. Values below 7 are acidic, and values above 7 are alkaline.

Podzolisation: A soil-forming process in which organic matter and minerals like iron and aluminium are usually, but not exclusively, released from weathered rocks and mixed to form compounds. These compounds are washed down from the topsoil and accumulate in deeper soil layers.

Sand dune: A hill or ridge of sand formed by wind or water movement, typically found in deserts, coastal regions and river valleys. Due to wind erosion and deposition, dunes can shift and change shape over time.

Sand blow: An area where strong winds have removed vegetation and loose sand, creating a shifting dune or an exposed sandy expanse. It often occurs in coastal or inland sandy regions, where wind erosion mobilises sand, sometimes burying surrounding landscapes. Sand blows can expand over time if not stabilised by vegetation or management efforts.

Silviculture: A forestry practice focused on managing forest regeneration, species composition, and growth, along with implementing appropriate harvesting techniques. Its aim is to sustain healthy and productive forests for various purposes, including timber production, biodiversity conservation, and ecosystem services.

Snigging: Refers to the process of dragging logs from the felling site to a landing or loading area using machinery such as a skidder, dozer, or tractor, or animals like bullocks or horses. This practice is common in logging operations to move timber efficiently while minimising damage to both the logs and the surrounding environment.

Widow-maker: A limb that has broken off and is left suspended in a tree, which could come crashing down with lethal force. Forest workers standing underneath can be killed, thus making widows of their spouses.

Wallum: An Australian term that refers to coastal, nutrient-poor sandy plains and heathlands, typically found in Queensland and northern New South Wales. Characterised by acidic soils, seasonal waterlogging, and fire-adapted vegetation, wallum ecosystems support a unique mix of shrubs, sedges, stunted eucalypts, and diverse wildlife, including many endemic species.

Wooden yoke: A part of the bullock harness. It is shaped to create a curved depression that allows it to rest across the necks of two bullocks and yoke them together.

Zeta curve: A shoreline that widens in the direction of beach drift and terminates where it meets a headland. When viewed from the air, it features a decreasing radius of curvature toward one end, resembling the Greek letter zeta (ζ).

NAMES

In this book, I use the singular term "Forestry" to collectively refer to the various iterations of the sub-department and department throughout the years, despite their changing names.

Forestry began in August 1900 as the Forestry Branch of the Queensland Department of Public Lands. In mid-1921, it was renamed the Queensland Forest Service, remaining within the same department. Following the passage of the *Forestry Act 1957*, it gained departmental status as the Department of Forestry. However, in 1989, after the election of a Labor Government for the first time in 32 years, Forestry was demoted to a service within the Department of Primary Industries and reverted to the Queensland Forest Service.

The long stretch of beach on the eastern side of Fraser Island, between Hook Point and Indian Head, is officially known as Seventy-Five Mile Beach. It is also referred to as the eastern beach and the back beach. The former name is the most commonly used for the beach, and I have employed it throughout the book.

Central Station was originally called the new Woongoolbver Creek camp, later renamed Scrub camp, and then Old Station. Today, it is known as Central Station. Chapter 16 provides insights into the origins of Central Station.

Many of the names on Fraser Island originate from Aboriginal place names, with the spelling aiming to reflect how the Aborigines pronounced those names. According to Dick Eckert, as a boy in the 1930s, he heard Aboriginal people speaking with a guttural tone from the back of their throats. However, there are many different spellings on maps because the names have been interpreted differently by Archibald Meston and later by surveyors and field officers.

Since 1979, some place names have changed entirely, or the Fraser Island Committee of the Queensland Place Names Board has adjusted the spelling. Their goal was to rationalise place names on Fraser Island by recognising both European and Aboriginal occupation, in preparation for the new edition of the Forestry Fraser Island map, scheduled for release in early 1980.

This indicates that some place names differed from the early Forestry maps. Nevertheless, I have opted for the names and spellings found on the 1951 Forestry maps, as they were predominantly used during the time the island was managed as a state forest by Forestry.

The following list includes some place names from the book that have historically had various spellings and are spelt differently or known by another name today:

Old Petrie camp – was the first forestry camp on the island and included a nursery. The old nursery was renamed to Dipuying.

Woongoolbver Creek – also spelt as Wangoolba, Woongoolba, and Woongoolver. It has been officially changed to Wanggoolba Creek on current maps.

Bun Bun Creek – changed to Boon Boon Creek.

Dundonga Creek – was also known as Dungonga Creek. However, Forestry maps clearly indicate that it has always been Dundonga Creek. There is also a Dundonga Logging Area.

Deep Creek – retained its name, with Dilgarring added in parentheses.

Lake McKenzie – retained its name, but Boorangoora was added in parentheses.

Lake Boemingen – was also known as Boemingan before the committee adopted Meston's spelling of Boomanjin.

A lake or swamp complex located near the AC8 Forestry area – renamed Woocoonba Lagoons, a term I used in the book since the Forestry maps did not provide a name for these waters.

Yankee Jack Creek – was recommended to be renamed to its original name, Tumbowah Creek. However, it was decided to retain the name with Tumbowah in parentheses.

NAMES

The following creeks, located south of Eurong towards Dilli Village, were part of the early grazing leases on the island called Grouyeah Run or Fraser Island Run:

First Creek – became Gerowweea Creek.

Second Creek – became Govi Creek.

Third Creek – became Taleerba Creek.

Fourth Creek – became Tooloora Creek.

There are some people named in the book associated with Fraser Island whose spelling is not confirmed. I have used what I believe to be the correct spelling. They include:

David Bracewell – also referred to as Bracefield, Bracefeld and Bracefell.

Patrick Searey – others have used Seary.

John "Yankee Jack" Pigott – others have used Piggott or Pigot.

Bill Seelke – others have used Selke.

Mathison – confirmed by members of the Mathison family. Others have used Mathieson or Matheson.

Andy Postan and Laurie Postans – are brothers, but they have different surnames because Andy changed his name by deed poll, omitting the final 's' from his business name. Apparently, it was much easier to change his surname than to alter all his business papers.

IMPORTANT STATISTICS AND FACTS
Forest Types

The extent of forest types on Fraser Island, located within the ex-state forest, were as follows:

Forest type indicator	Description	Area (acres)
1	Vine forest (rainforest)	1,640
1a	Vine forest with hoop pine	892
2	Tall closed forest 90 feet + with vine understorey	22,938*
3	Carroll scrub with satinay and eucalypt emergents	4,188*
3a	Carroll scrub plus hoop pine	1,089*
4	Blackbutt	34,382*
5	Blackbutt and other species	28,807*
5a	Low mixed hardwood	63,620
Others		101,901
Total		**259,457**

The majority of the 91,404 acres of commercial forest (indicated by * above) on the island consists of tall sclerophyll forest featuring blackbutt, satinay, and brush box emergents, often accompanied by an understorey of rainforest species. It accounted for about 35 per cent of the state forest area.

Land Tenure

The land tenure and areas of Fraser Island prior to the cessation of logging in 1991:

Land Tenure	Area (acres)
State forest	259,457
National park	129,483
Vacant and other Crown land, freehold land	13,838
Total	**402,778**

IMPORTANT STATISTICS AND FACTS

Sustained Yield

The first yield analysis was conducted in 1921, and the first detailed plots were established in 1952. A further and more comprehensive resource assessment was done in 1958, which established a sustained yield figure of eight million super feet per year.

A reassessment conducted in 1978 confirmed the data from 1958. The sustained yield remained at eight million super feet per year.

However, the sustained yield was lowered slightly to 7.8 million super feet per year in 1986 because of the extension of buffer strips around beauty spots and an expansion of the national park, which decreased the overall area of available commercial forest.

Actual volumes cut each year

The rate of timber cutting each year varied due to economic and market conditions. From 1952 to 1987, the average annual timber cut was 7.3 million super feet. In a typical year, logging occurred over 740 to 1,235 acres.

The following illustrates the volume harvested over a ten-year period:

Year	Volume cut (super feet)
1977–78	6,293,248
1978–79	5,760,435
1979–80	8,759,296
1980–81	6,842,368
1981–82	7,036,723
1982–83	4,424,576
1983–84	6,574,796
1984–85	5,821,337
1985–86	4,726,092
1986–87	8,420,505
Average	6,465,938

When logging stopped on the island, there were 19,770 to 22,240 acres of unlogged commercial forest remaining.

Timber products

The timber harvested from Fraser Island filled an important supply niche, primarily for south-east Queensland. For over 100 years, the island served as a unique source of high-quality materials used in specialised construction, such as wharves around the world and general structural applications. During the 1980s, products requiring further manufacturing, such as laminated beams, were successfully produced from hardwood sourced from the island.

Here are a few examples of the uses of timber sourced from Fraser Island:

(a) Structural framing

Blackbutt has been a popular timber for house frames and roofing. Its workability and desirability as a hardwood species commanded high prices. Blackbutt is found along the eastern seaboard, and the forests of Fraser Island feature some of the most productive stands of this species.

(b) Laminate products

Laminated beams and benchtops made from Fraser Island brush box and satinay exhibit a rich colour, texture and fine grain. They were favoured for their aesthetic appeal and serve as a typical example of value-added diversification in timber products.

(c) Flooring

Brush box was a popular choice for parquetry flooring. Its colour variations and durability made it ideal for this type of strip flooring.

(d) Furniture

Satinay became a well-known timber in the furniture trade, especially for lounge and dining room suites. Its aesthetic features were highly desirable and very appealing.

(e) Panelling

Brush box and satinay were considered two of the top choices of timber for panelling.

Since timber harvesting ceased on Fraser Island, the Wet Tropics in North Queensland, and the Conondale Ranges in the Sunshine Coast hinterland, Queensland is now a net importer of timber products. The purported substitution of plantation softwood timber has not succeeded in preventing this situation.

ACRONYMS

ACF – Australian Conservation Foundation

AHC – Australian Heritage Commission

ANU – Australian National University

CSIRO – Commonwealth Scientific and Industrial Research Organisation

FIDO – Fraser Island Defenders Organisation

ITM – Item Number from the Queensland State Archives filing system

MWBBHS – Maryborough Wide Bay and Burnett Historical Society

QNPWS – Queensland National Parks and Wildlife Service

QSA – Queensland State Archives

Botanical names of trees and plants mentioned in the book

The table below displays the botanical and common names of the plants mentioned in the book, organised by their respective plant families.

AIZACEAE	
pig face, coastal pig face	*Carpobrotus glaucescens*
ARAUCARIACEAE	
bunya pine^	*Araucaria bidwillii*
hoop pine	*Araucaria cunninghamii*
kauri pine, south Queensland kauri pine	*Agathis robusta*
ARECACEAE	
picabeen palm	*Archontophoenix cunninghamiana*
CASUARINACEAE	
coastal she oak, beach oak, horsetail she oak	*Casuarina equisetifolia subsp. incana*
CONVOLVULACEAE	
goat's foot vine	*Ipomoea pes-caprae subsp. brasiliensis*
pink bindweed	*Convolvulus erubescens*
CUPRESSACEAE	
cypress pine, white cypress pine	*Callitris columellaris*
CYPERACEAE	
rush	*Eleocharis spp.* or *Fimbrisylis spp.*
sedge	*Cyperus spp.*
DROSERACEAE	
sundew	*Drosera spp.*
ELAEOCARPACEAE	
blueberry ash, ash quandong	*Elaeocarpus reticulatus*
blue quandong	*Elaeocarpus angustifolia*
EUPHORBIACEAE	
wedding bush	*Ricinocarpos pinifolius*
FABACEAE	
black bean	*Castanospermum australe*
bacon wood, tulip siris	*Archidendron lovelliea*
dusky coral pea	*Kennedia rubicunda*
pea flowers	*Bossiaea spp., Dillwynia spp., Gompholobium spp.*
LAMIACEAE	
white beech	*Gmelina leichhardtii*
white teak	*Gmelina arborea*
LAURACEAE	
Camphor laurel*	*Cinnamomum camphora*
MELIACEAE	
red cedar	*Toona ciliata*
white cedar	*Melia azedarach*

	MIMOSACEAE	
wattle		*Acacia spp.*
	MORACEAE	
satine^		*Brosimum rubescens*
strangler fig		*Ficus watkinsiana*
	MYRTACEAE	
blackbutt		*Eucalyptus pilularis*
blue gum, forest red gum		*Eucalyptus tereticornis*
brush box, scrub box		*Lophostemon confertus*
carrol, cinnamon myrtle, grey myrtle		*Backhousia myrtifolia*
flooded gum, rose gum*		*Eucalyptus grandis*
grey ironbark		*Eucalyptus siderophloia*
Gympie messmate*		*Eucalyptus cloeziana*
Lemon-scented spotted gum*		*Corymbia citriodora*
midyim berry, midgen berry		*Austromyrtus dulcis*
Moreton Bay ash		*Corymbia tessellaris*
pink bloodwood		*Corymbia intermedia*
red bloodwood		*Corymbia gummifera*
red flowering gum*		*Corymbia ficifolia*
red stringybark, red mahogany		*Eucalyptus resinifera*
satinay, red satinay, turpentine, Fraser Island turpentine		*Syncarpia hillii*
scribbly gum		*Eucalyptus recemosa subsp. racemosa*
spotted gum*		*Corymbia maculata*
swamp mahogany		*Eucalyptus robusta*
swamp paperbark		*Melaleuca quinquenervia*
tallowwood, turpentine, tee, she-oak		*Eucalyptus microcorys*
tea tree		*Leptospermum spp.*
turpentine^		*Syncarpia glomulifera*
	ONAGRACEAE	
beach primrose		*Oenothera drummondii*
	OSMUNDACEAE	
king fern		*Todea barbara*
	PANDANACEAE	
pandanus palm, long-leaved pandanus		*Pandanus tectorius*
	PINACEAE	
Caribbean pine*		*Pinus caribaea*
loblolly pine*		*Pinus teada*
longleaf pine*		*Pinus palustris*
maritime pine*		*Pinus pinaster*
Norfolk Island pine*		*Pinus heterophylla*
Roxburgh pine*		*Pinus longifolia (now P. roxburghii)*
slash pine*		*Pinus elliottii*
weeping Mexican pine*		*Pinus patula*

BOTANICAL NAMES OF TREES AND PLANTS

POACEAE	
beach spinifex	Spinifex sericeus
buffalo grass*	Bouteloua dactyloides
saltwater couch	Paspalum veginatum
PROTACEAE	
coast banksia	Banksia integrifolia subsp. integrifolia
northern silky oak	Cardwellia sublimis
swamp banksia, broad-leaved banksia	Banksia robur
wallum banksia	Banksia aemula
RHAMNACEAE	
red ash	Alphitonia excelsa
RHIZOPHORACEAE	
mangrove species	Rhizophora spp., Bruguiera spp., Avicennia spp.
RUTACEAE	
crows ash	Flindersia australis
mauve-flowered forest boronia, forest boronia	Boronia rosmarinifolia
Queensland maple	Flindersia brayleyana
Wide Bay boronia	Boronia rivularis
SAPINDACEAE	
common hop bush, large-leaved hop bush	Dodonaea triquetra
foambark	Jagera pseudorhus
XANTHORRHOEACEAE	
grass tree	Xanthorrhoea spp.
ZAMIACEAE	
macrozamia, zamia palm	Macrozamia douglasii

*Denotes species introduced to Fraser Island.

^Indicates species not native to Fraser Island but referenced in the book.

Significant Timeline on Fraser Island

1770 Lieutenant James Cook named Indian Head and Sandy Cape due to two large patches of white sand. He also referred to the area as the Great Sandy Peninsula, unaware that it was an island.

1799 Explorer Matthew Flinders sailed along the western shores of the island from the north as far as Round Island, naming several prominent features.

1802 Flinders is believed to be the first European to set foot on the island.

1822 William Edwardson discovered that the peninsula is an island, and it became known as Great Sandy Island.

1836 *Stirling Castle* shipwreck survivors made their way to the island.

1842 Andrew Petrie explored the area alongside Henry Russell and others. Upon stepping onto the island, Russell named it "Frazers Island" in honour of Captain James Fraser of the *Stirling Castle*, who had died there in 1836.

1848 Maryborough was founded on the banks of the Mary River.

1862 Pettigrew and Tom Petrie explored timber in the Wide Bay region, including Fraser Island, and noted its timber resources.

1863 Pettigrew and Sim's sawmill began operating on the mainland at Dundathu, the indigenous name for kauri pine, near Maryborough. The first kauri logs from Fraser Island were sent to the mill.

1864 The first timber getter, John "Yankee Jack" Pigott, was killed by Aborigines.

1870 The Sandy Cape Lighthouse was built.

1872 The first Aboriginal agricultural mission was established by Reverend Edward Fuller, south of Ungowa.

1879 The first horses were brought to Fraser Island, becoming the ancestors of the brumbies. Cutting hardwood trees begins.

1882 Fraser Island was declared a reserve for a state forest, and the first nursery was established at Dipuying, near Bogimbah Creek.

1883 The first planting of trees in the state took place near Bogimbah Creek. Kauri seedlings were collected from locations near stumps of trees that were cut about ten years earlier.

1884 The first telegraph was constructed from the Quarantine Station at North White Cliffs to the Sandy Cape Lighthouse.

1897 An Aboriginal mission was established at North White Cliffs by Archibald Meston, later transferring to Bogimbah Creek.

1904 Aboriginal mission was abandoned.

1906 The first tramline was constructed.

1913 The first Forestry employee based on the island, Forest Ranger Walter Petrie, the grandson of Andrew Petrie, along with his family established the first forestry camp at Dipuying, approximately 2½ miles upstream from the mouth of Bogimbah Creek.

1916 Forestry established a new camp named Orange Tree along Woongoolbver Creek.

1919 The island's first and only sawmill started operations at North White Cliffs.

1920 Central Station camp was established, and the first successful trial regeneration burn occurred in a blackbutt forest.

1921–25 North White Cliffs School served families employed at McKenzie's operation.

1926 Forestry acquired McKenzie's tramline and jetty.

1934 Happy Valley Resort opened, but only lasted two years.

1935 The *Maheno* was washed ashore just north of Eli Creek. Andy Postans arrived to work on the island.

1937 Pile Valley and Lake McKenzie were declared beauty spots.

1948 Geological surveys confirmed the presence of commercial rutile and zircon deposits.

SIGNIFICENT TIMELINE ON FRASER ISLAND

1950 The first mineral leases were issued for sand mining on the island.

1962 The coastal strip, half a mile wide from Eurong to Happy Valley, was removed from state forest and designated as vacant crown land, to be managed by the Lands Department according to more appropriate provisions in their acts for leases, huts, and recreational activities.

1963 A new village was surveyed and subdivided at Eurong. Happy Valley was extended, and construction began on the Orchid Beach tourist resort.

1967 Gordon Elmer started the first vehicular barge operation to Fraser Island from Inskip Point.

1969 The Orchid Beach Resort opened. Jack Reville provided the first regular large group tours to Fraser Island.

1971 The northern part of the island was declared a national park, initially covering 61,306 acres, but it was expanded to 83,126 acres two years later. The Fraser Island Defenders Organisation was formed (FIDO).

1972 Sand mining operations commenced in January.

1974 The High Court unanimously upheld John Sinclair and FIDO's appeal against the successful sand mining applications granted to QTM.

1975 The Federal Government established an environmental inquiry into land use on Fraser Island.

1976 In October, the inquiry released its final report, recommending a halt to sand mining on Fraser Island and declaring that the island should be recorded as part of the National Estate.

1977 Fraser Island was added to the Register of the National Estate.

1978 A management plan was developed to establish land use priorities for the newly designated vacant crown land strip along the eastern beach.

1982 Forestry started licensing tour operators.

1985 The *Fraser Island Public Access Act* was enacted to authorise and regulate vehicle access to the island.

1986 A barge war erupted between Sid Melksham and Gordon Elmer, the two barge operators on Fraser Island.

1989 The Australian Labor Party formed government in Queensland for the first time in 32 years, promising to investigate the wisest use of Fraser Island through a public inquiry.

1990 Fitzgerald inquiry began, and environmental activists organised forest blockades.

1991 Inquiry recommendations were handed down. The government decided to end logging on Fraser Island after the industry refused to operate under the limited options available for economic reasons.

1992 In early February, forestry management on Fraser Island officially concluded after 120 years of sustainable stewardship. Despite allegations of environmental damage caused by logging operations, the island was designated a World Heritage Area for its natural beauty nine months later.

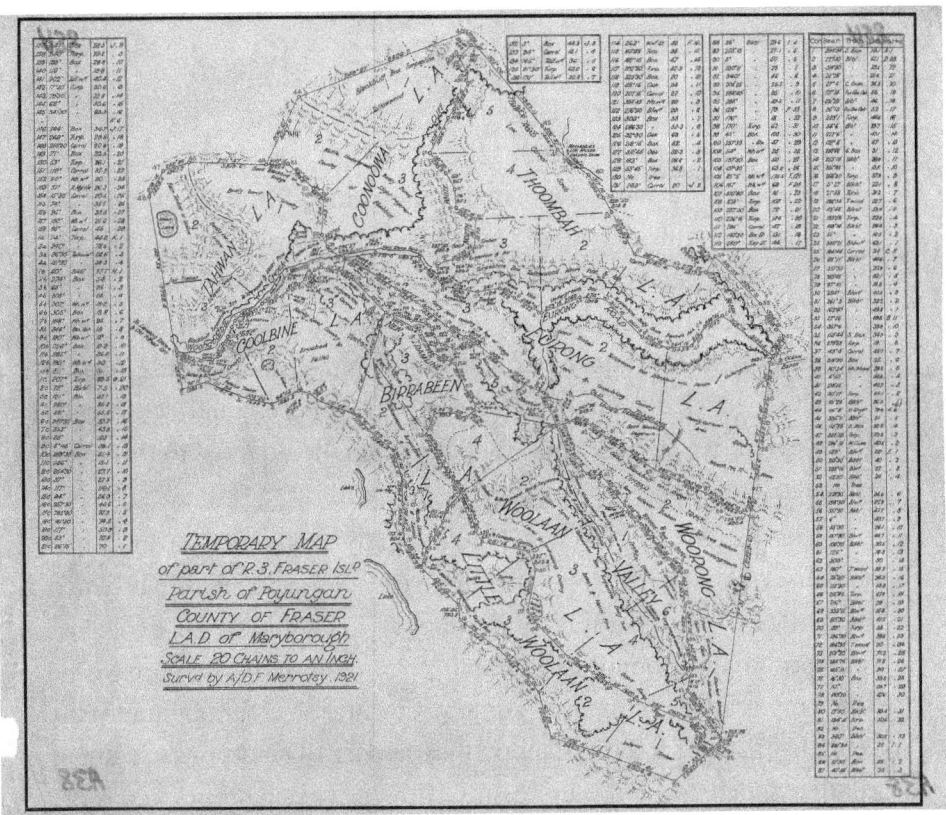

This 1922 map shows the detailed survey of Logging Areas around Central Station. It exemplifies the extensive survey work and meticulous mapping carried out by Forestry on Fraser Island and throughout the state.

The precise boundaries of different vegetation types illustrate how thorough forestry planning was and how it was guided by professional forest management.

Typically, a group of employees would reside in a bush survey camp made up of tents. Their primary tasks included road and tramline surveying, forest inventory, and documenting forest types or tree species associations. They often conducted strip surveys to record vegetation. After WWII, the process was made easier with aerial photography, which helped update and classify forest type changes.

(Queensland State Archives)

Foreword

The world's largest sand island is full of surprises. Sand, particularly the wind-deposited variety that forms the island, is very low in nutrients and generally very porous. A challenging substrate for plants to grow in you would think. Yet, almost all the island is thickly vegetated with a profusion of plants. From patches of rainforest to stately, wonder-inducing, cathedral-like stands of satinay and blackbutt, to drier eucalypt forest and scrublands comprised of a diverse mix of plants specially adapted to thrive on the poorer sands.

Then there is fresh water. Hypothetically, if stranded on an island, the first question that enters the mind of anyone practically oriented would be, "Where can I find water?" A hard task on an island composed almost entirely of sand, you might think. Paradoxically, not only are there streams – some with water so clear that under the dappled light of a forest canopy they appear to be dry watercourses until a touch reveals deep, calmly flowing water – but even more remarkably, there are lakes! Over 130 of them.

Unsurprisingly, the combination of vegetation, water and ocean has resulted in the island hosting fauna as rich as anywhere on the mainland and made it a prized hunting and foraging ground for the Kabi Kabi tribes who originally inhabited the region.

It is no wonder, therefore, that many books have been published about the island, variously covering its natural history, indigenous history, environmental battles, scenic wonders, and tourism potential. However, none of this literature aimed at the general public provides a full and honest appraisal of the positive impact that the often-demonised forestry industry has had. Robert Onfray has primarily set out to fill this void by writing a history of the island from a perspective shaped by his lifelong experience as a professional forester.

In some striking ways, the history of the island mirrors the history of the forested lands along Australia's eastern seaboard, particularly since European settlement. It reveals the same sad pattern of indigenous people enduring the inevitable impacts of first contact, the tragic conflicts, the end of their nomadic way of life, the exploitation of their communities, and the well-meaning attempts to assimilate them into modern society. There is a similar pattern of European exploration followed by the bold entrepreneurship of settlers who established enterprises to exploit nature's treasures, which is then succeeded by a more cautious approach that uses the knowledge gained from experience and the application of science to better shape and manage the land.

This included the realisation that even when Lieutenant James Cook and his crew first laid eyes on the island, there was nothing natural about the landscape. It was a landscape highly modified by that simplest and most ancient of tools, fire. The cessation of the practice of setting fire to the understorey whenever possible over tens of thousands of years by the indigenous people began to culminate in catastrophic wildfires. The purposeful use of fire had created a much-modified landscape and vegetation, favouring fire-resistant species and open woodland with a grassy understorey. From early on, it was obvious to settlers that non-intervention led to forests being choked with vegetation, resulting in hot, catastrophic fires during every drought cycle. It was also understood that many species relied on fire to regenerate, so foresters incorporated fire into their management.

The nation's development depended heavily on timber for building and infrastructure. Without the bounty provided by native forests, Australia's rapid and successful development would have been impossible. The forests of Fraser Island were no exception, providing a rich resource of kauri, blackbutt, and later satinay and brush box. The logistical hurdles involved in harvesting and transporting the timber over deep sand and water were quickly overcome. Their value also underpinned the efforts to transform the industry from a purely extractive one into a sustainable one, and in some cases even enhanced natural processes through applied science.

As the country's population became increasingly urbanised and removed from the often harsh realities of the primary industries fuelling economic growth, public sentiment drifted toward an idealised perception of the natural world – a world in which nature should be preserved in an undisturbed state. This sentiment was, in some cases, a legitimate reaction to instances where the long-term health and productivity of natural resources were compromised, resulting in timely corrections. However, regarding native forests, the belief that the appropriate form of preservation was to protect them in national parks and allow nature to take its course is, and has always been, logically flawed. This thinking continues to have devastating consequences today, both environmentally and economically.

The proud record of first-principle scientific study, which balances preservation and economic extraction, is in danger of being pushed aside by the ideological whims of an urbanised electorate ignorant of reality. Australian forests – unique, extensive, and well-endowed with high-quality timber resources – are at risk of being inexorably condemned to a worst-case scenario of a never-ending cycle of catastrophic bushfires during every drought.

As documented in this important book, timber extraction from native forests can be conducted sustainably in a manner that protects biodiversity and promotes healthier forests. However, "locking away" the island's forests with minimal management has inevitably led to poorer outcomes for the native flora and fauna. Additionally, it has compromised the island's tourism potential, which is already suffering from over-exploitation.

In 2023, the Queensland government changed the name from Fraser Island to K'gari (with a silent K), which comes from the name used by the Butchulla tribe, one of the main tribal groups of the Kabi Kabi people. This significant recognition of the former indigenous

FOREWORD

occupants hopefully heralds a shift towards also recognising the importance of active human intervention in managing forests and integrating principles of their traditional forest management practices into a modern context. It is hoped that this book will serve as a major catalyst in reassessing how our forests are better managed in the future.

Tim Macartney-Snape
April 2025

Introduction

Fraser Island is a land of contradictions. As the largest sand island in the world, it defies expectations by supporting towering forests that rival those on fertile mainland soils. Despite its foundation of shifting dunes, the island sustains a diverse ecosystem of freshwater lakes, rainforests, and windswept heathlands. This balance between fragility and resilience makes Fraser Island both a scientific marvel and a natural wonder.

It's hard not to fall in love with the island. I certainly did when my family moved to Maryborough in 1980. I spent numerous recreational trips exploring its forests, lakes, and beaches, but my time working there as a forestry student deepened my appreciation for its true beauty.

Instead of following well-trodden paths, I was fortunate to explore the island's most remote and inaccessible areas, witnessing landscapes that few ever see. This experience deepened my connection to the island and reinforced my dream of becoming a forester in Queensland, possibly living and working on Fraser Island – but life had other plans, leading me to work as a forester in New South Wales and Tasmania before ultimately returning to Queensland in a new industry late in my career.

After retiring and travelling around Australia for three years, my wife and I settled in Hervey Bay. I reconnected with the island through regular visits but discovered a different place than I once knew. The forests still stand tall, yet the history that shaped them is being erased. Today's managers and the government seem determined to bury the island's rich forestry legacy beneath a one-sided narrative that overlooks its role in shaping the landscape we see today.

This book aims to tell that story before it vanishes.

Forestry has been a fundamental part of Fraser Island for over

INTRODUCTION

a century, and it's easy to understand why. Despite being built on sand, the island's forests are home to some of Queensland's tallest and most commercially valuable trees. In the island's heart, a dense forest stretches for 37 miles, covering 90,000 acres, once a vibrant source of sustainably managed timber.

While large trees were removed during the early days of logging, 120 years of forest management have not diminished the island's natural grandeur. In fact, careful management has contributed to shaping the forests that visitors admire today. Tourists stand in awe of the towering satinay and brush box trees, yet few know their history or that the forests they walk through were once actively managed for timber production.

A prime example of this historical amnesia is the common claim that the forests around Central Station are "rainforests". They are not. Instead, they are a breathtaking satinay-brush box, wet sclerophyll forest. Much of it was never logged, as it was set aside as a beauty spot in 1937. Nevertheless, official narratives continue to misrepresent its history, erasing the legacy of those who worked to sustain and protect these forests.

This book aims to address that oversight by providing visitors, historians, and anyone interested in the island's true story with a record of how forestry has shaped the landscape they see today.

There are several historical quotations that contain words and expressions that are now considered offensive and unacceptable. They are reproduced here exactly as they were originally written or spoken.

These terms reflect the attitudes and language of their time, not those of the author or publisher. They are included solely to preserve historical accuracy and authenticity. Where such language appears, it should be understood in its historical context, and not as an endorsement of the views expressed.

Readers may wonder why this book refers to Fraser Island rather than its recently adopted Aboriginal name, K'gari. Originally called

Great Sandy Island, it was renamed "Frazer Island" in 1842 by explorer Henry Russell Stuart, after Captain James Fraser, who died there in 1836. The name was later adjusted to Fraser Island, which remained in use for nearly 180 years.

In 2014, the Badjala People were granted Native Title rights to the island. Then, in 2021, the World Heritage Committee officially recognised the name K'gari, and in June 2023, the Queensland Government formally adopted it.

I continue to use Fraser Island for a simple reason: the forestry history I write about took place when under that name. For those who worked in the industry and lived that history, Fraser Island is the name they knew and connected with.

Those discussing the island's more recent history under national park management may refer to it as K'gari, but that's another story altogether.

PART 1
THE BEGINNING

1

A LAND SHAPED BY SAND AND TIME

Fraser Island is old but not ancient, a testament to nature's quiet persistence. Its formation did not involve volcanoes or continental uplifts; instead, it resulted from the patient work of drifting sand carried by wind and tide over millions of years. This unassuming process crafted a landscape of unparalleled beauty and complexity, making Fraser Island the largest sand island in the world.

Erosive forces broke down exposed rock formations, releasing sand grains into rivers that carried them to the sea. These tiny sand particles began their journey northward, transported by a longshore coastal drift from the Tasman Sea.

Year after year, more than 17.6 million cubic feet of sand migrate along the coastline into Queensland, originating from locations such as the sandstone formations of the Hawkesbury area and the granitic tors of the New England Tablelands.

Around 50 to 80 million years ago, volcanic activity east of Maryborough created rocky outcrops of rhyolite, initially islands, that shaped the coastline for thousands of years. These outcrops, including Indian Head, Middle Head, and Waddy Point, became vital anchors for sand accumulation. As ocean currents approached these natural barriers, water movement slowed, allowing sand to deposit and gradually form the foundation of Fraser Island.

The sand that accumulated at the headlands covered the bedrock, forming dunes that stretched parallel to the coast. Onshore winds sculpted loose sand into tall parabolic dunes that advanced inland like waves, creating a sequence of overlapping formations. Even as sea levels rose and fell, this process continued, shaping a landscape in constant change.

The eastern beach showing Fraser Island's three rocky outcrops in the background – Indian Head, Middle Head and Waddy Point.
(Rulz.rishi, CC BY-SA 4.0 via Wikimedia Commons)

The eastern seaboard of Australia remains geologically stable, allowing this longshore drift system to persist for millennia. Despite its relatively recent formation – less than a million years ago – Fraser Island's dune systems are regarded as some of the oldest in the world.

Early research by CSIRO in the 1970s suggested that the dunes date back over 700,000 years, pointing to at least nine dune-building periods. However, more recent studies indicate that these parabolic dunes are significantly younger and formed rapidly during two key periods: before and after the post-flood Ice Age. Evidence from podzolic soil development on the exposed dunes along the west coast supports this updated understanding.[1]

Fraser Island's landscape reflects this dynamic formation story. The dunes follow a gradual ageing process from east to west. The youngest dunes near the eastern shore rise sharply to heights of 150 feet, while older, weathered dunes farther inland show gentler ridges and shallower hollows. In these older formations, water is

---

[1] Ellerton, D. et al. (2022) Fraser Island (K'gari) and initiation of the Great Barrier Reef linked by Middle Pleistocene sea-level change. *Nature Geoscience*, 15: 1017–1026, doi: 10.1038/s41561-022-01062-6.

more accessible, and the prolonged accumulation of nutrients has supported dense vegetation, including patches of rainforest that thrive in the island's centre.

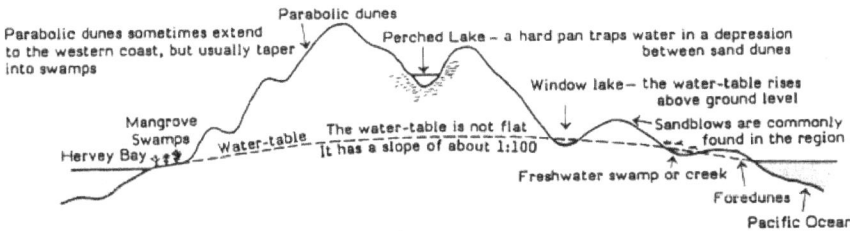

A diagrammatic cross-section of Fraser Island. Not drawn to scale.
(Department of Forestry Information Sheet 11 – Fraser Island Geography)

On the western slopes, the oldest dunes have been drained of nutrients over centuries by large trees. These dunes now support only smaller, twisted trees; their stark, broken stumps bear silent witness to once-flourishing forests. This region, characterised by smoother undulations and limited water, marks the transition to wallum country.

Sand dune on Fraser Island.
(John Robert McPherson, CC BY-SA 4.0 via Wikimedia Commons)

Driven by relentless onshore winds, the island's active sand blows continuously shift and reshape the landscape. These winds carve gaps through the vegetation and expose the skeletal remains of ancient forests buried beneath the shifting sands. Moving at a rate of three to six feet annually, these sand blows engulf everything in their path, creating an evolving environment that captivates visitors and researchers alike.

However, about 18,000 years ago, sea levels were significantly lower during the last Ice Age, and Fraser Island wasn't an island. Waddy Point and Indian Head emerged as solitary rocky hills amidst a vast coastal plain. As glaciers melted and sea levels rose, the Great Sandy Strait formed, eventually isolating Fraser Island from the mainland around 7,000 years ago.

Fraser Island currently hosts 36 active sand blows, showcasing nature's unceasing power to mould the landscape. Visitors can explore these formations at locations such as Hammerstone Sand Blow near Lake Wabby and Koorooman Sand Blow near the Cathedrals.

Some sand blows can rise over 164 feet near the eastern beach and accumulate to staggering heights of 790 feet further inland, often leapfrogging over one another. As these formations reach the water table, their movement slows, allowing pioneer vegetation to establish roots and gradually transform the barren landscape into lush terrain.

Relics of past sand blows create funnel-shaped parabolic dunes that extend from southeast to northwest under prevailing winds. Their ridges, shaped by wind erosion, become stabilised by vegetation over time, obscuring many from view. The island's northern section displays a younger dune system that overlays a once-flat landscape, highlighting the ongoing development of Fraser Island's geography.

Along the southeastern coast of Queensland, a series of rocky headlands that were once islands have greatly influenced the coastline over millennia. Each headland is accompanied by sweeping sandy beaches extending northward in a graceful reverse capital J-shaped curve, resembling the Greek letter zeta, and are known as zeta curves. Examples include Sunshine Beach, which terminates at Noosa Heads, and Rainbow Beach, which ends at Double Island Point.

One of the longest zeta curves in the world is located on Fraser Island's Seventy-Five Mile Beach, stretching from Hook Point to Indian Head. A shorter zeta curve also exists between Indian Head and Waddy Point, as well as between Waddy Point and Sandy Cape.

The zeta curve beach between Indian Head and Waddy Point.
(Liam Wille, CC BY-SA 4.0 via Wikimedia Commons)

Fraser Island marks the endpoint of a vast oceanic sand pipeline extending to Sandy Cape. Beyond this point, the sand vanishes off the edge of the continental shelf. This dispersal of sand away from the land has contributed to the formation of the Great Barrier Reef over the past 500,000 years. The unique shape of the coastline in this area, which curves northwest, also complicates the ongoing northward movement of the sand and establishes a natural endpoint for this geological phenomenon.

The sands hold wonders beyond their dynamic formation.

Strikingly coloured deposits, rich in mineral pigments like hematite, showcase hues ranging from red and pink to orange and brown, known as the Teewah Sands. Geologically distinct from the island's broader sand mass, these deposits are approximately 800,000 years old, similar to those found on the mainland along Rainbow Beach and Teewah Beach, south of Double Island Point.

Fraser Island's original area is believed to have a core of the Teewah Sands, which were formed by interglacial periods when sea levels were higher. The formation occupied a significantly larger area but was eroded and reworked during lower sea levels associated with glacial periods. Exposed sections of these sands have weathered into dramatic columns and cones, which are best viewed at Rainbow Gorge, The Pinnacles and Red Canyon.

The coffee rock outcrops found along the eastern beach at sites such as Poyungan and Yidney Rocks contribute to Fraser Island's geological intrigue. Despite their appearance, these structures are not true rocks; rather, they are hardened layers of sand cemented by organic acids from decaying vegetation.

When these organic acids percolate through the sand and encounter aluminium-rich groundwater, they create the distinctive dark brown colour of coffee rock. Although these formations resemble ordinary rocks along high-energy shorelines, they provide a unique glimpse into the island's ever-changing landscape.

Fraser Island's colourful sands, ancient dunes, and unique geological features showcase nature's artistry and resilience. With each gust of wind and grain of sand, the island continues to evolve, reshaping itself year after year, making it a truly natural wonder sculpted by time and the elements.

2

A WORLD-CLASS NATURAL WONDER

> Fraser Island is a sandheap clothed with forest vegetation varying with the moisture contents of the soil. The hillocky backbone carried a tremendous forest of turpentine, scrub box, blackbutt, tallowwood and stringybark.[1]

Fraser Island is not only a natural marvel but also a testament to the power of adaptation. Despite being composed almost entirely of nutrient-poor sand, this remarkable island sustains a vast amount of biomass. Various characteristics of this sandy environment reflect the challenges of living at the margins. For instance, the island is situated against the continental shelf and supports an unexpectedly dense cover of vegetation that thrives in sand. Moreover, it serves as the distribution limit for certain plants and animals.

The vegetation on Fraser Island thrives in conditions that would challenge most plant species. The island consists entirely of dunes, beach sand deposits, and a few small rocky outcrops, yet it sustains rainforests and tall eucalypt forests that develop on sand instead of traditional soil. There is an ongoing competition among various vegetation types to establish themselves on the dunes, contributing to their stabilisation.

While sand is recognised for its porosity and low nutrient content, the dune systems retain moisture due to the diverse vegetation that has developed. The nutrients in this ecosystem are closely linked to the degree of podzolisation in the soil.

Several factors influence the different types of vegetation on the island, including the age of the dunes, hydrology, topography, fire occurrences, and exposure to the elements.

---

[1] Forestry: Fraser Island experiments, *The Week*, 20 December 1920, p. 5. The quote is attributed to E.F.H. Swain.

Coastal vegetation: nature's first line of defence

The foredunes on the eastern beach, constantly battered by salt spray and shifting sands, can only support short, hardy plants such as beach spinifex, pigface and pink bindweed, which cling stubbornly to life here. These tenacious species endure harsh conditions as they struggle to stay above the sand that is constantly heaped on the dunes by the wind.

Coastal she-oak, pigface, beach primrose, saltwater couch, and goat's foot vine help stabilise the top and rear sections of the frontal dune, forming a protective barrier. This stabilisation shelters more sensitive plants, such as coast banksias and pandanus palms.

Wattles thrive in more sheltered spots over the foredune hills. Their height is restricted to avoid damage from salt spray, and they form dense thickets alongside midyim berries and smaller coast banksias. Shrubby plants like red and blueberry ashes, as well as tea trees, also flourish in this area, creating a buffer zone for taller woodland and forest species to establish themselves.

Further inland, woodlands dominated by Moreton Bay ash, white cypress pine and swamp paperbarks flourish in both wet and dry areas.

The forested heart

As one approaches the rise of secondary dunes, the first glimpse of an open forest appears, featuring a grassy understorey that supports blue gums and grey ironbarks. In contrast, the higher dunes are home to scribbly gums and bloodwoods, which dominate a large portion of the island. The vibrant colours and mottled patterns of the gnarled scribbly gums shedding their bark, along with an abundance of bloodwood blossoms, give these forests a natural charm.

These plants provide shade and help cool the sand. They add leaves, bark, and decomposing woody material to the surface. Over hundreds of years, this plant litter mixes with the sand to form humus, which enhances moisture retention. Plants need moisture to thrive; few can survive in dry, highly porous sand.

As leaves and other litter decompose, they form a soil-like layer. She-oaks and macrozamias are plants that fix nitrogen in sandy soil. Once the leaves and bark break down, the plants' roots quickly absorb and recycle the nutrients produced. Over thousands of years, the accumulation of humus and litter fosters conditions favourable for larger trees to establish and thrive. These trees have greater moisture and nutrient needs.

As the dunes rise and shelter increases, taller vegetation types take hold. Large blackbutt trees grow beyond the secondary dunes on the high hind dune system, where they enjoy better protection against salt-laden winds.

The tall blackbutt forests are among the most valued commercial forests, spanning approximately 34,000 acres, or eight per cent of the island.[2] These forests also feature the equally valuable tallowwood and red stringybark, which grow to impressive sizes.

Another important commercial forest community is the awe-inspiring satinay–brush box[3] wet sclerophyll forest, which exists as an ecotone – a transitional area between eucalypt stands and rainforests. Satinay is an extraordinary tree, notable not only for its imposing size but also for its limited distribution.[4] It is found solely on the island and in a small, isolated area in the northern part of the Cooloola Sand Mass.[5] While brush box grows naturally across extensive regions on the mainland, it never attains the impressive sizes seen on Fraser Island.

---

[2] Chapter 14 provides a detailed description of the utilisation and silvicultural practices in these forests.
[3] In Queensland, and certainly in the Maryborough district, brush box was commonly called scrub box.
[4] The timber utilisation history of satinay is outlined in Chapter 11.
[5] There are also outlier locations on Moreton Island and North Stradbroke Island, as well as an isolated location near Tewantin.

Blackbutt forest. (Department of Forestry)

Stand of satinay-brush box forest.
(State Library of Queensland)

In the most sheltered swales of the hind dunes, rainforest thrives, supporting hoop pine, kauri pine, white beech, picabeen palm and strangler fig. Rainforests and adjacent areas were targeted for logging when it began on the island in 1863. Kauri pines were particularly sought after for their attractive, straight trunks, while durable white beech was also favoured. As kauri stands were nearly exhausted a decade later, hoop pine logging began. This tree species occurs over mainly 2,000 acres, with its natural distribution extending north of Eli Creek.

One common tree in the understorey of the rainforest is the medium-sized shrub known as carrol. It is also found quite extensively throughout the wettest areas of satinay-brush-box and hoop pine forests. This shrub is related to lemon myrtle and emits a fresh, musky aroma.

An interesting feature is that several tree species – blackbutt, tallowwood and scribbly gum – reach their northern distribution limit on the island. Bacon wood (or tulip siris), satinay and macrozamia are found almost exclusively on Fraser Island, with a very limited range on the mainland.

Specialised plant communities

Beyond the towering forests, heaths, or wallum, along with the swamps in the low-lying dunes on the island's northern part and the extensive sections on the oldest dunes to the western side, are home to various specialised plant communities.

The western dunes boast a rich variety of flowering plants, resulting in vibrant wildflower displays throughout the year that add splashes of colour to the island's landscape. Among these are the lemon-scented tea trees, which bloom with waxy white flowers. Found only in the Great Sandy Region, the Wide Bay boronia produces an abundance of waxy purple flowers in seasonal bursts and thrives in wetter areas. The mauve-flowered forest boronia is commonly found in open forest areas and is known for its highly scented leaves. The wedding bush showcases a profusion of small, five-petalled white flowers from August to September. Additionally, numerous pea flowers, primarily yellow, and many small-leaved heaths bloom at various times throughout the year.

The western dunes also host cypress pines, three species of banksia (wallum, coast, and swamp banksias), grass trees, along with several sedges and rushes.

Many sheltered inlets and bays along the west coast, especially between Moon and Snout Points, host significant mangrove communities that support hundreds of animals, including fish, crabs, birds and bats. Mangroves are also located north of Moon Point at the main creek estuaries, such as Wathumba.

Peat swamps, situated near sea level on the western side, developed alongside the mangrove forests. These are the only known examples that flow into tidal wetlands anywhere in the world.

Some plants have developed unique adaptive features that enable them to thrive in sandy environments. For instance, in the low-lying dunes and swamps, carnivorous sundews capture insects to obtain the nitrogen that the sandy soil lacks. Certain trees have evolved to store nutrients in bulbous lumps on their trunks when necessary. Other trees have adapted by developing aerial roots to respond to the shifting sands.

A complex community of soil fungi exists in the sand dunes. These fungi form beneficial relationships with plant roots helping to make the limited minerals in the sand accessible to larger plants in exchange for carbohydrates. Additionally, they assist in breaking down plant litter, which enhances the sandy soil's ability to retain water.

The wild residents

The island is home to over 40 species of mammals. One of its most iconic residents is the dingo, recognised as one of the purest strains in Australia. However, it poses potential dangers due to an increase in attacks on humans. Dingoes primarily feed on the swamp wallaby, northern brown bandicoot, sugar glider, and squirrel glider. They also scavenge on any dead animals washed up on the beach, such as whales and turtles.

Nine species of rodents live on the island, including the bush rat, pale field rat, water rat, web-footed water rat, grassland melomys, and fawn-footed melomys. Additionally, the small marsupial and carnivorous dasyurid, the yellow-footed antechinus, is also found there.

Since whaling operations ceased in the early 1960s, the humpback whale population has experienced significant growth. These whales migrate past the island annually, with many stopping in Platypus Bay during their southward journey. They typically begin to arrive in mid-August and remain until mid-October before continuing their migration to Antarctic feeding grounds. Several species of dolphins are occasionally observed, including the bottlenose dolphin, common dolphin and Indo-Pacific humpbacked dolphin.

The Great Sandy Strait is a vital habitat for dugongs, a species that relies on the seagrass beds in the area. Past hunting has significantly diminished their numbers, but they are now making a comeback. The substantial population in the southern Hervey Bay region is considered the most significant along Queensland's coastline.

There are 12 different species of bats found on the island, all of which are insectivorous. These include the common bentwing bat, Gould's long-eared bat, hoary bat, and large-footed mouse-eared bat.

The island is particularly exciting for bird watchers, showcasing a diverse range of over 300 species. Even casual observers can spot white-bellied sea eagles, ospreys, and kites that often soar over the eastern beach. Common seabirds such as gulls, terns, pied oystercatchers, and small dotterels can also be seen on the eastern beach.

Reptiles are often observed on the island, with reports of 79 species. The two most common reptiles are carpet pythons and goannas.

Other non-venomous snakes include the green tree snake and the small-blotched python. The venomous snakes consist of the death adder, the taipan, the eastern brown snake and the red-bellied black snake.

The waters around the island are home to both freshwater and sea turtles. The lakes support Kreftt's river turtles, short-necked turtles, and broad-shelled turtles. Green sea turtles and loggerhead turtles inhabit the surrounding ocean, coming ashore to lay their eggs.

Of particular interest are four species of "acid" frogs that have adapted to the unique acidic waters of the wallum regions: the Cooloola sedge frog, the wallum rocket frog, the wallum sedge frog, and the wallum froglet. Fraser Island contains the largest number of acid frog habitats in eastern Australia.

The jewels of the island

The lakes on Fraser Island are a remarkable natural phenomenon resulting from the unique composition of the sand and its environmental influences. The sandy soil is typically very porous, allowing water to filter through the large spaces between the grains. However, on Fraser Island, the sand can retain as much as 30 per cent of its volume in water near the surface due to capillary action within the humus layer. This layer acts like a plastic sheet, similar to those used for mulching, and helps maintain a higher water table than normally would be the case.

Further down, decomposing leaves and organic matter mix with the sand over many years to create a hard pan that traps surface water, ultimately forming numerous lakes. Fraser Island boasts over 130 lakes, mainly located in the northern section above Orchid Beach.

Three distinct types of lakes are found on the island, each with unique characteristics. Fraser Island is especially renowned for its perched lakes, which are situated high in the sand dunes. Very few of these lakes are found outside Queensland's Great Sandy region. They are rare elsewhere and formed in places where water tables are higher. Water accumulates in depressions, and these lakes also form when one parabolic dune overtakes another, creating a depression that traps water like a saucer. They do not receive inflow from any streams and have no outlets.

An aerial capture of the stunning Freshwater Lakes west of The Pinnacles. (Gypsy888, CC BY-SA 4.0 via Wikimedia Commons)

Boomerang Lake and Lake Boemingen are notable examples of perched lakes. They rank among the highest and largest in the world. Furthermore, while Lakes McKenzie and Wabby are popular with tourists, Lake Boemingen is especially renowned for its picturesque shores lined with paperbark trees and its stunning white sandy beaches.

Lake McKenzie, however, stands out as the island's most celebrated lake, admired for its breathtaking beauty. The shimmering white sand surrounding the lake enhances its vibrant sky-blue colour, creating a truly spectacular sight.

A panoramic view of Lake McKenzie.
(Korkut Tas, CC BY-SA 3.0 via Wikimedia Commons)

More than 40 of these remarkable freshwater lakes are located on the island, with many still lacking names. Most of these lakes sit south of Lake Bowarrady and maintain their water levels well above the local water table.

Due to the low concentrations of ions such as calcium, sodium and potassium, the perched lake is remarkably fresh. Nonetheless, organic acids from decomposing vegetation make the lakes quite acidic, with pH levels as low as 4.5. As a result, fish populations are sparse, although turtles can thrive in these unique environments.

The second type of lake is known as the water window lake, prevalent in the island's northern and more isolated regions. These lakes form when the land surface dips below the local water table, exposing the stored water and creating a window to the aquatic depths below. Lake Garawongera and Basin Lake are easily accessible examples of this type.

Lastly, barrage lakes form when shifting sands block a creek or stream from flowing into the ocean, creating a barrier that pools water and gradually deepens into a lake. Lake Wabby is the most prominent example of this type. It is the deepest lake on the island and is beautifully coloured emerald green due to algae.

The sand blow responsible for forming Lake Wabby is called Hammerstone. As the active dune continues to shift inland, it is expected to eventually engulf the lake.

The veins of life

Fraser Island receives an average of 59 inches of rainfall annually. Although the intensity of rainfall is much greater than on the mainland, water does not flow over the surface except on some heavily compacted roads. The mountains of loose sand act as a reservoir, retaining the rainfall until it percolates through the sand to a few feet above sea level, beyond which it cannot pass. At that point, it is forced into the low flats and valleys, forming creeks of continuously flowing water that return to the ocean from which it originated.

Rain does not influence creek levels because they are continuously supplied by a permanent reservoir. The stored water may take many years to reach sea level through the numerous creeks on the island. Fraser Island is one of the best-watered areas in Australia. In fact, the entire island operates like a giant sponge, saturated with an immense body of the purest fresh water imaginable.

The island's most impressive creek is Eli Creek, located on the eastern beach. Remarkably, its flow remains unaffected by seasonal rainfall fluctuations, as the sand mass functions as an aquifer, releasing water from the water table at a constant rate. It is estimated that water from this creek flows into the ocean at a rate of one million gallons every hour.

Towards the northern limit of the timber belt runs Bowarrady Creek. It begins in the highest dunes and flows towards the west coast. The water is tinted by the tannins from the bark of the trees that line its banks. Near the creek's mouth, there is a tranquil lagoon and swimming hole. The dunes above the creek at the coast offer stunning views of Platypus Bay.

Eli Creek is the largest creek on the eastern side of the island.
(UrbanDruid, CC BY-SA 4.0 via Wikimedia Commons)

The lagoon at the mouth of Bowarrady Creek.
(Keith Sinclair, CC BY-SA 4.0 via Wikimedia Commons)

Another spectacular waterway is Wathumba Creek, situated on the west coast. This short creek channels water from Wathumba Swamp to the ocean. Its beautiful estuary is a popular all-weather refuge for boats and fishermen, showcasing remarkably clear water and notable tidal variations.

Finally, there is Woongoolbver Creek, which flows from Central Station to the western coast. Surrounded by a narrow strip of rainforest scrub, the water in the creek is crystal clear. The land gently slopes down toward the west coast, where flat alluvial mangrove plains border the short streams that feed into the creek.

3

THE ORIGINAL GUARDIANS

> Man did not create the land or the fish or the fowl or any animal, vegetable or mineral found on it or beneath it. These were given to us as bounties to use, and to not abuse.[1]

Carbon dating indicates that Aboriginal people have lived on the island for up to 30,000 years, with more active usage for at least the past 7,000 years. However, the history of Aboriginal occupation on the island remains unclear and, at times, controversial.

The Wide Bay area was home to 19 subgroups of the Kabi Kabi people. Fraser Island was seasonally inhabited by the Badjala,[2] Ngulungbara, and Dulingbara tribes, who also lived on the mainland and spoke a dialect from the Mary and Wide Bay region.[3]

The Badjala people referred to the island as Gurrie or Curri, which means "paradise" in honour of a creation spirit that could not leave the area's beauty and slept in the local waters. Other tribes called it Moonbi and Talboor.

The Dulingbara inhabited the southern end from Hook Point to Woongoolbver Creek, migrating freely from Inskip Point across the Great Sandy Strait. Hook Point was an important campsite.

The Badjala occupied the central part of the island, from Woongoolbver Creek to Yidney Creek. Lake Wabby, regarded as the home of the rainbow serpent, was a sacred site. According to a Badjala Aboriginal who continued to live on the island, a beautiful

---

[1] Badjala elder Olga Miller at the Fraser Island Environmental Commission of Inquiry 1975.
[2] I have chosen to use the female form of the tribal name, rather than the male form of Butchulla.
[3] This is a very contested subject. Elder of the Batjala, Olga Miller, claimed there was only "one nation" on the island. They separated into six clans, each of which controlled a section of the island. Miller was from the Wondunna clan which was based at North White Cliffs and possessed a strong local oral history of the island from her grandfather.

girl died there one day, and despite giving her water and wongs,[4] she still passed away. The Aborigines held a negative view of the place and rarely visited it. North White Cliffs, known as Balarrgan, was a ceremonial area, while the mouth of Bogimbah Creek served as their main campsite and feasting ground.

The Ngulungbara occupied the northern half of the island, including Bowarrady, Indian Head, and Sandy Cape. Coongul and Bowarrady Creeks functioned as the main camping and fishing spots. The rhyolite at Indian Head was utilised for tools, and James Cook named it in May 1770 after observing Aborigines gathered there. He described it as:

> ... a black bluff head or point of land, on which a number of the natives were assembled, which occasioned my naming it Indian Head.[5]

The archaeological and social significance of Aboriginal use is evident through large midden heaps, campsites, fish traps, bora rings, scarred trees and stone tools. Middens reveal remnants of seafood and tools used for preparing food. Seafood such as wongs, along with fish, crabs, oysters, turtles, dugongs and large flat pearl shells were common staples. From the freshwater creeks, they caught eels and fish. On land, they hunted wallabies, possums, and bandicoots, and gathered yams, macrozamia nuts, roots, seeds, tree grubs, honey, and various fruits.

Permanent camps were established in more sheltered areas, and stone tools from the mainland have been discovered. Bora rings near Lake Wabby, Yidney, and Bogimbah held sacred importance for men-only ceremonies.

---

[4] Wongs are shellfish, the local name for pippies, eugaries or cockles, depending on where you come from.

[5] Cook, J. (1968) *Captain Cook's Journal during his First Voyage round the World made in H.M. Bark "Endeavour" 1768-71. A Literal Transcription of the Original MSS.* with Notes and Introduction, edited by Captain W.J.L. Wharton, p. 256.

Portrait of an unidentified Fraser Island Aboriginal man, c 1900.
(State Library of Queensland)

Early encounters with Europeans

As he sailed towards Sandy Cape on 27 July 1802, Flinders documented seeing "a number of Indians, fifty as reported, looking at the ship".[6]

Andrew Petrie[7] wrote after his expedition in 1842 that he was:

> ... met by a great many natives, who were fishing at the mouth of the passage.[8]

---

[6] Flinders, M. (1814) *A Voyage to Terra Australis* (Volume II). G & W Nicol, London, p. 6.
[7] More details about Andrew Petrie will be introduced in the next chapter.
[8] Petrie, A. (1842) *Journal of an Expedition to the "Wide Bay River" in 1842*. Extract from an old diary reproduced in C. C. Petrie (1904) *Tom Petrie's Reminiscences*, Watson, Ferguson & Co., Brisbane, p. 266.

The first recorded contact between Aborigines and Europeans occurred in 1802 when Matthew Flinders anchored the brig *Investigator* south-west of Sandy Cape. On 30 July, he wrote:

> In order to give the botanists an opportunity of examining the productions of Sandy Cape, I determined to remain here a day; and some natives being seen upon the beach, a boat was sent to commence an acquaintance with them; they however retired and suffered Mr Brown to botanise without disturbance.[9]

The following morning, Flinders anchored his brig within a quarter of a mile from the shore to support the three landing parties, exchanging goods with the Aborigines they met. Flinders' group of six, including Bongaree, his Aboriginal friend from Sydney, experienced a somewhat awkward yet friendly encounter:

> Bongaree stripped off his clothes and laid aside his spear as inducements for them to wait for him; but finding they did not understand his language, the poor fellow, in the simplicity of his heart, addressed them in broken English, hoping to succeed better. At length they suffered him to come up, and by degrees our whole party joined; and after receiving some presents, twenty of them returned with us to our boats, and feasted upon the blubber of two porpoises, which had been brought on shore purposely for them ... we then quitted our new friends after presenting them with hatchets and other testimonials of our satisfaction.[10]

Another party returned later in the day with scoop nets that the Aboriginals used to catch fish after exchanging goods.

Perhaps the most documented and contentious incidents between Aboriginal peoples and Europeans took place in 1836 when the surviving crew from the *Stirling Castle*, which had shipwrecked on a reef further north, landed just north of Waddy Point.

The writings of Eliza Fraser, one of the survivors, and the

---

[9] Flinders, M. (1814) Op. cit., p. 9.
[10] Ibid, p. 9.

captain's wife, have been the subject of much debate. Recent writers have characterised her accounts as exaggerated and primarily focused on the negative treatment she faced from the Aborigines while on Fraser Island. This depiction aims to connect to the slaughter, displacement and mistreatment the Aborigines received.

While Aborigines faced significant hardship due to the colonisation of their lands, there is no evidence to suggest that Eliza Fraser's published accounts contributed to this suffering.[11] The conflicts at the frontier arose primarily from Aboriginal resistance to losing their lands for traditional purposes, compounded by the introduction of disease, opium and alcohol.

In 1850, the Aboriginal population on Fraser Island was estimated at around 2,000. An escaped convict, David Bracewell, who lived among the Aborigines, recounted witnessing them "at their great fights" along a four-mile stretch of beach.

The alleged massacre

The European encroachment onto Fraser Island was marked by tensions and the eventual displacement of Aboriginal populations.

In August 1848, the governor of New South Wales formed a small native police corps to suppress the "collisions" between Aborigines and settlers in areas "beyond the settled districts".[12] A division consisting of an officer and 12 troopers was stationed in the Wide Bay-Burnett region.

In 1847, a river port was established at Maryborough, which has a close connection to the history of Fraser Island in many ways. Almost immediately, conflicts broke out between Europeans and local Aborigines as squatters started settling in the Mary Valley. John Bidwill, the first Commissioner of Crown Lands for the area, wrote to the Chief Commissioner in Sydney detailing an attack on

---

[11] More details about the fate of the *Stirling Castle* and her crew are outlined in the next chapter.
[12] Queensland was still part of the New South Wales colony, becoming its own colony on 10 December 1859.

his property in Tinana. By February 1851, following numerous incidents – some quite violent – locals sent affidavits to the Magistrates Court accusing several Aborigines of murder.

Locals were aware that Aborigines often raided stations and frequently sought refuge on Fraser Island afterwards. The most controversial and debated incident happened in December 1851, when an alleged massacre of up to 100 Aborigines took place after a 23-man native police force, led by Commandant Frederick Walker, was dispatched to the island to suppress Aboriginal raids on settler farms and reclaim stolen property, following warrants issued against several Aboriginals, using the best names to describe them.

Walker sought the governor's approval to proceed to Fraser Island and arrest the offenders under the warrants. The island had become a sanctuary for those Aborigines who were aware they would face reprisals for their actions against the new settlers. The governor requested the attorney general's advice on the legality of Walker's plan before granting approval.

The Attorney-General, in considering the matter, wrote:

> It must, unhappily, be expected that the proposed attempt at arrest may lead to a warlike conflict and perhaps to loss of life, but the aim of the law must not be paralysed by the expectation of such results. If the offenders were white men engaged as bandits in committing attacks upon life and property of their fellow subjects, an armed force would necessarily be employed against them.[13]

After eight days on the island, Walker wrote a report about his trip while in Maryborough. This report included descriptions of several encounters with Aborigines, including the deaths of two individuals following Walker's men firing on a boat that had been stolen from a squatter.

In 2017, Professor Lyndall Ryan from the University of New-

---

[13] Queensland State Library, Oxley Microfilm Reel A2.23.

castle launched a webpage, funded through the Australian Research Council, detailing frontier massacres of Aborigines in eastern Australia. The site documents a massacre of 100 Aboriginal people as part of the trip to Fraser Island in late 1851. The entry says:

> Aboriginal people were 'driven into the sea and kept there as long as daylight and life lasted' Lauer (1977). Lauer estimates that 100 Aboriginal people were killed.[14]

According to Walker's report of the trip to the island, Aboriginal sergeants Edgar and Willy, along with several troopers, left camp and set out on foot to track a group of Aborigines they had previously encountered. Following one of their trails to the eastern beach, they returned three days later and claimed they drove the group into the sea. No fatalities were mentioned. However, they made a gruesome discovery: the remains of one Aboriginal, who had apparently died and allegedly been dismembered by his companions for food, with the remaining parts found in dilly bags.

Since no commissioned officers accompanied the group, contemporary historians have largely dismissed the recorded account, although they accept such an event occurred. Claims of a massacre involving a hundred Aborigines are unfounded, as no evidence supports such assertions. Moreover, no credible oral histories from the island's Aboriginal descendants mention a massacre.

It is highly plausible that the Aborigines, with their superior knowledge of the terrain, easily evaded the troopers on foot who were in unfamiliar territory. The sergeants' claim of driving them into the sea may have been a convenient way to avoid admitting failure to Walker.

The quote attributed to Dr. Peter Lauer comes directly from a letter written anonymously to the editor of the *Moreton Bay Courier*, signed with the pseudonym of "A SQUATTER" from

---

[14] Ryan, L. et al. (2019) *Colonial Frontier Massacres in Australia, 1788 to 1930.* V3.0, University of Newcastle (Trove). Accessed 6 February 2024; Lauer, P. (ed) 1977, Fraser Island, *Occasional Papers in Anthropology, no. 8.* Anthropology Museum, University of Queensland, St Lucia.

Burnett River. This letter admits that the information originated from unverified sources in Sydney regarding a rumoured massacre.[15] It was also penned nine months after the event. This account differs markedly from Walker's first-hand report, in which he makes no suggestion that any of the Aborigines who were chased and ended up in the sea, met their death. Dr. Lauer's conclusion that a massacre occurred appears implausible because it lacks firm evidence to support it.

Paul Dillon, an author of several books on Queensland history, meticulously examined the evidence, distinguishing between primary and secondary sources.[16] He considered Walker's report as the most reliable source, refuting exaggerated accounts of mass slaughter:

> Therefore, Commandant Walker's report is the only probative evidence available, that two Aborigines were killed. Consequently, there was no massacre.[17]

A list of massacres against Aborigines is outlined in a 2017 report by the Anti-Discrimination Commission Queensland. One of these events allegedly took place on Fraser Island around the same time as mentioned earlier:

> 1851-52: Native Police engaged in 'hunting expeditions' over the Christmas period, with the biggest massacre of Butchella people occurring at Indian Head on K'gari (Fraser Island).[18]

However, no evidence has been provided to support the claim. I am not aware of any material linking the deaths of Aborigines at the hands of the Native Police to anywhere near Indian Head.

---

[15] Letter to the Editor, *Moreton Bay Courier*, 18 September 1852, p. 2 (Trove). Accessed 6 February 2024.

[16] Dillon, P. (2022) *Fraser Island: Vrai ou Faux*. Connor Court Publishing, Brisbane.

[17] Ibid., p. 80.

[18] Anti-Discrimination Commission Queensland (2017) *Aboriginal people in Queensland: a brief human rights history*, p. 9. < https://www.qhrc.qld.gov.au/__data/assets/pdf_file/0013/10606/Aboriginal-timeline-FINAL-updated-25-July-2018.pdf> Accessed 11 February 2025.

The Europeans arrive

Timber harvesting, oyster fisheries, and cattle and sheep grazing began on Fraser Island in the 1860s. These activities restricted the movement of Aborigines and disrupted their traditional and social practices on the island. By 1870, the Aboriginal population was estimated to be around 1,600.

Many historians argue that the island was declared an Aboriginal reserve in 1860 to prevent European occupation, citing no sources other than an article in The *Maryborough Chronicle* written years later, which described the island as:

> ... a place swarming with very wild and savage blacks who regarded it as their last sanctuary against the fast encroaching tide of white settlement, and fiercely resented any entrance by white men.[19]

However, there is no evidence in official government documents that such a gazettal ever occurred.

In 1843, the local Land Commissioner, Dr Simpson, recommended that Fraser Island would be an excellent location for a missionary station since it supported many Aborigines. However, nothing was done to establish a mission and over the next 20 years, the Aboriginal population on the island declined dramatically.

By 1864, there was a belief that Aborigines in the Wide Bay and Burnett districts should be gathered and settled on Fraser Island. The proposal suggested:

> Let us suppose that all the blacks in the Wide Bay, Burnett, and all other districts in which they could be collected, were transported to Frazer's [sic] island. Let them there be placed under strict surveillance and strong guard. Let them be fed with food sufficient at the State's expense, and encouraged by rewards – compelled, if necessary, by the infliction of corporal punishment – to cultivate the

---
[19] Old Pioneer Passes, *Maryborough Chronicle, Wide Bay and Burnett Advertiser*, 6 January 1926, p. 8 (Trove). Accessed 6 February 2024.

ground; in fact, made compulsory apprentices to habits of civilisation.[20]

This thinking led to the idea that Fraser Island could become a model penal settlement to control Aborigines, which missions were expected to achieve. The first such attempt was established in 1870 by Methodist minister and bush missionary Reverend Edward Fuller near a logging camp called Piersen's camp, half a mile south of South White Cliffs or Ungowa.[21] The underlying principle held by German and English evangelists at the time was to encourage Aborigines to settle in one place and engage in productive work to "civilise" them and make them behave similarly to Europeans.

The missions

However, Fuller soon realised that Fraser Island was unsuitable for an agricultural missionary settlement, especially without any government funding, and his attempts to grow vegetables were unsuccessful. He also faced challenges with the Aboriginal tendency to wander, as they only took part in the mission for religious and literacy lessons when it suited them and did not interfere with their tribal activities. Ultimately, Fuller had to abandon his mission and returned to the mainland in 1873.

On the mainland, frustration persisted regarding how effective the native mounted police were in dispersing Aborigines, often resulting in accusations of unreported murders.

As Europeans settled more land, the Aboriginals struggled to

---

[20] *Maryborough Chronicle, Wide Bay and Burnett Advertiser*, 30 June 1864, p. 2 (Trove). Accessed 6 February 2024.

[21] Alice Wilson studied Fuller's papers and letters, compiling a report on the Aboriginal missions at Fraser Island. Fuller mentions the Pierson brothers and their logging crew operating near his mission site. Wilson cites a reliable source indicating Pierson's camp as three miles north of Snout Point. While Bill Seelke was based near Snout Point during WWI, cutting cypress and satinay, I doubt Pierson's camp was that far south as only softwoods were harvested during the 1860s and early 1870s, and it is highly improbable that commercial kauri pines were found in that area. Also of note is that Fuller's mission commanded a full view of every vessel that entered or left the Mary River. He couldn't get that view from Snout Point.

provide for themselves, and their hostility to European settlers diminished as their resistance was broken. Many were coerced into working for the settlers, often receiving payment in alcohol, tobacco, tea and flour. This situation fostered a cycle of dependency on settlers for survival, frequently in exchange for alcohol and opium.

As Fred Williams writes, toward the end of the century, the Aborigines:

> ... were doomed to become a totally demoralised race. Mentally, morally and physically they became weak shadows of what they had once been.[22]

In February 1897, Archibald Meston[23] urged the home secretary to urgently relocate the "unwanted" Aborigines from Maryborough to Fraser Island. He inspected the island the previous year and identified at least two sites he considered suitable for Aboriginal reserves: Stewart Island and North White Cliffs.

Meston argued that Fraser Island was an ideal location for unemployed and "degraded blacks" from the settled districts. He believed the remaining Aborigines in these areas should be relocated to a place free from contact with Europeans, which would allow them to practice their traditional lifestyles.

Meston provided a damming assessment of their condition:

> The men had lost their manhood and self-respect, were depraved slaves of opium, listless and aimless, and spiritless, living under some horrid enchantment, half-starved clothed in rags, careless of life and death.
>
> The women and girls were in the same condition. They had become a public nuisance in Maryborough, the children begging money in the streets, and the older people soliciting food. The women and girls frequented the opium

---

[22] Williams, F. (1982) *Written in Sand: A history of Fraser Island*. Jacaranda Press, Brisbane, p. 41.

[23] Meston was acting in his position as special commissioner to inspect Aboriginal reserves and ration stations. The following year, he was appointed as the southern protector of Aborigines.

dens of the Chinese, and also cohabited with white men and kanakas.[24]

In response to these issues, the government passed *The Aboriginals Protection and Restriction of the Sale of Opium Act* in 1897. This legislation aimed to gather the remaining Aborigines and included provisions for their removal, primarily by force, to missions and reserves so they could be entirely isolated from contact with Europeans.

Once he received approval, Meston gathered 51 fringe-dwelling men, women, and children from Maryborough and transported them to North White Cliffs, where they occupied the deserted Quarantine Station buildings. He reported positively that after supplying them with food and resources for hunting and fishing, their overall health and condition improved within the first two months. Over the following years, 165 Aborigines from across the state were added to the reserve.

The reserve site had become a "favourite resort for pleasure parties" among local settlers who had enjoyed sailing across the strait to North White Cliffs for the past 20 years. However, several incidents involving European visitors and picnickers detracted from the seclusion and peace that Meston desired.

Tensions escalated when 20 youths arrived in two sailing boats for the 1897 Easter weekend. One of them, after Meston informed him he could not access the reserve without permission, responded, "Go and attend to your niggers."[25]

In response, Meston instructed his son to take some inmates from the mission to drive the troublemakers away from the shore.

> Two white men ran for the boats, two were thrown down and one or two were struck by the blacks.[26]

---

[24] Meston, A. (1897) *Report on Aboriginal Station recently formed on Fraser's Island*, 2 April. ITM 18308, QSA.

[25] The White Cliffs Affair, *Maryborough Chronicle, Wide Bay and Burnett Advertiser*, 27 April 1897, p. 2 (Trove). Accessed 1 December 2024.

[26] Meston, A. (1897) *Letter to W. H. Ryder, Under Secretary*, 22 April. ITM 18308, QSA.

This incident marked another step in the long, tragic decline of the once proud local Aborigines.

During subsequent legal actions, public petitions and meetings, it was revealed that the Lands Department had gazetted North White Cliffs as a public reserve in 1894. The government overlooked this fact when sanctioning the Aboriginal reserve for the mission. Meston had no authority to expel holidaymakers from the area. The public demanded that the Aboriginal reserve be relocated to a more remote part of the island, believing that North White Cliffs was "essentially a Maryborough resort".

Surveyor-General Archibald McDowall[27] suggested that Meston relocate the reserve to the Bogimbah Creek area, about nine miles to the north. This location would place the Aborigines closer to the kauri pine nursery, where some had previously assisted when it first operated in the early 1880s and "could be made useful" for forestry work. Despite Meston's objections, the home secretary ordered the creation of an initial reserve of 43 square miles or 27,520 acres at Bogimbah for the Aborigines in May 1897, a decision to which Meston reluctantly accepted. The reserve was extended in 1901 to 196 square miles (125,440 acres).

Materials from two old houses at the Quarantine Station were transported to Bogimbah Creek to construct huts. Meston purchased the six-room house occupied by Ronald Mitchell and his son near the pine nursery and relocated it to the mission site to serve as the superintendent's house. This was a two-bedroom, weatherboard building with an iron roof, an eating recess and a kitchen, and a full-width front verandah.

The Aborigines were free to move anywhere on the island and were encouraged to maintain their traditional lifestyle as much as possible, preserving ancient customs, songs and corroborees. Selected men were sent to the mainland as trackers, while other

---

[27] McDowall was the District Surveyor at Maryborough in the early 1880s when he set up the first attempt at reforestation and silviculture on Fraser Island. More details are provided in Chapter 13.

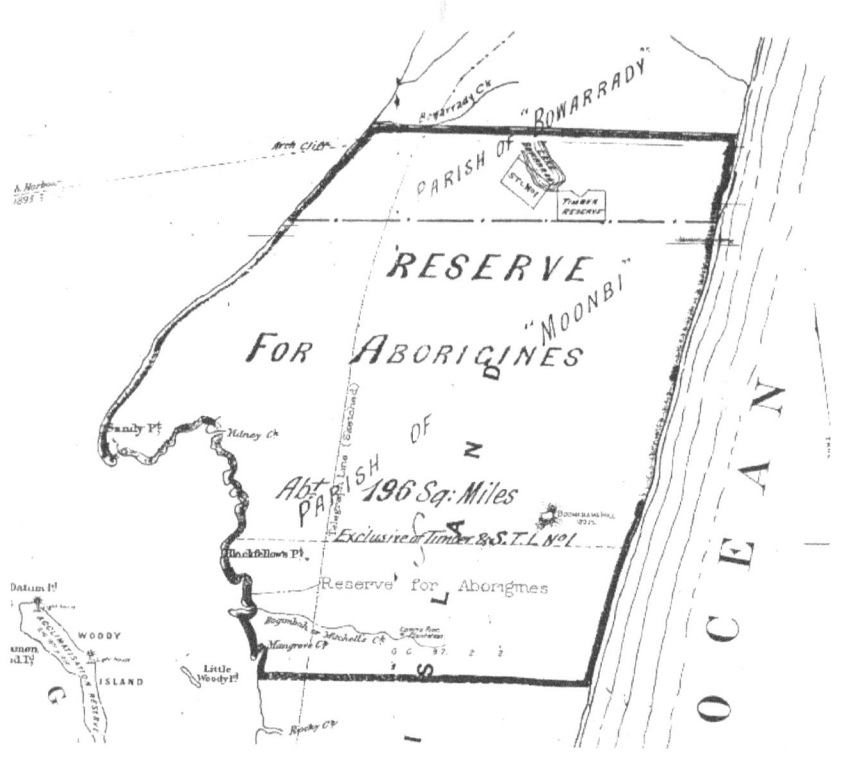

Map showing the Aboriginal Reserves in the Bogimbah Creek area. The original area went as far north as the broken line running across the island immediately above Blackfellow's Point. (Queensland State Archives)

trusted individuals were permitted to work there for up to 12 months. Groups were also allowed to hunt for honey, possums, koalas and kangaroos on the mainland. They were even allowed to earn income by collecting gum from eucalypts for the Brisbane Tanning Company, which patented a new process for tanning leather products. They spent what they earned shopping in Pialba and Maryborough.

When the mission at Bogimbah Reserve began, 76 Aborigines were present there. In September 1899, the premier, the governor, and the home secretary visited the site. However, they gave an extremely unfavourable report, raising concerns about using fear and violence to enforce discipline. They believed the Aborigines were bored, deprived, and dissatisfied with their circumstances.

Under missionary Ernest Gribble, the Anglican Church ran the Yarrabah Mission in north Queensland, which was viewed favourably by the government. Consequently, the management of the Bogimbah Reserve was transferred from Meston and his son to the Anglican Church in February 1900, and it was renamed the Bogimbah Mission.

When Gribble first visited Bogimbah, he also raised concerns about the cruel treatment of the Aborigines. Meston, however, argued that the missionaries would be unable to control the behaviour of the Aborigines under their care.

Nonetheless, the change in discipline did not lead to a sharp decline in the circumstances of the Aborigines.

A tragic legacy

The mission's population grew to 180, while the supply of rations remained unchanged. Under Meston, the Aborigines were actively involved in hunting and fishing, supplemented by a minimal supply of rations, including tea, flour, tobacco, sugar, and soap. However, under Gribble's regime, greater emphasis was placed on religious instruction and educating children. The Aborigines were limited to just one day for hunting and fishing as a recreational activity, turning it from a necessary dietary requirement to a pastime. Gribble greatly relied on maize meal as a staple food, along with small amounts of flour, sugar, and tea.

The welfare of the Aborigines declined dramatically. The introduction of clothing and exposure to diseases – mainly hookworm infestation, influenza, and tuberculosis – increased. Their diet was high in sugar and starch, and the lack of discipline led to increased alcohol consumption and opium use. In July and August 1901, 29 Aborigines died out of 150. In contrast to Meston's regime, the relaxation of discipline meant as many as 26 could escape the mission.

The ingestion of white clay was a symptom of the malaise

faced by the Aborigines and contributed to their tragic demise.[28] It became quite clear that the mission would not be the success the Anglican Board of Missions had anticipated after taking over. It eventually closed in late 1904. The surviving Aborigines were forcibly relocated to the Yarrabah Mission near Cairns, the Durundur Mission near Woodford and Barambah[29] near Murgon. This decline marked a sorrowful chapter in the island's history.

From an estimated population of over 2,000 healthy, once mighty and proud Fraser Island Aborigines, only about 20 individuals from three families remained 50 years later. These individuals and their descendants became forestry workers to support their families.

---

[28] People suffering from hook worm infestation, or ancylostomiasis, develop insatiable cravings to eat clay, ashes, even charcoal, to replace the missing elements in their diet.
[29] Now called Cherbourg.

4

THE ELIZA FRASER SAGA

Since it pleased the Father of Mercies to deliver me from the hands of barbarians, and to restore me to the arms of my surviving friends, I have been strongly urged by some of them, to furnish for the press, a Narrative of my Capture, Sufferings, and Miraculous Escape from Bondage; together with other remarkable events, that have attended me since the fatal period of my unfortunate shipwreck; a request which I now attempt to comply with, with no small degree of reluctance, through fear that more may be expected from me, than what I shall be able to perform; having never received but an indifferent education, and having been by the hands of unmerciful savages deprived of my husband, and thereby of that aid that would have been of essential service to me in this my undertaking, I cannot therefore but flatter myself that for reasons mentioned, my readers will expect no more from me, than a plain, unvarnished tale; exaggerating nothing, but recording truly and faithfully the particulars of such events as most deeply impress my mind at the present moment, and which are esteemed by me the most worthy of record.[1]

The shipwreck of the *Stirling Castle* and the trials and tribulations faced by its surviving crew undoubtedly form Fraser Island's most infamous story following European settlement. What captured the world's attention was the ordeal of the captain's wife, Eliza Fraser – her detainment and treatment at the hands of "primitive natives" and her alleged witnessing of her husband's fatal stabbing. The story climaxed with a dramatic rescue involving convicts who had lived among the local Aborigines.

Despite being deeply embedded in Australian folklore, the

---

[1] Fraser, E. (1837) *Narrative of the capture, sufferings, and miraculous escape of Mrs Eliza Fraser*. Charles S Webb, New York, p. 5.

story has become highly contentious, especially concerning its supposed but unproven effect on the fate of the island's original inhabitants.

The only formal accounts of events are found in a limited number of primary sources: the testimonies of five survivors – Eliza Fraser,[2] John Baxter,[3] Harry Youlden,[4] Robert Darge[5] and Robert Hodge[6] – along with reports from the convict rescuer John Graham,[7] Lieutenant Charles Otter,[8] and Captain Foster Fyans.[9] My research has relied heavily on the exhaustive analysis of these sources by Barry Dwyer and Neil Buchanan[10] and Michael Alexander.[11] Unfortunately, the lack of any recorded accounts from the Aboriginal individuals involved has made it difficult to establish an accurate version of events.

Eliza Fraser's differing accounts have only added to the uncertainty, with many believing she embellished her story to profit

---

[2] Fraser, E. (1836) *Mrs Fraser's Narrative*. Archives Office New South Wales SZ976, COD 183. Appears as Appendix 7 in Dwyer, B. & Buchanan, N. (1986) *The rescue of Eliza Fraser*. Cooroora Historical Society, Gympie, pp. 35-6. This is the first written account of Eliza's version told to the Moreton Bay Penal Settlement clerk on 6 September 1836.

[3] Baxter, J. (undated) *John Baxter's report for the Colonial Secretary*. It is reproduced as Appendix 6 in Dwyer, B. & Buchanan, N. (1986). Op. cit., pp. 33-34. Also, *Evidence to Lord Mayor Inquiry*, published in Curtis, J. (1838) *Shipwreck of the Stirling Castle*. George Virtue, London.

[4] Youlden, H. (1853) Shipwreck in Australia. *The Knickerbocker,* 41(4):291-300.

[5] Darge, R. (1837) *Evidence to London inquiry*. Appears as Chapter 14 in Alexander, M. (1971) *Mrs Fraser on the Fatal Shore*. Simon and Schuster, New York, pp. 142-8.

[6] "Shipping Intelligence", *Sydney Gazette*, 13 September, p. 2 (Trove). Accessed 24 February 2024.

[7] Graham, J. (1836) *Report to Commandant Captain Foster Fyans*, 6 September. Archives Office New South Wales 4/2325.4. It is reproduced as Appendix 5 in Dwyer, B. & Buchanan, N. (1986) Op. cit., pp. 28-32.

[8] Otter, C, (1836) *Report to Commandant Captain Foster Fyans, 27 August*. Archives Office New South Wales SZ976, COD 183. It is reproduced as Appendix 4 in Dwyer, B. & Buchanan, N. (1986) Op. cit., pp. 26-27.

[9] Fyans, F. (1836) *Letter to Colonial Secretary, Sydney* (accompanied with Lt Otter's report), 6 September. Archives Office New South Wales SZ976, COD 183. It is reproduced as Appendix 8 in Dwyer, B. & Buchanan, N. (1986) Op. cit. p. 37.

[10] Dwyer, B. & Buchanan, N. (1986) Op. cit.

[11] Alexander, M. (1971) Op. cit.

from the ordeal. Notably, all survivor testimonies – except that of an embittered Youlden – were published immediately after the event. In contrast, Youlden's account emerged 17 years later and has been heavily relied upon by Eliza's critics.

News of the shipwreck and its aftermath first reached the public through newspaper reports based on survivors' statements upon their return to Moreton Bay and Sydney. A charitable fund was quickly established for Eliza, however, she was understandably reluctant to recount her traumatic experiences in detail.

Two books were published soon after Eliza returned to England: a brief compilation of events written by Eliza in 1837 and a more authoritative account by John Curtis,[12] a London court reporter who covered the Lord Mayor's inquiry into her captivity. While often described as Eliza's biographer, Curtis' book draws not only on her testimony but also on the accounts of Baxter and Darge.

Contemporary analyses of Eliza's differing accounts have been widely criticised as exaggerated, unreliable and racist. However, it's easy for these critics to judge from afar – none of them had to endure what she went through.

The wreck of the *Stirling Castle*

In October 1835, the 350-ton brig *Stirling Castle* departed London under the command of Captain James Fraser. Fraser suffered from severe chronic stomach ulcers, faced poor health, and his wife Eliza believed her presence and care could alleviate his condition. Leaving their children in the care of a local minister in Scotland, a pregnant Eliza joined the journey at the last moment, embarking on what would become an ill-fated expedition.

The ship faced numerous challenges on the way to Sydney, burdened by an unhappy crew and an ailing captain. The crew resented Eliza's authoritative attitude, viewing them more as servants than sailors. It was no surprise that most of them absconded upon

---

[12] Fraser, E. (1837) Op. cit.; Curtis, J. (1838) Op. cit.

arrival in Sydney, choosing to forfeit their pay rather than endure a return voyage under Eliza's de facto command. This discontent foreshadowed the troubles that lay ahead.

Captain Fraser was left with First Mate Charles Brown, Second Mate Baxter, Boatswain Edward Stone, Carpenter Jacob Schofield,[13] his wife, and nephew John Fraser. He needed to recruit a new crew before departing Sydney on 15 May 1836, bound for Singapore to load cargo for the return voyage home.

With his ulcers inflamed, Captain Fraser was short-tempered and abusive to his crew, eventually relinquishing command to his two officers, Brown and Baxter. However, no sooner had the boat left Sydney Heads than discontent among the crew began to surface. Eliza continued her demands for service from the sailors.

Portrait sketch of Eliza Fraser. (State Library of Queensland)

Even though Fraser was determined to give the notorious Great Barrier Reef a wide berth, a fatal miscalculation in navigation by

---

[13] According to Alexander (1971) Op. cit. p. 24, Schofield joined the crew at Sydney along with the other sailors.

his officers led the ship directly into the dangerous reefs. On the night of 21 May, the *Stirling Castle* struck a reef in the Swain Reefs at the southern end of the Great Barrier Reef. The ship was severely damaged, and the crew frantically worked to keep it afloat. The next day, realising the ship could not be saved, they prepared to abandon her using the longboat and pinnace, both of which were hastily repaired and loaded with limited supplies.

A poorly disciplined and disgruntled crew, lacking clear directions from the captain, only made things worse. When Fraser ordered the provisioning of the rescue boats after deciding to abandon ship, Youlden and Darge refused to go below for water casks and barrels of salted beef and pork. Instead, the others hurriedly loaded bread, salted beef, some pork, three gallons of brandy, and an 18-gallon cask of beer from the harness casks on the deck.

It wasn't until 4 pm that they were ready to launch the two boats. Since the *Stirling Castle* listed towards the sea, they had to lift the boats over the raised upper rail into the calm waters inside the reef.

Survival at sea

The survivors faced immediate hardships once they were at sea. The longboat, carrying Captain Fraser, Eliza, and several crew members, began to take on water, requiring constant bailing to stay afloat, but thirst and exhaustion soon weakened them.

Captain Fraser experienced severe pain from his ulcers, and Eliza, who was eight months pregnant, took over most of the bailing work for her husband. She endured considerable physical strain and collapsed into the scuppers, resulting in the baby being born underwater and drowning shortly after birth.

The boats drifted for days, battling rough seas and dwindling supplies. On one occasion, they arrived at a small island where they found fresh water.[14] However, the respite was short-lived as the crew's morale deteriorated, leading to conflicts over the little resources they had.

---

[14] Believed to be Lady Musgrave Island.

On the island, Eliza clambered over some rocks to a seeping fissure that soaked her gown. She then squeezed her gown to collect water into a bottle for her ailing husband, only to have it snatched and drained by Youlden, who claimed the captain wasn't the only one worthy of water. She scolded him, and Youlden replied:

> Damn you, you she captain, if you say much more, I'll drown you![15]

After reaching another island and carrying out repairs with makeshift materials, the decision was eventually made to head for Moreton Bay, but the journey was fraught with challenges. The longboat and pinnace separated, with the latter – a faster and better-designed boat – commanded by Stone. The groups hoped to reunite later, but they did not.

Landing on Fraser Island

The longboat carrying Eliza, Captain Fraser, and the remaining crew crept along the coast by oars, lacking food and water. The crew wanted to land ashore after seeing smoke along the coastline, but Captain Fraser refused. He was obsessed with the fear of being confronted by "cannibals". However, after Youlden, Darge, and other sailors got drunk on brandy and ale, they threatened to throw Fraser overboard. Facing a mutiny, he finally relented and allowed them to row ashore.

The longboat eventually reached the shores of Fraser Island, just north of Waddy Point, watched by a group of Aborigines above the dune. Overcoming their fear of these apparitions from the sea, they approached, casting a piece of kangaroo meat between them. Exhausted, hungry and desperate, the crew grabbed the food, believing it was a charitable gift. For the Aborigines, it was a typical barter ritual expecting payment in return. They approached the Europeans, removing items of their clothing.

A few days later, a larger group of Aborigines approached the shipwreck party. Items of clothing rescued from Eliza's trunk,

---

[15] Fraser, E (1836) Op. cit., p. 35.

valued more than food and water, were traded for fish. This exchange continued until the sailors had no more currency left to trade freely.

Meanwhile, Captain Fraser, Brown and Baxter repaired the longboat – the sailors refused to help – and Fraser waited for the prevailing south-easterly winds to subside before they could launch again.

The physically stronger crew members, led by Youlden and Darge as the ringleaders, were hostile toward the Frasers. They were frustrated by the lack of action and emboldened by the last of the brandy. Not knowing they were on an island, they decided to walk down the eastern beach towards Moreton Bay and refused to help launch the longboat. Following their initial interaction with the Aborigines, they felt assured of a safe passage. This choice signified the start of a harrowing period of captivity for those who remained.

Captain Fraser decided to launch his boat after facing harassment from the Aborigines, who were likely emboldened by seeing the remaining smaller group. However, they could not go ahead; the boards had dried and warped, rendering their boat unseaworthy.

Captivity and harsh treatment

Interactions with the Aborigines quickly turned hostile. The following night, the remaining crew began walking south along the eastern beach, setting their longboat ablaze. They moved slowly as Captain Fraser struggled. In the morning, the Aborigines surrounded them. At first, the encounter was cordial, with the Aborigines showing them how to find fresh water after Baxter indicated they were thirsty. Soon after, the Aborigines were eager for a return of their generosity. Baxter was beaten to surrender his uniform coat, and all were stripped naked. Eliza tried to maintain her modesty by wrapping entwined vines around her loins as best she could.

After that encounter, the group managed to walk along the beach without harassment for two nights, but they were then accosted by another clan of Aborigines near Yidney Rocks. All except Eliza were compelled to follow them to their camp behind the foredune.

They were forced to gather food and firewood, tasks typically assigned to women. The Aborigines punished them for their slow work by prodding them with a firestick or the point of a spear.

Eliza was taken to a camp by a group of women the next morning. Her account describes unfriendly treatment, including being made to act as a wet nurse, fed scraps such as entrails, fish heads and bones at mealtimes, which the children or dingoes invariably took before her. She was often punished with firebrands to expedite her work and taunted mercilessly.

When Eliza saw her husband again, he was severely emaciated after being forced to haul logs for the fires ever since his capture. He pleaded with her for help, but she couldn't assist him as she was exhausted from her experiences. Eliza also claimed that an Aborigine had forcefully prodded her husband in the back with a spear in her presence. Baxter wrote that Eliza told him:

> He [Captain Fraser] was speared in the back of the shoulder, which had been inflicted upon him for not making any progress with the wood. Mrs F. remained with her husband until sundown, when he expired of his wounds, his last words were, 'Eliza, I'm gone!'[16]

The Aborigines quickly removed the body and buried it in a shallow grave.

---

[16] Loss of Stirling Castle, *The Australian*, 18 October 1836, p. 2. Based on memorandum from Second Mate John Baxter (Trove). Accessed 9 February 2024.

Artwork depicting the spearing of Captain Fraser. (State Library of Queensland)

Eliza's account of this event is one of the most controversial aspects of her story, and other survivors have provided differing versions.

In Eliza's first and most direct account, the remaining men, including Brown and seaman Michael Denny, also endured severe hardships. She believed these hardships arose from their rebellion against the treatment of their captain and their inability to carry wood due to weakness. Brown suffered burns on his legs and back after the Aborigines allegedly rubbed them with firebrands and he died an agonising death. While deeply troubling, these accounts are crucial for understanding the full extent of their ordeal.

Meanwhile, Youlden reported that shortly after starting their walk, Aborigines stopped them and forced them to surrender all their possessions, receiving nothing in return. Later, they encountered another clan and went to their camp to seek food, but all they got was water, and their blankets were taken. The Aborigines pelted them with stones as they departed. In another incident, an Aborigine eagerly wanted to acquire the quadrant one of the men carried and struck him hard in the face with a heavy club. As the bedraggled group continued towards Hook Point, they suffered from the weather, exposure, harassment from the Aborigines and a lack of food:

> We staid [sic] here some days, and were joined by the longboat party, who had experienced no better treatment than ourselves from the savages.[17]

Eliza, Baxter and sailors William Elliot and Michael Doyle were the only survivors left on the eastern beach after Youlden's group departed. They, along with Youlden's group, were separated into different Aboriginal groups. They crossed the Great Sandy Strait to Inskip Point in canoes at different times. Elliot and Doyle attempted to escape by swimming across the strait but drowned. Baxter remained on the island, too weak to travel. He was compelled to help with the fishing nets and missed out on the feasts, rarely getting more than a fish head to eat. He recounted speaking to another "wild white man" named Tallboy, who was later identified by Darge as Banks, having lived with the Aborigines for six years; initially as a slave and then accepted by the tribe.

On the mainland, Youlden's group of five men was taken south along the Noosa River as far as Lake Cooroibah, where Dayman and Carey stayed. Youlden, Darge, and ship steward Joseph Corralis were taken to the mouth of the Noosa River, where they managed to escape along the beach. They encountered another tribe of Aborigines, not associated with those from Fraser Island.

Corralis convinced them that the white ghosts would reward them with iron if they took them to Moreton Bay. The Aborigines led them across Pumicestone Passage to Bribie Island. Exhausted, Youlden was left behind to rest his torn feet at an Aboriginal camp while the other two starving sailors continued.

The rescue

Meanwhile, Lieutenant Otter and his friends hunted on Bribie Island while on leave. On 8 August 1836, Darge and Corralis encountered Otter. Shocked by their condition and hearing their story, Otter sent

---

[17] Youlden, H. (1853) Op. cit., p. 296.

a small group of men accompanied by an Aboriginal guide to locate and rescue Youlden.

At Moreton Bay, Corralis was very forthcoming about the fate of a white woman held by Aborigines. Not surprisingly, neither Youlden nor Darge were reticent, both seemingly wishing the Fraser party ill. However, Corralis was helpful and urged the commandant to send out a search party. The Commandant, Captain Foster Fyans, ordered Otter to lead the men in rescuing Eliza and other survivors. Otter quickly assembled a rescue party comprising only three soldiers and 14 volunteer convicts.

One of the first volunteers was convict John Graham. He had escaped from Moreton Bay Penal Settlement and spent six years living with the Aborigines, learning to speak their language and becoming familiar with the territory. He returned to Moreton Bay after the death of his Aboriginal wife, seeking freedom and believing his sentence had expired. The success of the expedition relied solely on his local knowledge.

By coincidence, around the same time that Youlden, Darge, and Corralis arrived at Moreton Bay to share news of their ordeal, Graham heard from local Aborigines about the arrival of "ghosts", including a "she-ghost".

The rescue party departed on 11 August 1836 in two whaleboats, almost three months after the shipwreck of the *Stirling Castle*.

Graham travelled overland alone and discovered that Eliza was with a group of Aborigines heading south to meet with another tribe, 35 miles away, and he knew where to find her.[18]

At Double Island Point, Graham rejoined the rest of the party and told Otter about the predicament Eliza was in:

> ... but what was his disappointment and apprehension of horror for that suffering female when I gave him a description of where and how she was carried to be the

---

[18] Otter, C. (1836) *Report to Commandant Captain Foster Fyans*, 27 August. Archives Office New South Wales SZ976, COD 183. It is reproduced as Appendix 4 in Dwyer, B. & Buchanan, N. (1986) Op. cit., pp. 26-7.

shew and mock of wild savages upwards of 40 miles from where we were.[19]

Graham first rescued Baxter at Hook Point, where he was near death from starvation. Graham nursed him all night by the fire with food. The next morning, he convinced the Aborigines to help take Baxter to the whaleboats waiting at Double Island Point, promising rewards like tomahawks, bread, potatoes and honey.

Graham then walked south from Double Island Point along Teewah Beach to look for Eliza near their favourite camping spots on the Cooloola Sand Mass.

He left the beach where the high dunes of coloured sands end to travel to Lake Cootharaba, leaving a message for Otter's group, who set off down the beach the next morning to wait for Graham. It was here that Eliza was a prime exhibit at a large corroboree – for some, it was the first time they had seen a white woman.

Graham reached the lake and waded to the northern end at Fig Tree Point, where he found Eliza in a guarded hut. Aborigines with spears blocked his way to the hut. He had to rely on his relatives among the Aborigines, who helped him trick the guards and rescue Eliza.

Illustration of Eliza Fraser being rescued from her captives.
(State Library of Queensland)

---

[19] Ibid., p. 29.

Otter's description of Eliza was included in his official report:

> Although only 38 years of age she looked like an old woman of 70, perfectly black and dreadfully crippled from the sufferings she had undergone.[20]

The rescue of Eliza Fraser and the other survivors involved significant risks and was marked by controversies, particularly regarding the roles of convicts Bracewell and Davis. Bracewell, who had previously lived among the Aborigines, apparently played a crucial role in negotiating Eliza's release. However, Eliza later accused him of rape, although these accusations remain disputed and undocumented in official reports.

Impact and legacy

The shipwreck of the *Stirling Castle,* the fate of the survivors, and the rescue of Eliza Fraser are integral parts of our history. This is supported by documents held in our national archives as well as books and reports published in newspapers. Of the 20 crew members who set sail from Sydney, only eight survived.

The entire saga has profoundly influenced Fraser Island's historical and cultural landscape. It brought international notoriety to the tranquil island and ultimately resulted in its renaming in honour of Captain James Fraser, despite the contentious circumstances surrounding his death. Eliza's varying accounts and the absence of Aboriginal perspectives complicate the narrative, resulting in numerous interpretations of what is true. Her earliest statement to Fyans remains the most genuine description of her time with the Aborigines.

Modern scholars continue to debate the implications of Eliza's story. Some argue that Eliza's stories support negative perceptions and treatment of Indigenous people. However, many have drawn these conclusions without verifying the historical context, often relying on records and interpretations while remaining in libraries.

---

[20] Quoted in Burger, A. (1986) *Fraser Island*. Self-published, p. 32.

The limited primary sources and varying accounts from survivors such as Youlden, Baxter, and Darge further complicate the historical context.

The story has been dramatised in various forms, ranging from literature to film, often highlighting the more sensational aspects of Eliza's captivity and rescue. While keeping the story alive, these dramatisations have also perpetuated myths and inaccuracies, complicating efforts to understand what truly occurred.

5

THE NEW ARRIVALS

Early European observations

Lieutenant James Cook's journal contains the earliest recorded European observations of Fraser Island. While sailing past in May 1770, he mistakenly thought the island was part of the mainland, naming it the Great Sandy Peninsula. As he charted the region, he documented landmarks such as Indian Head, Sandy Cape and Breaksea Spit, writing:

> This point I have named Sandy Cape on account of two large white patches of sand upon it.[1]
>
> This shoal I call Breaksea Spit, because we now had smooth water whereas upon the whole coast to the southward of it, we had always a high sea of swell from the south coast.[2]

Almost three decades later, Matthew Flinders navigated the same waters aboard the *Norfolk* in mid-1799. Unlike Cook, Flinders sailed further into Hervey Bay, mapping the western shores of what was still thought to be a peninsula. Sandbanks near Round Island hindered his voyage, but he successfully identified and named prominent features such as Arch Cliff, Sandy Point and North White Cliffs.

During a subsequent expedition aboard the *Investigator*, Flinders became the first European to set foot on the island, landing at Bool Creek, west of Sandy Cape, on 31 July 1802. He documented the first contact between Aborigines and Europeans on the island, and the event resonated profoundly with local Aboriginal groups, who later commemorated it through corroborees, embedding the meeting into their cultural storytelling.

---

[1] *Captain Cook's Journal.* Op. cit., p. 95.
[2] Ibid., p. 96.

Flinders speculated that "the head of Hervey's Bay might communicate with Wide Bay," suggesting that the Great Sandy Peninsula was indeed an island. However, he abandoned further exploration to meet up with his slower companion ship at Sandy Cape.

Flinders' instincts were confirmed nearly two decades later. In June 1822, Captain William Edwardson, sent from Sydney in the cutter *Snapper* to find a new site suitable for a penal settlement, discovered the Great Sandy Strait, proving that Cook and Flinders' peninsula was an island. Edwardson renamed it Great Sandy Island. Had he also discovered the Mary River, it might have become the site of a new penal settlement, which the New South Wales Governor was eager to establish. Ultimately, this could have resulted in the capital of Queensland being centred around Maryborough and the Wide Bay region.

1822 sketch of the passage from Wide Bay to Hervey's Bay rendering the Great Sandy Peninsula and island by William Edwardson. Scale half an inch to the mile.
(Queensland State Archives)

THE NEW ARRIVALS

Over the following decades, several runaway convicts and shipwreck survivors arrived on the island's shores, marking the beginning of colonisation in a region where it had already begun to the south at Moreton Bay.

By 1823, several runaway convicts, including John Graham, David Bracewell, James Davis, George Mitchell and John Fahy, roamed the Wide Bay area, living among and forming close bonds with Aboriginal groups, including those on Fraser Island.

Graham was fortunate to be accepted as the deceased husband of Mamba, an Aboriginal woman from a clan near Tewantin. Between 1827 and 1833, he primarily lived in the lower Noosa area. David Bracewell escaped from Moreton Bay multiple times and was recaptured almost as often. After one escape in 1831, he remained free until 1837, when he resided with Aborigines in the Cooloola Sands and Tin Can Bay area. He earned the nickname "Wandi", meaning "great talker". He eventually returned when Andrew Petrie and his party found him at Noosa Heads in 1842.

James Davis arrived in Moreton Bay in 1829 as a teenager. Soon after his arrival, he absconded and joined a tribe near the Mary River, where he lived for 14 years. His tribal name was "Durrumboi," and he underwent the bora initiation rites, bearing chest cicatrices as marks of his tribal status.[3] He married an Aboriginal woman and fathered a son before being "rescued" at Tiaro by the Petrie expedition in 1842.

The Petrie expedition

Andrew Petrie, the Superintendent of Government Works at Moreton Bay, played a crucial role in exploring and developing the region. Dispatched from Sydney in 1837, he oversaw the construction of new buildings due to the inadequacies of earlier efforts by junior military officers.

---

[3] The practice of cicatrisation among the Fraser Island Aborigines was common among the men and carried out as an initiation rite on young men at bora ring ceremonies. The open wound was filled with fat and powdered charcoal to keep it open. The stinging jumping ants were sometimes applied to raise the weal.

Petrie often explored the bush with companions. On many of his early trips, they would get lost in the bush, prompting him to develop his navigation skills to find his way back to "civilisation".

MR. ANDREW PETRIE.

Photographic print of Andrew Petrie. (State Library of Queensland)

He discovered the bunya pine in "bunya bunya country", recognising its value as both timber and an essential food source for Aboriginal tribes during their annual festivals. Concerned about potential hostility from Aborigines if white settlers harvested the trees, the government issued a ruling in April 1842 prohibiting the cutting down of bunya pines.

NEW SOUTH WALES
GOVERNMENT GAZETTE,
Published by Authority.

TUESDAY, APRIL 19, 1842.

Colonial Secretary's Office,
Sydney, 14th April, 1842.

HIS Excellency the Governor has been pleased to appoint ALEXANDER FULLERTON MOLLISON, of Melbourne, Esquire,

to be a Magistrate of the Territory and its Dependencies.

By His Excellency's Command,
E. DEAS THOMSON.

Colonial Secretary's Office,
Sydney, 18th April, 1842.

ONE HUNDRED POUNDS REWARD;

OR,

A FREE PARDON AND PASSAGE TO ENGLAND.

WHEREAS it has been represented to the Government, that on the night of the 23rd

Colonial Secretary's Office,
Sydney, 14th April, 1842.

IT having been represented to the GOVERNOR that a District exists to the Northward of Moreton Bay, in which a fruit-bearing Tree abounds, called Bunya, or Banya Bunya, and that the Aborigines from considerable distances resort at certain times of the year to this District for the purpose of eating the fruit of the said Tree: —His Excellency is pleased to direct that no Licenses be granted for the occupation of any Lands within the said District in which the Bunya or Banya Bunya Tree is found. And notice is hereby given, that the several Crown Commissioners in the New England and Moreton Bay Districts have been instructed to remove any person who may be in the unauthorised occupation of Land whereon the said Bunya or Banya Bunya Trees are to be found. His Excellency has also directed that no Licenses to cut Timber be granted within the said Districts.

By His Excellency's Command,
E. DEAS THOMSON.

Government Gazette notice about bunya pine.

With the closure of the Moreton Bay Penal Settlement in 1842 and the colony opening up for free settlement, Governor Gipps instructed Petrie to explore potential settlement areas and timber resources. This included the Maroochy River,[4] which flows into the sea north of Bribie Island, as well as the surrounding region for future free settlement and timber harvesting. He was also tasked with exploring an unmapped river rumoured to enter the Great Sandy Strait behind Fraser Island, seeking the main ranges where the bunya pine grows – a personal interest of Petrie's – and recovering the two escaped convicts, Bracewell and Davis.

Squatter Henry Russell was eager to find a grazing run in the promising northern lands after his brother established one in

---

[4] Then known as Morouchidor River.

the Darling Downs on the Condamine River. He joined Petrie's expedition along with former Royal Navy sailor William Joliffe. Petrie purchased a seven-oared mongrel whaleboat built by a prisoner, which he named the *Commandant's Gig*. Walter Wrottesley, a newcomer to Brisbane seeking adventure, also enlisted for the trip, accompanied by a crew of five convicts and two Aborigines from the Brisbane River who manned the oars.

The expedition left Brisbane on 4 May 1842 and sailed north. They could not enter the Maroochy River due to the dangerous bar at its entrance. Petrie wanted to investigate and report on a bunya pine forest. Instead, they continued north and arrived at what they believed was Hervey Bay, only to discover it was the Noosa River mouth. At Noosa Heads, they heard that the escaped convict Bracewell was "only a short way off," living with the local Aborigines. The next day, Petrie sent a letter with some Aborigines they had met by chance, urging him to return to Brisbane. Bracewell and an Aboriginal friend joined the expedition as guides two days later.

After crossing the treacherous Wide Bay Bar at the southern end of Fraser Island, the expedition entered the Great Sandy Strait. Petrie observed numerous shoals and inlets before landing on Fraser Island on 10 May.[5] From a vantage point atop a sand dune, he discovered the entrance to a river, which he named Wide Bay River.[6]

They reached the mouth of the river at sundown that day and set up camp on the northern side of River Heads. It was here that Petrie noted:

> ... a species of pine not known before. It is similar to the New Zealand Cowrie pine and bears a cone. It forms a valuable timber. The blacks make their nets of inner bark of this tree.[7]

---

[5] Relieving forester in the early 1940s, Jules Tardent, wrote they camped near Geewan Creek, south of Snout Point. However, that area is too far south to see the mouth of the Mary River.

[6] Later renamed Mary River.

[7] Petrie, A. (1842) Op. cit., p. 261.

He discovered the kauri pine, a valuable timber resource that grows on Fraser Island and became a key part of the island's early logging history.[8]

Following the expedition and reports from Petrie and Russell, pastoral settlement expanded in the Wide Bay region. Jolliffe wasted no time in leaving the Hunter River with livestock and established a run on the Mary River at Tiaro. Other settlers followed, relying on supplies from the port at Maryborough, and the region was proclaimed the Wide Bay Commissioner's District.

Settlement and the quarantine facility

The discovery of gold in Gympie in 1867 spurred a rush of immigrants seeking wealth. The port of Maryborough quickly became a bustling commercial centre, with ships from Europe making direct trips up the Mary River.

In 1872, Richard Sheridan, the Sub-Collector of Customs for the port of Wide Bay, wrote to the Colonial Secretary's office recommending a quarantine facility for Maryborough's port. He proposed using Duck Island in the Great Sandy Strait for this purpose. However, after an area at North White Cliffs was reserved for quarantine purposes in 1873, one larger weatherboard building, and three smaller ones were built the following year on the flat ridge on the northern side of North White Cliffs. This location was favoured because it provided smooth water anchorage and deep, protected shelter for ships.

The quarantine station was overseen by an elderly navy veteran, Mr. Watson, and his wife, who acted as matron. They enjoyed:

> … perhaps as enviable a lot as any being gifted with the natural taste for idleness need aspire to.[9]

Larger ships visiting the area could not navigate the Mary River

---

[8] See Chapter 6 for more details.
[9] The Sketcher – Jottings from Hervey Bay, *The Queenslander*, 17 August 1878, p. 621 (Trove). Accessed 8 April 2024.

while fully loaded. Instead, they would disembark their passengers at North White Cliffs, where immigrants were taken to the barracks at the quarantine station before being transported up the Mary River to Maryborough by local steamers. Although there was anticipation of a significant influx of immigrants following the first wave, it ultimately did not materialise.

Despite the activity linked to the Gympie goldfields, there is scant evidence that the site operated effectively as an immigration and quarantine station. Although immigrant shipping passed through the area, no records exist of arrivals or the number of people processed.

The station became the main housing for up to 12,073 South Pacific Islanders, known as "kanakas", who were indentured labourers brought in for sugar cane farming. The Quarantine Station closed in 1886, and by 1896, the abandoned houses had fallen into disrepair. Still, "well-to-do" visitors from Maryborough occasionally used these structures while on holiday, and there were ongoing requests for the government to repair them.

Overcoming the navigational challenges

As Maryborough became a crucial port and trading centre, accessing the Mary River proved challenging. Ships had to navigate the treacherous Wide Bay Bar near Inskip Point or sail around the vast Breaksea Spit at the island's northern tip, which became notorious for its shipwrecks. Many vessels are recorded as lost in or around these waters.

Beacons and buoys were set up in the Great Sandy Strait south of the Mary River to assist vessels. However, markers for crossing the Wide Bay Bar were often obscured during inclement weather. There were repeated appeals to establish a lighthouse at Inskip Point and to connect it to Maryborough with a telegraph service, but these requests were consistently denied.

In 1866, two substantial fixed lights were established on Woody

Island to serve as long-distance leads, guiding ships approaching the Great Sandy Strait channel from the north and to navigate the numerous sandbanks and shoals.

After the Queensland colony was established in 1859, there was a realisation of the necessity to build lighthouses in the most exposed and dangerous coastal areas for shipping. Lieutenant George Heath,[10] the newly appointed Portmaster and Marine Surveyor, was tasked with surveying the Queensland coast to identify the best locations for the highest-priority lighthouses.

His search, along with reports from two independent Select Committees and input from an engineer, determined that Bustard Head, located further north, and Fraser Island were the top priorities to meet the colony's immediate trade and commerce needs. Sandy Cape was identified as an ideal site for a lighthouse due to its position and elevation.

Sandy Cape was described as:

> ... the site from its position and elevation, the most eligible for erecting a lighthouse and from which a powerful dioptric light would command the danger.[11]

The danger was Breaksea Spit – a long, low-lying shoal extending nearly 25 miles north of the island to the edge of the continental shelf. This area is particularly hazardous, consisting of dead coral and sandbanks where the sea often breaks heavily.

Although Sandy Cape Lighthouse was originally intended to be Queensland's first and tallest lighthouse, delays in receiving materials from England delayed its completion.[12] The lighthouse was finally completed in 1870, two years after the Bustard Head Lighthouse was finished. Both lighthouses are notable for their

---

[10] He reached the rank of Commander before he was placed on the retired list of the Royal Navy in 1869.

[11] Thorburn, J. H. (1964) Major lighthouses of Queensland Part 1. *Queensland Heritage*, 1(1):18-29.

[12] Moreton Bay lighthouse was built first but when the colony was still part of New South Wales.

construction techniques, which utilised bolted prefabricated segments of cast iron shipped from England, marking a new era in lighthouse construction in Australia.

The lighthouse was designed by William Pole of Kitson and Company in England and built by the Maryborough firm J and J Rooney. It was originally powered by kerosene before being converted to electricity in the 1930s.

The lighthouse was constructed before cranes and heavy-duty vehicles existed. Consequently, materials for the lighthouse were shipped to Rooney Point (originally known as Panama Point) and transported by bullocks. They were moved piece by piece along the beach to a three-quarter-mile wooden tramway, which facilitated the transportation of materials up steep dunes nearly a thousand feet above sea level by horse-drawn trolleys.

Sandy Cape Lighthouse, 1907. (State Library of Queensland)

The accommodation was built for a head lightkeeper, three assistant lightkeepers, their families, and a schoolteacher. Besides residences, the site included a school attended by approximately 30 children. Apart from a few itinerant forestry camps, this small and isolated community represented the first permanent European settlement on the island.

In 1878, a staffed light and semaphore station was established at Hook Point, situated inside Wide Bay Bar at the southern end of the island. This station supplemented a similar one across the strait at Inskip Point. A cottage for the light attendant was constructed at the Hook Point site.

Two white leading lights were positioned at the top of North White Cliffs in conjunction with the Woody Island lighthouse. These lights provided safe passage between the Mary River mouth and access to the northern and southern reaches of the Great Sandy Strait. Initially established in 1880, the kerosene lights needed weekly refilling and servicing. In 1976, they were replaced with electric lights powered by solar-charged batteries, but they were removed in 1984 after port and starboard navigation buoys were installed.

A telegraph line was installed to connect the mainland via Woody Island, ensuring communication between the Sandy Cape lighthouse and the mainland. The first line ran from the Quarantine Station at North White Cliffs to Sandy Cape in 1884, and a telegraph office opened at the quarantine station a year later. Patrick Searey served as the resident line keeper stationed at Bogimbah Creek, responsible for regular line patrols on horseback. In 1890, local dugong fisher Johann Heinrich (Harry) Bellert replaced Searey.

However, the original telegraph line fell into disuse after the quarantine station closed. The cable consisted of seven copper wires enclosed in Gutta Percha, wrapped in galvanised wire, with an outer layer of tarred hemp. It didn't take long to deteriorate, and by the turn of the century, it had become so rotten that it could not be picked up without breaking.

In 1902, plans were made to lay a telegraph cable from Hervey Bay to connect with the Sandy Cape telegraph line. The government accepted a successful tender for an undersea cable that extended from Urangan to Woody Island, then along the entire length of the island to Jeffries Landing. From there, it was laid across the Great Sandy Strait to Bogimbah Creek. Between 800 and 1,000 iron poles were delivered to Fraser Island via a punt to replace the original timber poles for the overhead telegraph line. This new line carried a plain eight-gauge copper wire.

Once completed, Sandy Cape had a telephone service linked to Maryborough. In 1914, Bellert bought a T-Model Ford for his patrols, the first vehicle on the island. His family called the car "Leapin' Lena".

The telegraph line continued to operate until World War II. Unfortunately, little evidence of it remains.

Early agricultural ventures and the brumby legacy

In 1879, Walter Hill, the curator of the Brisbane Botanic Gardens, inspected Fraser Island and identified abundant herbage suitable for cattle grazing. He observed:

> There is a belt of country running inland on the eastern coast along an irregular line averaging about two miles deep, watered by numbers of small creeks which flow into the ocean; the herbage here is of exceedingly rich and nutritious character, and is the principal place available to the settlers for spelling their horses and cattle.[13]

George Dicken was already managing the land which Hill described as an ideal location for resting horses and cattle, in 1878. The Lands Department mapped this area as the Grouyeah Run, although it was locally known as the Fraser Island Run. It extended from present-day Dilli Village north past Lake Boemingen to Eurong. Dicken and his wife lived in a homestead nearby in Yarong,

---

[13] Hill, W. (1879) *Timber &c. On Frazer's Island*. A Report to the Legislative Assembly, 17 May. Government Printer, Brisbane, p. 3.

just north of the current settlement of Eurong. All the horses were grazed southwards towards First, Second, and Fourth Creeks. Near modern-day Eurong, buffalo grass and three coconut trees were planted.

Dicken, raised in India, soon partnered with Harry Aldridge to crossbreed Walers for gun carriages and remounts for the Indian Army. Aldridge, the son of Maryborough's first European settler, was a keen breeder of Arab horses, while Dicken specialised in breeding Suffolk Punches and Clydesdales. They began their partnership by barging 20 horses and 40 head of cattle to the island.

Portrait of Harry Aldridge. (State Library of Queensland)

In 1882, Aldridge expanded his interests on the island by leasing 25 square miles known as the Indian Head Run, which extended from above Akuna Creek to the present site of Orchid Beach township.

However, they couldn't keep the horses on the island for too long, because their hooves became too large and soft to handle the sandy conditions. Aldridge would transport the horses back to the mainland from Moon Point, swimming alongside his boat.

A few horses ran wild on the island. Shortly after leaving the island, one shipload of horses went down south of Sandy Cape. Some survived and swam back to roam freely. When Aldridge and Dicken gave up their runs, some horses and cattle escaped into the bush. In 1906, 12 horses owned by Mr W. Reid were taken off the island and sent to Gympie.

Retired policeman and expert tracker Tommy King ran approximately 60 horses and cattle on the island, which grazed on the Aboriginal Mission reserve at Bogimbah and Eurong. He acquired his herd of horses from Ronald Mitchell's breeding stock.[14]

Later, timber cutters used draught horses to pull logs, primarily along the early tramlines and drag scoops for road maintenance.

Aldridge and Dicken also kept many cattle on the island, but their enterprise was likely unsuccessful. Although the cattle fattened reasonably well, the birth rate remained low.

In mid-1902, reports of "abundant grass" in the north-west section of the island during the Federation Drought on the mainland prompted Edward Morgan, a squatter from Warwick, to inspect the island along with the former Surveyor-General McDowall before obtaining an occupation licence in the Bogimbah Creek area and near Eurong. Morgan sent around 10,000 sheep and 750 head of cattle to the island until the drought broke. Drover Joseph Brumby managed the herd. After the sheep were hand-shorn in October 1902, Searey transported 86 bales of wool from Eurong to Yankee Jack Creek for loading onto punts.

---

[14] Chapter 13 introduces Ronald Mitchell and his son.

By 1910, there were two grazing selections on the island. One comprised 1,637 acres under an Agricultural Homestead lease held by Lars Benson near Sandy Point.[15] The other was an unconditional selection granted to Isabella Henderson, wife of Sandy Cape lighthouse keeper Duncan, who continued horse breeding near Wathumba Creek.

Horses were employed for mustering cattle until the 1950s. The cattle were transported to and from the island by punt, mainly to the Yidney and Figtree Creek areas where cattle yards were situated.

The brumbies observed on the island up until 1992 were descendants of these early horse breeds. Estimates indicated their population peaked at over 2,000 in the early 1900s, but their numbers gradually declined due to natural causes, dingoes, and challenges posed by the sandy environment. The ingestion of sand while grazing shortened their life expectancy.

In the early 1970s, the Queensland Beach Protection Authority identified brumbies as the primary cause of foredune erosion and sought to eliminate them. However, due to a widespread public outcry, the plan was eventually abandoned. A culling and removal program in the early 1990s ultimately removed the brumbies from the island.

---

[15] Now known as Moon Point.

PART 2

UTILISING THE TIMBER

6

EARLY TIMBER EXPLOITATION

The first timber getters

Many attribute Fraser Island's timber exploitation to Petrie's 1842 visit and his glowing descriptions of its forests. His diaries, however, contain only a single notable reference to timber:

> ... the timber is a great deal superior [*to Moreton Island*], and also the soil; the cypress pine upon Frazer Island being quite splendid.[1]

That is it!

While Petrie's brief mention may have sparked some interest, the driving force behind timber exploitation was Queensland's post-1859 immigration boom. Scottish immigrant William Pettigrew, who operated Brisbane's first steam sawmill in 1852, discovered that the supply of logs around the Moreton Bay region was limited and struggled to meet the demand for sawn products.

Pettigrew saw an opportunity further north and persuaded Petrie's son, Tom, to join him in August 1862 to explore the area's timber potential.

Tom Petrie grew up among Aborigines in Moreton Bay. In later years, he relied on their knowledge of pathways and forests in southeastern Queensland and employed many Aboriginal people as timber getters. This made him an invaluable resource for Pettigrew's expedition. After taking a steamer to Maryborough with Pettigrew, Tom successfully enlisted the help of local Aborigines, who were willing to guide them to the locations of the large timber stands.

Pettigrew was impressed by the extensive stands of majestic kauri pines at Susan River, Tin Can Bay and Fraser Island. Consequently, he purchased land along the Mary River at Dundathu, on the

---
[1] Petrie, A. (1842) Op. cit., p. 266.

outskirts of Maryborough, for a new sawmill. He partnered with his foreman, William Sim, to establish Pettigrew and Sim, which began operations in late August 1863.

Softwoods were valued for their quality and ease of cutting. In late 1863, expert American axeman John "Yankee Jack" Pigott began logging kauri and white beech trees on Fraser Island to supply logs to the Dundathu sawmill. He had a crew of four men and established a camp at Tumbowah Creek, which was later renamed Yankee Jack Creek.

After felling trees, his team debarked the logs to prevent sand from dulling the saws and cut the logs into lengths using an axe. The men utilised the bark as a building material and, in later years, it was used on tracks to prevent vehicles from getting bogged down in the sand.

The logs were dragged through the bush using winches and then rolled down the banks into the creek. The creek was dammed, allowing the logs to float to its mouth with the tide. They were then manually manoeuvred into position with cant hooks and tied together into rafts. Utilising the tides, they floated across the Great Sandy Strait to the mouth of the Mary River, where tugs hauled them up the river to Dundathu.

A year later, tragedy struck. Pigott was murdered under mysterious circumstances. The reason for his death remains unknown, but speculation continues even today. He died a week after a cyclone struck Port Curtis further north, with gale-force winds battering the coast around Fraser Island. Both the American barque *Panama* and the brig *Fayaway* were wrecked on the northern part of the island. The latter ran aground on Breaksea Spit on 1 February, laden with a substantial load of sawn timber from the Dundathu sawmill. The former became stranded off Rooney's Point on 18 March.

Jack Barry provided an implausible account during the magisterial inquiry into Pigott's death. He claimed that both men left their camp on the island to travel to Maryborough for supplies. They spent the night at the southern head of the mouth of the Mary River. Somehow, they ended up much further north the next day, past Rooney Point, many miles away from the river:

> … started the next morning for Maryborough but mistook the way, and instead of coming up the river got blown away to the north end of Frazer's Island, where we landed about sundown … [2]

Despite the strong winds and rough waters from the recent cyclone, it's quite strange that both men ended up on the northern part of the island, far from their camp at the mouth of the Mary River.

Upon landing, an Aboriginal spear struck Pigott, while Barry was battered on the head with Pigott's rifle and left for dead.

Pigott was a large man with a flaming red beard, and some believe his death was retribution for how he treated Aboriginal women. Many colourful stories and rumours surrounded Pigott; he was said to have engaged in "blackbirding" or "gin jockeying", supposedly shot local Aborigines from his horse, and underpaid those who worked for him.[3] However, no primary source information confirms these claims, though it was reportedly common knowledge around Maryborough that Pigott harboured a dislike for the local Aborigines.

A more credible reason for why they veered so far off course is that Pigott was enticed by the prospect of plundering timber from the stricken ship, *Fayaway*.[4] A surviving sailor who reached

---

[2] Magisterial inquiry, *Maryborough Chronicle, Wide Bay and Burnett Advertiser*, 7 April 1864, p. 2 (Trove). Accessed 7 April 2024.

[3] Tales from the Dead, *The Sydney Morning Herald*, 1 October 2006. Accessed 6 April 2024. The article mistakenly assumes there were many logging operations in 1863 when, in fact, there was only Pigott's operation. This contemporary account of Pigott is typical of the current narrative, displaying an erroneous caricature of him, totally dependent on circumstantial evidence rather than fact. It is replete with modern attitudes and mindsets not relevant to what life was like 160 years ago.

[4] I thank Geoff McWilliam for sharing information about *Fayaway* and Pigott's interest.

Urangan reported that *Fayaway* was in sound condition, and news quickly spread about the valuable timber stranded on the Breaksea Spit.

Renowned for defying authorities and the law, Pigott found the temptation to stealthily procure valuable timber irresistible, particularly since the owners could easily reclaim their cargo by floating the pine out of *Fayaway's* hold when the weather permitted.

As Pigott and Barry rounded Rooney's Point, they were observed by the Chief Officer of *Panama*, who was sailing past in the distance. One of *Panama's* seamen testified:

> A blackfellow came to the wreck and told me that two white men had come on shore the evening before – had shewn fight to the blacks and that 'blackfellow have kill him'.[5]

The Chief Officer decided to send some crew members ashore to investigate. Upon their return, they reported that they had discovered Pigott's body. No mention was made of him being buried "headfirst with his feet sticking out", as some "historians" have claimed.[6]

Barry survived the attack and escaped along the western beach. Three days later, he met a friendly Aborigine named Jemmy, who sought help at North White Cliffs. Barry was then taken to a hospital in Maryborough.

The remainder of Pigott's logging crew, worried about their boss's delayed return, departed the island for Maryborough a few days later and did not come back. Consequently, logging activities on the island ceased.

Following the magisterial inquiry, the Lands Department considered banning logging on the island and designating it as an Aboriginal Reserve, but this never materialised.

---

[5] Magisterial inquiry, Op. cit.
[6] Queensland, *The Sydney Morning Herald*, 12 April 1864, p. 3 (Trove). Accessed 7 April 2024.

The Harbour Master and Police Magistrate, who distributed blankets, tobacco and other goods to the Aborigines, attempted to withhold their supplies until he could identify who had slain Pigott. This approach proved ineffective, and he was never able to identify the murderer or murderers.

The next wave of timber utilisation

The discovery of gold at Gympie later that decade sparked a rise in timber demand, and in 1868, logging resumed on the island.

Timber getters loading felled logs onto wagons pulled by bullocks c 1870.
(State Library of Queensland)

Pettigrew was well-equipped to confront the unique challenges of sourcing timber from the island. He understood the difficulties of transporting logs to his mill after establishing a fleet of steam tugs and barges to make the transport to the Dundathu sawmill profitable.

The first timber getters to venture onto the island after Pigott's murder were 17-year-old Patrick Searey, Harry Bristow and George Dempster. Bristow scorned the saw and only cut down his trees with an axe.

Man standing beside kauri tree, nd. (State Library of Queensland)

Searey, a former ferryman on the Brisbane River at Petrie Bight, attempted to float pine logs to the mouth of Woongoolbver Creek by damming the creek along its banks. Unfortunately, his plans failed because the open, porous sand absorbed the water and did not raise the water levels.

He used draught horses to haul the logs, but they proved uneconomical in the challenging conditions. Consequently, he brought bullocks to the island despite an official prohibition. He stood firm against bureaucratic opposition, agreeing to obtain a permit from Brisbane.

In 1879, an old steam-powered lighter named *Muriel Bell*

transported the bullocks to the island. It is believed to have been the last boat to use Waterspout Creek to fill its tanks.[7]

The bullocks were harnessed to jinkers, each loaded with a log, and pulled through the forest to loading areas at creeks on the island's western side. A team of bullocks could haul a load four to five miles daily, and on shorter trips, they could manage two loads per day.

Each bullock team comprised 12 to 18 bullocks linked in pairs by wooden yokes, connected to the log jinker with heavy chains. Bullocks were paired with others of similar size, strength, and temperament to create a more efficient working unit. The leaders were positioned at the front, while those at the back acted as polers, and those in between served as body bullocks.

Bullocks were cheaper than horses, and their maintenance costs were lower because they could thrive off the land. However, finding enough feed on the island posed a problem, making it too costly to hand-feed them. Therefore, the bullocks couldn't work every day. Two teams of bullocks worked on alternate days, with the resting team allowed to roam freely to graze; they typically headed straight to the eastern beach in search of food and water.

Searey and Bristow worked at Woongoolbver Scrub, near what would later become Central Station, while Dempster felled a magnificent stand of kauri trees in the Yidney Scrub. While the rainforest pockets and the surrounding hardwood forests supported scattered kauri trees, Searey told Walter Petrie in 1913:

> He extracted 300,000 super feet from the area of about five acres of scrub at and embracing the present area No. 5 Wungoolba *[Woongoolbver]*. The area is, comparatively speaking, low scrub, and Mr Searey stated that the kauri on it was not of great length but was a very even-sized stand of usually three-foot diameter trees.[8]

---

[7] Waterspout Creek is an inconspicuous creek that is not marked on modern or tourist maps. It is the first creek southwards of Buff Creek, south of Ungowa. A pipe ran from the creek to the sea, enabling small steamers to tie up in the deep water very close to shore and fill their tanks directly.

[8] Petrie, W. (1922) *A Note on "Dundathu" kauri* (Agathis robusta). Forestry Bulletin No. 4. Queensland Forest Service, p. 4.

Searey and Bristow moved to the magnificent stand of kauri in the Bowarrady Scrub further north, where hoop pine was also abundant. They also harvested white beech, although it was not as favourable as the two pine species for general building purposes. While it was ideal timber for boat decking and flooring due to its resistance to termites, it could not be "freshed", and they could not export it in log form.[9]

The cypress stands from Yankee Jack to Yidney Creeks, located on the western part of the island, were also mainly harvested for wharf piles; however, they were stunted compared to the mainland cypress trees.

The island featured large trees. A kauri pine at Yidney Scrub reached nearly 80 feet to the first limb, while another tree had a stump diameter of 10 feet 6 inches. A white beech had a stump diameter of 6½ feet, a tallowwood measured 7 feet 2 inches in diameter, and a satinay was 80 feet to the first limb with a stump diameter of 8 feet 3 inches.

These men had to be tough and independent. They built good relationships with the remaining Aborigines on the island, exchanging tea and flour for fish and crabs. They even organised friendly boxing matches with them. Searey's wife accompanied him, and it is common folklore that she never left the island for 15 years. She made do living in a simple hut constructed of hardwood frames and bark from cut logs for the roof and walls.

There is an extraordinary story about the spearing of newly arrived timber cutter John Cunningham in 1877. Cunningham and his colleague Jeremiah Shea were searching for a young Aboriginal worker of another timber getter, known as Jack Smart, who allegedly speared one of Cunningham's horses. They went to another timber cutter's camp near the young man's campsite. Early

---

[9] Freshing was used in early timber getting when chasing red cedar, mainly along creeks in very isolated areas. Felled trees were left on the ground until a flooding event arrived to float the logs closer to sawmills. Freshing wasn't practised on Fraser Island as red cedar didn't occur there. However, as mentioned earlier, creeks were dammed to carry logs to the creek mouth before bullocks arrived on the island.

EARLY TIMBER EXPLOITATION

the next morning, they raided the Aboriginal camp. Shea caught hold of the alleged perpetrator during the commotion, awakening the Aboriginal's wife. As a struggle ensued, she kept tripping Shea by repeatedly thrusting a yam stick between his legs. Her father, Toby, arrived soon after, armed with spears, and threw one at both men, piercing Cunningham's groin. After attempting to remove the spear, Cunningham cried out, "I am dead, Jerry, the niggers have speared me."[10]

Cunningham managed to fire his gun into the air, scattering the Aborigines into the surrounding bush, including young Jack, before collapsing into Shea's arms, who supported his head on his knee. Shea sent some Aborigines to report the incident at the logging camp. Cunningham's older brother, Charles, and James Tucker quickly arrived, and they took the critically injured man to Maryborough for treatment. He died three weeks later from an infection of the wound.[11]

A second sawmill after Pettigrew's was built in 1866 by Andrew Wilson, James Bartholomew and Robert Hart, who later formed Wilson Hart & Co. Fairlie & Sons was built in 1868, and Hyne and Son in 1882.

Searey was the first to cut hardwood timbers for the other sawmills in Maryborough. He used bullocks to haul the first logs onto ramp skids in the Bogimbah – Poyungan area, transporting large tallowwoods to the Urang Creek landing.

In September 1878, the local newspaper reported that 41 men were involved in removing timber from Fraser Island, accompanied by 12 women and 36 children. Approximately 40 Aboriginal workers also helped with the work. Supporting these timber activities were 112 horses and 270 working bullocks, essential for hauling the

---

[10] From the Courier, *Maryborough Chronicle, Wide Bay and Burnett Advertiser*, 16 October 1877, p. 2 (Trove). Accessed 9 April 2024.

[11] Toby was hunted by renowned policeman Constable King for weeks "from scrub to scrub". His wanderings took a toll on his powerful frame and he was a wreck of his former self. After camping at Sandy Cape lighthouse he was captured without offering any resistance and charged with wilful murder five months after Cunningham died.

felled timber. About 450,000 super feet of kauri and hoop pine were extracted monthly from the island.

In the late 1870s, the felling of the tall and attractively straight satinay trees,[12] along with nearby brush box trees in areas referred to as "scrub," began with high hopes. The satinay and brush box forests are widespread on the island's southern half, covering the high sand ridge country in a central belt, as far north as Lake Bowarrady. However, the logging of satinay and brush box didn't last long.

Satinay's cousin on the mainland, turpentine, had already been cut to produce thousands of sleepers for export to South Africa. However, it wasn't long before the sawmillers noticed that boards cut from satinay were prone to warping and shrinking easily. Similarly, they found brush box difficult to work with due to its density, interlocked grain, and the presence of silica. As a result, they considered both satinay and brush box to be useless timbers, which led the sawmillers to instruct the fallers to bypass these trees.[13]

Until 1886, large quantities of kauri pine were cut under special timber licences, but since then, the only timber harvested has mainly been hardwoods. The relatively scattered and limited distribution of kauri on the island did not support intensive logging for long. In other areas on the mainland in south-east Queensland, the Forestry Branch described native stands of kauri as "almost trees of the past" by 1912.

Timber contractors such as Bill Seelke, Tom Berthelsen (Snr), Peter Sorrensen, brothers George and John McLiver, and August and Henry Wilschefski[14] arrived in the early 20th century. In 1944, Seelke told forester Ron Whale that he was the first to cut

---

[12] Prior to the 1920s, satinay (*Syncarpia hillii*) was known as Fraser Island turpentine and then red satinay and now just satinay. It shares the genus with the mainland species known as turpentine (*Syncarpia glomulifera*). The leaves are aromatic and when crushed have a taste and smell reminiscent of turpentine, although others argue the smell is due to the odour of their resin.

[13] Chapter 11 provides more details about the fascinating rise of the satinay timber into a premier timber species and dispels some myths about its use.

[14] They were known as "the twins", and both were champion axemen. August had a creek named after him south of Figtree Creek.

tallowwood in 1902 in areas previously logged for kauri and white beech by Ronald Mitchell 20 years earlier, hauling the logs to the Urang Creek dump.

The problem faced by timber cutters and sawmillers was that hardwood logs didn't float, unlike pine logs. Flat-bottomed punts, propelled by large sweeps, were necessary to transport them to the mainland. Loading and unloading these logs was hard work, and the crews had to cross the Great Sandy Strait with the tide. They also needed to reach the landings at the creeks during high tide to get loaded during the next low tide, allowing them to depart at the subsequent high tide.

The first of the towing punts, the paddle steamer *Culgoa*, was pulled by a steam launch named *Dagmar*, owned by Captain Jack Blue. Edward "Ned" Armitage, with his small steamer *Geraldine*, and brothers Christie and Matthias Mathison in their wooden barge *Slave*, arrived a little later.[15]

---

[15] Chapter 12 provides more details about the logging barges and punts used to transport logs from Fraser Island to the sawmills in Maryborough.

7

CHASING FOREST CONSERVANCY

Unlike much of Queensland, Fraser Island's forests escaped the pressures of agricultural development that required permanent tree clearing. However, the sawmillers and timber-getters, who operated before professional forest management, mirrored the wasteful practices observed throughout the colony in the late 19th century.

Early settlers depended on the island's forests for crucial materials such as housing, mining supports, and railway sleepers. However, the unchecked exploitation of kauri and hoop pines demonstrated a resource-rich colony that was unaware of its limits.

Proposals for a definitive forestry policy were frequently outlined but ultimately ignored, as the government consistently failed to act. Although Parliament generally recognised that the colony's most valuable timbers were vanishing rapidly, decisions were always deferred to a later time.

Anyone could cut timber if they held a licence and paid a modest fee. This system was effective because timber cutting relied entirely on manual labour. However, licence holders typically felled only the best logs, resulting in significant waste from indiscriminate cutting and the destruction of younger trees that could have been potential future resources. At the same time, the government focused on supporting settlement and introduced legislation in 1860 and 1868 to encourage land purchases and clearing for agriculture, which further diminished the availability of timber.

Concerns about dwindling forest resources and logging practices were raised in the 1860s, coinciding with the arrival of timber cutters on Fraser Island. At that time, the only measure for forest conservation was the establishment of timber reserves. Timber could be harvested from these reserves during their interim holding period before the lands were opened for selection and clearing. However, many of these reserves were revoked after fulfilling government timber supply requirements.

The forest and timber resources were under attack not only from pastoralists; the sawmiller's exploitation was both rapacious and wasteful. Few changes were made to forest management when this issue was highlighted, aside from a new regulation requiring that felled pine be removed from the forest within 12 months, which was later shortened to three months.

In 1864, the government introduced a new Special Licence for sawmillers, who argued that they needed to invest significant capital, conduct surveys, and cut tracks to access timber, yet lacked security of supply. The licence fee was £12 per square mile, granting holders exclusive rights to cut and remove timber within their designated area, typically near a dedicated sawmill. Wilson Hart held about seven miles under Special Licence on Fraser Island. However, the Land Commissioner stopped issuing further Special Licences on the island in 1874.

The Acclimatisation Society of Queensland was the first to officially raise concerns about indiscriminate logging with the government in 1870, yet their efforts yielded little success in prompting change:

> It was merely the first cry of a newborn child the awakening of a sense of public responsibility in this matter.[1]

Their calls for public accountability in tree clearing went unheeded until a Select Committee was established in 1875 to explore effective methods for preserving timber growth and conserving forests for "useful purposes".

The Chief Engineer of Roads, Fred Byerley, testified during the

---

[1] Thomas, A. H. (1931) Forestry in Queensland – Tragic history of apathy and ruthless sacrifice. *Telegraph Literary Staff*, pp. 3-4.

inquiry that he had recently recommended reserving Fraser Island because it supported timber resistant to "cobra".[2] He referred to a provision in the *Crown Lands Alienation Act of 1868* that allowed the government to reserve areas of preferred timbers for public works, such as bridges. Holders of timber licences could cut trees in these areas without permission. By 1875, approximately 50,000 acres of such reserves had been proclaimed. Byerley also mentioned tallowwood on the island, although it was often referred to as turpentine at that time, which added to the confusion.[3]

In April 1879, Walter Hill was asked to prepare a report on forestry and timber utilisation. This request followed his critical response to a questionnaire in 1874, where he expressed strong concerns about timber wastage due to poor logging practices and widespread ringbarking. As part of his responsibilities, Hill inspected Fraser Island. He was alarmed to find that the department had not implemented any regeneration efforts in the forests after kauri pines had been felled. However, he was impressed with the hardwood forests of blackbutt, tallowwood and satinay, believing they offered better prospects for a continuous supply than kauri pine.

Hill recommended immediate actions to conserve the state's valuable forests. He proposed separating forest management from the Department of Lands and placing it under the guidance of a qualified conservator. He also suggested reserving more land as state forests and implementing a timber export duty to prevent logs from being squared and sold for export rather than processed for domestic use.

The Officer Administering the Government issued a circular

---

[2] Cobra refers to the molluscan borer known as Teredo or shipworm. It is a bivalve mollusc that has a worm-like appearance and can destroy wooden-hulled ships or wooden harbour installations. In later years, satinay became a valuable pile timber when it was recognised as being resistant to marine borers.

[3] There is some confusion about the use of common names in the early days. Tallowwood was called turpentine, tee and even tea-tree. It was believed to be resistant to marine borers, as Maryborough sawmillers used it as piles for their loading wharves with the bark still on.

to Parliament, urging politicians to take action to ensure that the department replanted trees and minimised waste in the forest. They also provided examples of similar initiatives undertaken by other British colonies worldwide.

Meanwhile, timber reserves gradually expanded following advice from the department's limited survey staff. One notable area was the central commercial timber belt on Fraser Island, which was designated as a timber reserve in 1882. It stretched from Yankee Jack Creek in the south to Bogimbah Creek in the north.

At that time, little information was available about the ecology of Australia's unique forests and how to manage them for future generations. Most ideas about forest management stemmed from European experiences, which had been utilising their forests for over 400 years in a more simplified and organised manner. However, the methods for regenerating Australian trees after logging were largely unknown. Raising seedlings and planting them in cut-over areas was considered the best practice. On Fraser Island, the stands of kauri pine – the most sought-after tree in the rainforest scrubs – were nearly exhausted, raising concerns about the future timber supply.

In 1882, under the guidance of Maryborough's District Surveyor Archibald McDowall, Fraser Island was chosen for a trial to grow seedlings in nurseries and plant kauri pines in cleared scrub areas at minimal expense.[4]

By 1901, only a few commercial-sized pines remained on Fraser Island, after sawmillers had removed large quantities of kauri pine for nearly two decades in the 1860s and '70s. Consequently, the department stopped issuing timber licences for kauri pine on the island after 1883.

The issue of royalty payments was first raised in 1882. Two years later, the government introduced new regulations requiring payment of royalties on the Ordinary and Special Timber Licences: three pence per 100 super feet for hardwood and sixpence per 100

---

[4] More detailed information about this pioneering work is provided in Chapter 13.

super feet for pine. Unsurprisingly, the timber industry vigorously opposed this, claiming it would ruin their businesses as it directly affected their profits.

However, as the supply of native pines became increasingly scarce and demand surged, sawmillers found it difficult to argue for a policy that allowed them to extract as much timber as they wanted for a single pound in annual licence fees rather than paying for the amount they removed. Nonetheless, they managed to persuade the government to scrap the royalty fees just two years later.

In 1888, Maryborough sawmiller and parliamentarian Richard Hyne actively sought recognition of the dwindling supply of valuable timbers, mainly native pines. He advocated for a separate Forestry Department and the permanent declaration of timber reserves. He even voiced concerns about the rapid rate of timber cutting:

> Anyone engaged in the industry, as I am, cannot help noticing the rapid rate at which our timber forests are being cleared of marketable timber; pine, cedar, and ironbark especially. I look upon it with great alarm. I am not one of those who say there is plenty of timber for our time, and that the future can take care of itself.[5]

Although Hyne's appeals did not result in immediate change, the government assembled a group of experienced individuals to report on forest conservation and forestry management. Their recommendations aligned with Hyne's call for a separate department and staff, the reservation of valuable timbered lands, increased revenue from timber sales, and the establishment of nurseries and enrichment planting programs.

In the 1890s, each annual report advocated for a return to a royalty system despite the challenging economic conditions at the time. The timber regulations and licences were administered by the local Land Commissioner, who was primarily employed to address closer settlement issues rather than forestry matters.

---

[5] Queensland Parliamentary Papers LVIII 1889, pp. 1,444-5.

The government argued that the colony did not receive a fair return for the timber removed. In his 1894 report, Walter Hume, the Under Secretary for the Department of Lands, expressed this concern:

> ... the present system under which a party of men on payment of a few pounds licence fees are permitted to take possession of thousands of pounds worth of national property can only be described as faulty.[6]

In 1900, a separate Forestry Branch was finally established within the Department of Lands. Leonard Board was appointed as the first Inspector of Forests, assisted by two forest rangers: Gilbert Burnett in the south and Frederick Lade in the north. Both had previously worked as Crown land rangers. Burnett conducted several timber surveys on Fraser Island and the mainland, which resulted in a doubling of timber reserves by 1906, after which the department phased out the licence system.

By 1905, Board's workload was becoming increasingly difficult as he was also responsible for the Pastoral Occupation Branch. The previous curator of the Botanic Gardens, Philip Mac Mahon, was appointed as the new Director of Forests. He continued to face challenges in forest administration within the larger Lands Department, which had a singular focus on land settlement. Daily operations were governed by timber regulations established under the *Land Act 1902*, making forest management challenging due to a lack of coherent policy.

As the timber supply became a critical issue and the value of forests was recognised, calls increased to reserve high-quality forested land as state forests in perpetuity for ongoing forestry purposes. Mac Mahon summarised this sentiment in his first annual report:

> ... it would hardly seem too much to ask that at least half the forest revenue be earmarked for the purposes of forest demarcation, conservation and development.[7]

---

[6] Hume, W. C. (1894) *Annual Report of the Department of Public Lands for the Year 1894*. 22 April 1895, p. 2.

[7] *Report of Director of Forests* (1906) Appendix II, Department of Public Lands. Govt Printer, Brisbane, p. 52.

Although the government finally drafted forestry legislation in December 1906, known as the *State Forests and National Parks Act 1906*, it was fairly brief. It outlined the creation of state forests and national parks, the appointment of staff, and certain restrictions on the alienation of forested land and timber rights. Forestry administration still relied on the regulations of the *Land Act*, which remained in place until 1914, when the *Forestry Act* was finally gazetted.

Fraser Island was among the first to benefit from the 1906 Act when the central timber belt, stretching from Yankee Jack Creek north to the Bogimbah Aboriginal Reserve, was declared a state forest in 1908.[8] There was optimism that policies promoting sustainable and proper timber utilisation were finally being implemented, overseen by a ranger from the Forestry Branch rather than by the Land Commissioner.

Revisions to the *Land Act 1902* and Timber Regulations represented efforts to gain more control over the utilisation of forests on Crown land. However, the changes were minimal, as the nascent Forestry Branch was still part of the Lands Department, which focused on opening land for settlement. This meant that policies promoting land settlement and agriculture remained the main priority.

However, for Fraser Island, this was less of a concern, as the sandy hills offered few opportunities for closer settlement and farming. The island's majestic forests attracted the primary focus.

---

[8] Between 1908 and 1923, the commercial timber areas up to Lake Bowarrady were progressively declared state forest.

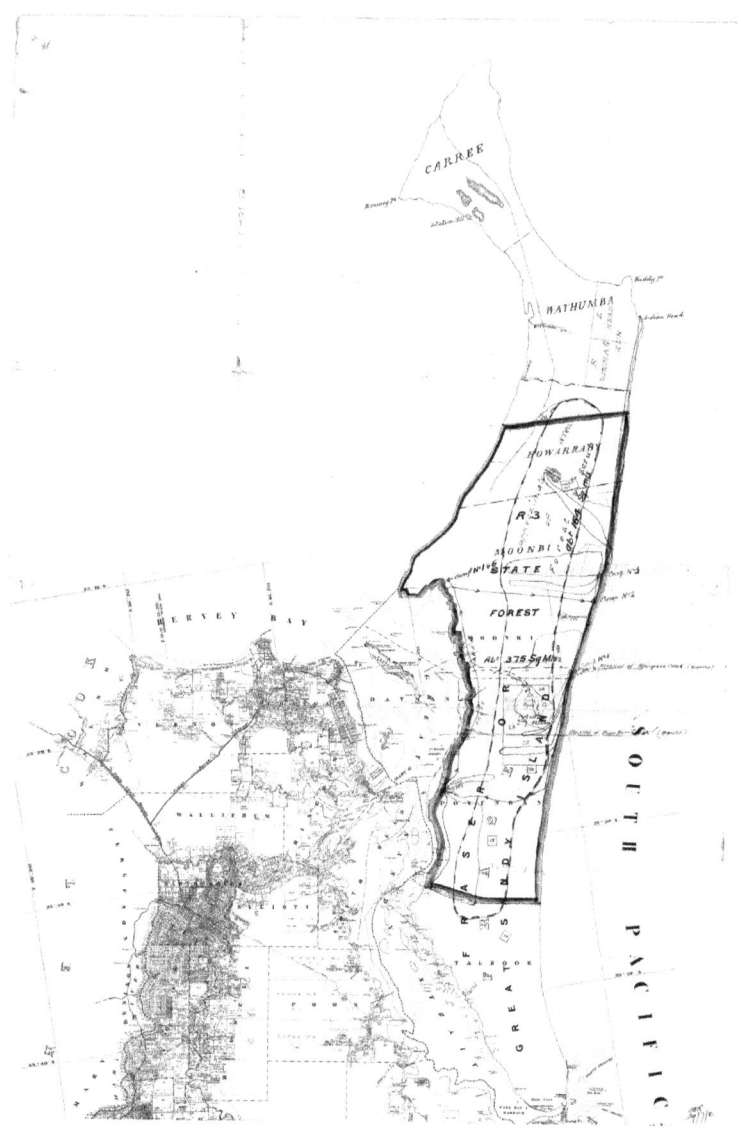

Map showing the full extent of R3 State Forest as of 1910.
(Queensland State Archives)

8

Some action taken:
Greater control of forestry operations

> ... an island which is merely a barren sand heap, except for the timber.[1]

The challenge of sand and distance

Fraser Island's vast stretches of sand posed significant challenges for timber cutters long before pneumatic tyres made the hauling easier. As timber stands became more distant from the landings on the west coast and the main sandy tracks, logging grew more labour-intensive. This work was demanding for bullock and horse teams, as they struggled to move logs over longer distances of shifting sands. Timber getters often used up to ten teams at a time, but the lack of suitable pasture made their work even harder and affected their ability to keep the livestock healthy for work.

Most areas had only a sparse cover of very coarse grass. While working bullocks had strong digestive capabilities that allowed them to stay healthy for about a year, their condition rapidly declined if they were not taken to mainland pastures for sustenance. They also ingested large amounts of sand while feeding, which ultimately led to many of them dying. By 1903, only two bullock teams remained operational on the island.

Wilson Hart, a key figure in the local timber industry, threatened to abandon logging on Fraser Island entirely. However, their ultimatum rang hollow, as sourcing timber on the mainland was just as tough due to large areas being cleared for agriculture.

Forest Ranger Gilbert Burnett discovered a magnificent stand

---
[1] Letter from Wilson Hart to Minister for Lands, 24 March 1905. LAN/AK23 Batch 36, QSA.

of tallowwood at the head of Bogimbah Creek, primarily located within the Bogimbah Aboriginal Reserve. However, the stand's location further inland from the island's western coast rendered conventional hauling methods impractical. A tramline was the only economically viable method to access the timber.

Battles over timber rights

At that time, Wilson Hart and Hyne & Son proposed an ambitious solution to the government: they requested a substantial block of hardwood to justify the capital investment needed for a tramline.

Negotiations over an appropriate block were intense and prolonged. The sawmillers lobbied for a reduced royalty of four pence per 100 super feet, citing the high costs of constructing a tramline up to seven miles from the coast. In contrast, the Lands Department pushed for six pence per 100 super feet.

Under the new policy of auctioning blocks to encourage competition and set a minimal reserve royalty rate, Wilson Hart and Hyne & Son requested that an area on the island be marked out in coordination with their overseers to assess a route and determine costs for the tramline.

In December 1904, Burnett delineated approximately 4,330 acres outside the Bogimbah Aboriginal Reserve, which featured fine stands of prime tallowwoods, blackbutt and a small quantity of kauri pine at the head of Urang and Poyungan Creeks, an area known as Poyungan Scrub. He estimated that the block contained three million super feet of timber. Burnett also recognised the presence of satinay, an "unknown timber", which he hoped would be similar to the mainland turpentine tree, commonly cut for sleepers, and, due to its straight boles and size, could be used for piles. However, as sawmillers did not favour satinay, he suggested that the auction only include "millable timber", acknowledging that satinay could be utilised later for sleepers and piles.

This block marked the first timber sale auction by the Forestry

Branch in the state and heralded a new era of timber operations on the island. It was based on conditions negotiated with Wilson Hart and Hyne & Son over the preceding year. Unsurprisingly, their joint application was successful, and the hardwoods were sold at an upset royalty rate of five pence per 100 super feet. They were required to construct five miles of tramline within 12 months and held the rights to the timber on the block for a minimum of five years.

A few months later, Edward Morgan, a squatter with an occupation permit to graze sheep and cattle on the island, sought exclusive rights to the island's timber, offering to establish steam-driven sawmills in exchange.

Morgan had previously inspected the island with McDowall in 1902 and argued that the current harvesting practices were wasteful because many undersized trees were being felled. However, the Inspector of Forests, Leonard Board, denied his request for exclusive rights and encouraged Morgan to bid for timber blocks at auction like everyone else.

Meanwhile, the new tramline constructed by Wilson Hart and Hyne & Son became a crucial lifeline for the timber industry in Maryborough.[2] George Gorlick was the first to snig logs on the tramline, initially with horses and later with bullocks. The logs were then transported to Urang Creek for loading onto punts.

As previously mentioned, finding suitable grazing areas was a significant challenge. Wilson Hart tried to allocate all appropriate grazing areas for their contracted bullock teams between Bogimbah and Moon Point, which had historically been used for grazing during drought periods on the mainland.

However, most of the feed supplies had to be transported by rail from the Darling Downs to Maryborough, shipped to the island, and then carted over eight miles along the tramline to the holding area.

---

[2] More information about this tramline is provided in Chapter 10.

Although they finalised access arrangements to a vast forest on the island with their tramway and newly acquired block, Wilson Hart and Hyne & Son needed timber more quickly than it could be supplied. They financed work teams under a bill of sale, allowing them to use bullocks regularly on alternate days after resting.

Twenty men were employed as timber cutters, including two who only cut firewood for the locomotive. Their living conditions were very primitive; they slept on logs with sheets of iron above them. The workers stayed on the island for four months before returning home to Maryborough. The first communication with the mainland was via smoke signal, and later by telegram once a line connected Sandy Cape lighthouse to the mainland. Initially, sailing boats served as the primary means of transport, but motorboats eventually replaced them. Consequently, the men could go home once a month, and later, every fortnight.

Southern exploiters and local defenders

After Wilson Hart and Hyne & Son settled in to build their tramline and began harvesting their newly auctioned block, tensions escalated when "southern exploiters" from outside Queensland tried to access timber to cut sleepers for international markets. This further complicated operations on the island, as these new players offered double the royalty rates and proposed building essential infrastructure, such as sawmills, tramways, and wharves. This provoked fierce opposition from Wilson Hart and Hyne & Son, who depended on Fraser Island's timber for their survival.

The southern exploiters faced their own issues. Philadelphia Hanley, a prominent merchant, successfully selected an area of approximately 14 square miles (8,960 acres) to the west and south of the Wilson Hart and Hyne & Son block, which featured significant quantities of blackbutt and satinay, as well as tallowwood. However, Burnett noted that the trees were old and "piped", making them only suitable for sleepers.

Hanley faced problems when the government insisted on charging for the total timber cut instead of just the sleepers produced. His plans faltered, and another southern merchant, J T Caldwell, encountered similar resistance. Representing the British firm McEuen & Co., Caldwell aimed to harvest 50 million super feet from a designated area of 24 square miles (15,360 acres), which included the former Hanley block. He planned to harvest at least 100,000 super feet each month, but claimed he could achieve 250,000.

Forestry rejected Caldwell's request for exclusive use and instead auctioned the area in March 1908 as two separate blocks (Blocks 24 and 25).

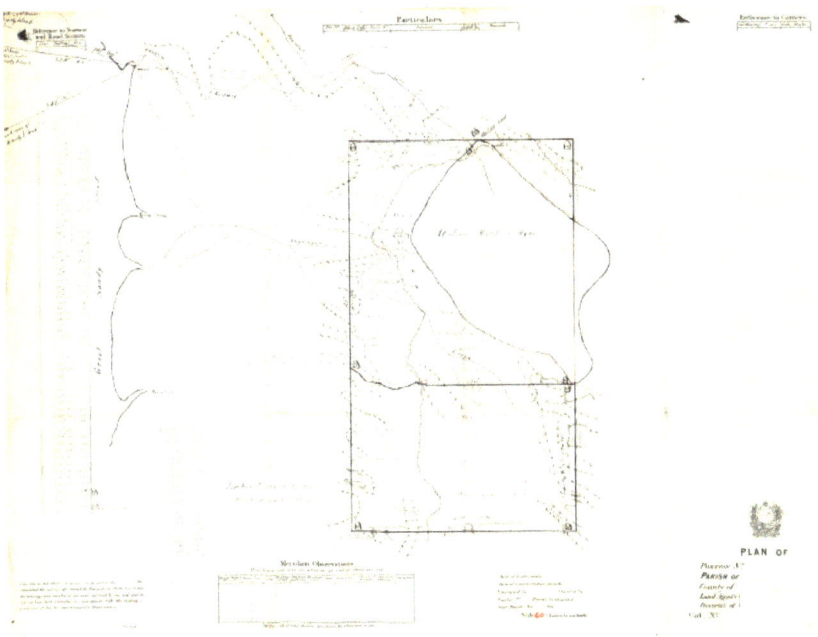

1908 plan showing the Wilson Hart-Hyne & Son logging area surrounded by Blocks 24 and 25. (Queensland State Archives)

The local sawmillers, led by Harry Hyne, lobbied fiercely to keep outsiders out, arguing for the protection of the local industry and sustainable harvesting practices. In a letter to the minister, Hyne claimed that all the timber was only suitable for sawmilling, was needed for the Maryborough sawmills, and should not be used for railway sleepers. His local parliamentary members, William Mitchell and John Adamson, met with the minister to outline their concerns and keep "outsiders" off the island to ensure it could remain a:

> ... happy hunting timber ground for themselves, their heirs, executors, and assigns for ever.[3]

While both Wilson Hart and Hyne & Son enjoyed the privilege of ignoring the excellent satinay and brush box trees, as they were not suitable for milling at the time, they wanted to save them from being used as sleepers, since they might prove suitable for milling in the future.

Caldwell complained that local sawmillers paid a lower royalty to access the finest timber on the island. The local sawmillers disagreed. Hyne, specifically referring to Hanley and Caldwell, told the minister, "If you get an adventurer, he may promise you anything."[4]

The debate unfolded publicly when Archibald Meston, representing Caldwell, exchanged letters with Mitchell and Adamson in the newapapers. Meston launched an extraordinary attack on them, which they dismissed as rhetorical grandstanding:

> One has a feeling of reverence for the dexterity with which the two Maryborough legislators promptly extricated themselves from the quicksands into which they walked when introducing that deputation, and their ingenuity in the construction of the aeroplane on which they suddenly soared from the earth-born advocacy of an unscrupulous timber monopoly to the Chimborazo summit of an assumed, pure, unsullied patriotism, which clasped its hands on the sunlit heights, and thanked goodness that it was not as other legislators and common mortals, but was concerned

---

[3] Fraser's Island Timbers, *Brisbane Courier*, 26 May 1908, p. 7 (Trove). Accessed 12 April 2024.

[4] A Timber Concession – Protest from Maryborough – Deputation to the Minister, *Brisbane Courier*, 4 April 1908. p. 10 (Trove). Accessed 12 April 2024.

entirely with Queensland obtaining the best possible price for her timber! ... They are opposed to the exportation of our timber to other countries because it is required for the State and the Commonwealth, and conclude by saying that their sole anxiety is for the State getting the best possible price! And yet they acted as innocent pilot fish, leading the Maryborough timber people to ask the Minister for Lands to give them the whole of the timber on 656 square miles of Fraser's Island at 5d. per hundred feet, when the Southern buyers were offering a shilling![5]

Caldwell accused Hyne of subtly manoeuvring behind the scenes. Hyne mentioned the John Callan Park Hospital in Sydney when a representative of McEuen & Co. wrote to him, saying they had heard about good timber on the island and inquired whether they could obtain any. He replied:

> There was none. Any person who respected timber knew so. Anyone thinking otherwise was a fit subject for the Callan Park Hospital as an imbecile.[6]

Hyne allegedly wrote this as his joint venture with Wilson Hart extracted 14 million super feet from one of the state's best stands of hardwood in an area of the island now known as the "Valley of the Giants". Seven years later, they opened another large block at the head of Woongoolbver Creek near Central Station to harvest another 18 million super feet. There was so much timber available that perhaps Harry was the one who should have been admitted to Callan Park!

Continued exploitation

Wilson Hart and Hyne & Son were also eager to access another block since the construction of their tramline proved much more

---

[5] Fraser's Island Timber, *Brisbane Courier*, 5 June 1908, p. 6 (Trove). Accessed 12 April 2024.
[6] This is a second-hand recollection found in a letter from Caldwell to the Minister of Lands dated 18 April 1908. ITM 25184, QSA. The Callan Park Hospital was an insane asylum from 1878-1914. It was the first purpose-built hospital for moral therapy treatment in Australia.

expensive than expected. They were looking for additional timber nearby to help reduce those costs, despite having already removed about four million super feet, primarily tallowwood, in the first two years. Mac Mahon, the newly appointed Director of Forests, visited Fraser Island to inspect the area and agreed to auction off the extra timber that Wilson Hart and Hyne & Son needed.

Local politicians advocated for using available timber supplies for local sawmillers in smaller quantities to align with their business profiles. They strongly supported the sawmillers, arguing that Fraser Island timbers should not be harvested for overseas export, particularly since reports suggested that 900,000 railway sleepers would be sent to India each year. They justified the lower royalty they paid for the timber while recognising that Queensland should receive the best price for its timber resources.

In 1907, timber cutters supplying various sawmills in the Maryborough district leased several small timber blocks of 640 acres without going to auction. According to the 1904 Timber and Quarry Regulations, local Land Commissioners had the authority to sell without competition when the total royalty payable was less than £10.

Logging on the island in 1908. (Department of Forestry)

The boundaries for these blocks were not marked on the ground. Peter Sorrensen leased a block east of Leading Hill, above the headwaters of Bun Bun Creek, and Sim & Co. leased the 80-acre Block 24a. Bristow was still cutting on the island in his seventies and, in 1904, moved into the former Bogimbah Mission superintendent's house with his wife after the mission closed.[7]

These small timber getters struggled to survive. They worked in remote areas with costly supplies and provisions, and the mills they supplied charged timber royalties on their accounts. Consequently, Forestry reduced the royalty on the small blocks to six pence per 100 super feet.

Because an area of 240,000 acres on Fraser Island was declared a state forest under the new *State Forests and National Parks Act 1906*, the timber regulations that governed the timber sales did not apply to state forests. This meant that Forestry could not issue licences until new regulations were enacted. After thoroughly surveying the resources, Mac Mahon used the opportunity to develop a new long-term plan. He emphasised that the timber resource on Fraser Island was immensely valuable and should be managed within a well-considered system rather than arbitrarily through applications made to Forestry.

The progress of this plan was delayed for over three months until Mac Mahon inspected the island. Meanwhile, three teamsters, dependent on logging on the island, had their applications for small new areas held up because of Mac Mahon's emphatic direction. They complained bitterly in the newspapers, which forced Mac Mahon to concede that Forestry could still offer month-to-month sales as a temporary solution.

By the end of 1909, nearing the conclusion of the original five-year term of the Wilson Hart and Hyne & Son timber sale, most of the easily accessible commercial timber had been removed, including 15 million super feet of predominantly tallowwood. The remaining

---

[7] This house is described in Chapter 3.

areas were situated in challenging locations that required hauling timber up steep inclines with wire ropes and other equipment. Although this was an expensive endeavour, the timber must have been valuable to pursue, as they sought a one-year extension to their permit. It was approved; however, the royalty increased to six pence per 100 super feet.

The following year, after slow progress in cutting and hauling the more difficult sections, they reapplied for a one-year extension, which was granted. However, the royalty was further increased to nine pence per 100 super feet in line with the upset price for recent auctions in the Maryborough district. They objected, and the minister agreed to lower the upset price to eight pence per 100 super feet.

Wilson Hart and Hyne & Son applied to harvest a block of blackbutt located immediately to the north and east, which could be accessed by a new tramline branch. Forestry granted them 12 months to remove an estimated 240,000 super feet of timber. However, after only 60,000 super feet had been removed, they needed to apply for an extension due to a consistent lack of grass throughout the year. The teamsters were forced to work their teams intermittently as the horses pulled the bogies along the tramway.

In July of the following year, Wilson Hart and Hyne & Son won the auction for the 3,000-acre adjoining block known as Quandong Scrub at the head of Urang Creek. This area predominantly consisted of blackbutt and was estimated to contain eight million super feet. Operations did not commence until 1913 when Burnett inspected the block and found that only 730 acres had merchantable timber. By the following year, after removing four million super feet, they were left with just a few more months of cutting.

Towards the end of that year, both sawmillers applied for their respective blocks, as did Sim & Co. and Dempster. Although these blocks were smaller, Forestry reverted to its policy of opening them to auction at a minimum price of nine pence per 100 super feet.

Locomotive deep in the forest on the Wilson Hart-Hyne & Son tramway from Urang Creek.
(Armitage family collection, courtesy Tess Patterson)

After Norman Jolly[8] inspected the island in June 1912, he argued that while hauling over sandhills is "of course difficult", he believed the challenges were overrated and that the royalty paid was too low. He asserted that the snig distance was not long and described the timber as being of the best quality, noting that felling one tree produced three sawlogs, compared to just one on the mainland.

Jolly asked Gilbert to prepare a report comparing the costs of delivering wood to sawmills from the forests on the island with those on the mainland. The report indicated that the cost difference

---
[8] Jolly replaced Mac Mahon as Director of Forests in 1911.

could be as high as one shilling and three pence per 100 super feet. Jolly acknowledged that there was:

> ... apparently no room for a higher royalty but I am inclined to think that the charge for haulage [on Fraser Island] is high.[9]

As the focus of timber operations was on the highest sandhills of the leading timber belt, which extended up to nine miles inland from the barge loading areas on the west coast's creek estuaries, it became clear how critical a tramline was for transporting the logs. Jolly believed that sales of small blocks to independent teamsters should only occur where it was not economical to lay a tramline. There were nine such blocks, with one each allocated to the Berthelsen,[10] the McLiver and the Wilschefski brothers, two to Wilson Hart, and another to Hyne and Son.

Table 1

Small Blocks allocated to various sawmillers and cutters

Sale No	Block No	Purchaser	Volume	Expire
857	43	August Wilschefski	150,000	13/3/14
858	44	Tom Berthelsen (Snr)	100,000	13/3/14
859	45	Albert Berthelsen	100,000	13/3/14
860	46	Henry Wilschefski	100,000	13/3/14
861	19	Hyne & Son	100,000	13/3/14
862	47	George McLiver	100,000	13/3/14
863	36	Wilson Hart	60,000	13/3/14
864	48	John McLiver	100,000	13/3/14
865	49	Wilson Hart	150,000	12/11/14

Only one other stand of tallowwood and blackbutt justified the construction of a tramline. It was in the southern part of the island at the head of Woongoolbver Creek, approximately six to nine miles inland. This area had previously been applied for successfully by

---

[9] Jolly, N. (1914) Report to Minister of Lands, 24 March. ITM 25184, QSA.
[10] The brothers were Christian Albert (known as Albert) and Thomas Edward (known as TE).

Map showing the various blocks listed in Table 1.
(Queensland State Archives)

Ned Armitage's son, Norman, a few years earlier but was never taken up.

In April 1914, Wilson Hart and Hyne & Son sought to have the Woongoolbver Creek block marked and put up for sale as soon as possible. They clarified that their interest was solely in the tallowwood and blackbutt timber, reiterating that the satinay and brush box:

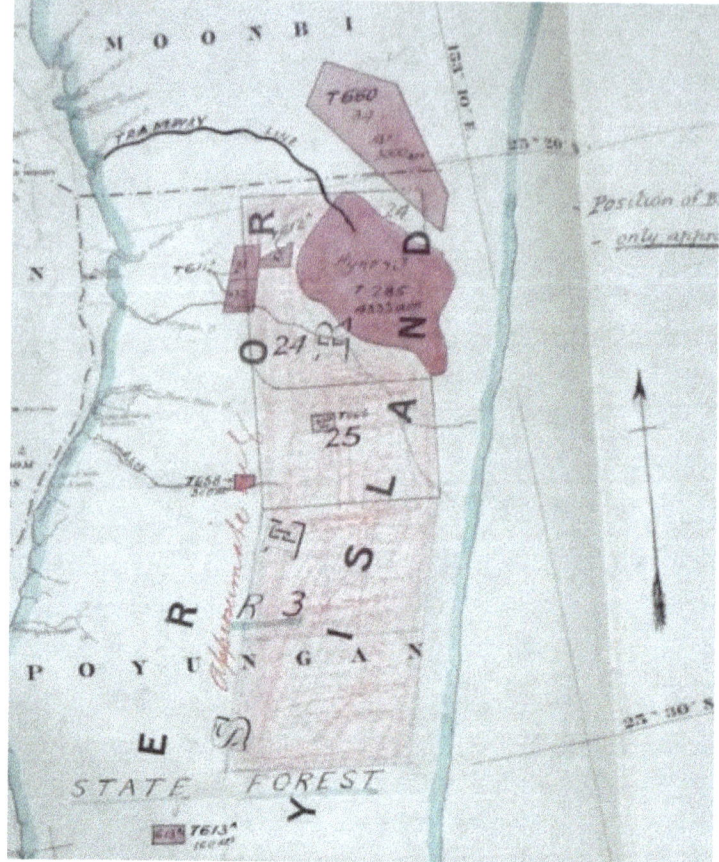

Dark shaded areas show the blocks being worked in 1913.
The northern block of 3,000 acres is the Quandong Scrub.
(Queensland State Archives)

... have proved to be quite useless for building purposes, and although we have gone to considerable expense in trying to place these varieties on the Queensland market, we have been unsuccessful, and in most cases have had to take the timbers back, as builders positively refuse to use them.[11]

They pointed out the significant costs of running the current tramline and expected to be granted a valuable timber block like the one under consideration to help offset these high expenses.

---
[11] Wilson Hart and Hyne & Son (1914) Letter to the Minister of Public Lands, 16 April. ITM 25184, QSA.

With new Timber Regulations established under the *State Forests and National Parks Act 1906*, Jolly was eager to tighten the conditions of the timber sale and implement forest improvement silviculture. To achieve this, he wanted to manage timber operations through a forest officer under his control instead of the usual arrangement under the Land Commissioner based in Maryborough.

In October 1914, the Woongoolbver Creek block was auctioned at an upset price of one shilling per 100 super feet for five years, with an option to extend the term if a tramline was constructed. Wilson Hart and Hyne & Son won the auction but remarked:

> Through the actions of outsiders who were in no sense legitimate timber merchants, we were forced to protect our interests and bid as high as 2/7 [2 shillings 7 pence] per 100 super feet.[12]

Realising they couldn't afford to work the block at such a high royalty, they relinquished it a few months later. Confident there was enough interest, Jolly decided to re-auction the block in April 1915 and raised the upset price to one shilling six pence per 100 super feet. However, there were no bids, resulting in another auction a fortnight later at a lower starting price of one shilling per 100 super feet.

Wilson Hart and Hyne & Son were successful and quickly dismantled their existing tramline, relocating it south to access the Woongoolbver Creek block.

* * * * *

Despite decades of intense harvesting activities, supported by tramway haulage, and concerns voiced by Jolly, the forests remained remarkably impressive. Armitage, referring to himself as "Old Citizen", wrote about the forests in 1929:

> The traveller strikes a living wall of giant timber trees up to 150 foot high buried in the jungle scrubs so thickly growing

---

[12] Hyne & Son (1915) Letter to James Tolmie, Minister for Lands, 5 May. ITM 25184, QSA.

that roads and tracks must be cut to enable one to get through. Giant [*trees*] 100 to 120 feet clear to the first limb, are there in thousands, straight as an arrow ... can only be used as sawmill logs up to about four or five feet in diameter, containing from five to six thousand feet in each tree.

Then beyond that limit again come the super giants so big that no sawmills at present in use in Queensland have any machinery capable of handling them ... these great monarchs of the forest are from six to ten feet in diameter and contain from seven thousand to thirty thousand feet of timber in each tree.[13]

---

[13] Nature's Bounty, *Maryborough Chronicle*, 8 June 1929, p. 14 (Trove). Accessed 2 May 2024.

9

McKenzie's Fraser Island gamble:
timber, triumph and turmoil

Hepburn McKenzie, a Scotsman and Sydney-based timber merchant, started his own business in the early 1890s after gaining experience working in a timber yard. He initially supplied red cedar directly to Chinese furniture makers in Sydney before purchasing a yard in Pyrmont, where he built a sawmill. The mill's success prompted him to relocate to a larger five-acre site in 1900, where he installed one of Australia's first bandsaws, increasing production sixfold compared to traditional steam-driven vertical frame sawmilling.

McKenzie expanded his operations by acquiring land across the road from his mill, establishing a planing mill, a box-making factory and a storage area. Receiving over 100 horse-drawn jinkers and dray loads of timber daily, the site produced approximately 1.75 million super feet of timber each month. Unfortunately, a fire destroyed the mill in 1906. Undeterred, McKenzie purchased a six-acre property on Glebe Island to build another sawmill powered by electricity generated from a motor alternator connected to a steam engine.

In 1907, after experiencing a shortage of hardwood supply, he constructed a bush mill at Ourimbah on the Central Coast of New South Wales. By the end of 1909, McKenzie had acquired 860 acres of forest at Kioloa on the south coast of New South Wales. He built a three-mile horse-drawn tramway with timber rails to then transport the timber to his mill in Sydney until a sawmill was established in the forest in 1912. He also constructed six or seven cottages and a school for his workers and their families.

Fraser Island ambitions

In June 1911, McKenzie, accompanied by Sydney banker Robert Lewers, visited Fraser Island and was impressed by the timber resources they observed. They met with the minister to seek rights to cut timber on the island over at least 20,000 acres. Additionally, they requested rights to at least 200 acres to build a jetty, sawmills, and workers' cottages, similar to what McKenzie had done at Kioloa. Due to the capital involved, they requested a lengthy "fixity of tenure".

Lewers informed the Land Commissioner in Maryborough that they planned to ship timber to Sydney but were also willing to sell in the Queensland market. Following a departmental inspection of the proposed area, it was reported that blackbutt and satinay were the principal timbers, with the best stands found in patches of large trees. However, as with Caldwell and Hanley's previous similar applications, concerns arose that if their proposal was approved, it would adversely impact the sawmilling interests in Maryborough.

Forestry considered offering a smaller block of 5,000 acres, like Block 25, which was estimated to contain five million super feet. Ultimately, McKenzie received notification that the government had decided against selling any further large timber areas on Fraser Island.

Two years later, McKenzie approached the minister again to seek access to 15 to 20,000 acres of timber on Fraser Island. He emphasised his intention to utilise all the merchantable timber, including satinay and brush box, while adhering to a minimum girth limit of 72 inches.

Jolly was enthusiastic about the proposal, particularly the offer to purchase satinay, brush box and other "unsaleable scrub woods". He had consistently advocated raising the minimum girth limit from 60 inches to match the standards of other states, such as New South Wales. He expressed frustration that, after 40 years of timber utilisation on the island, the forests were in poor condition:

Magnificent satinay-brush box forest near Woongoolbver Creek.
(Photo the author)

Teamsters buy small lots of blackbutt and tallowwood when situated close enough to the beach (western), but when patches of tallowwood and blackbutt have been found large enough to warrant a tramline, large sales have been made, one having been affected this year. All these sales leave the so-called inferior species untouched with the result that economic forestry cannot be attempted.

Last year's experiments with the sowing of blackbutt and tallowwood seed gave very fair results but necessitated the destruction of the inferior species at a cost of £2 per acre which expenditure should be avoided. If the position were reversed by the department obtaining a revenue of £2 per acre from the sale of these species, forestry would be possible. For this reason, I am very much in favour of a large sale of these timbers together with such blackbutt and tallowwood as are scattered throughout the block.[1]

Forestry informed McKenzie that his proposal was still excessive and required modification. In a revised proposal, McKenzie continued to pursue a substantial block. Jolly outlined the conditions of a sale, specifically an area of approximately 8,000 acres, with the minimum girth limit set at 54 inches for satinay and brush box to encourage their removal and facilitate the regeneration of blackbutt and tallowwood.

Forestry allowed McKenzie to specify any area for cutting rights. After revisiting the island in January 1916, McKenzie selected a site at the head of Bun Bun and Bennett Creeks. Forestry organised an auction in October 1916, offering the right to cut all satinay, brush box, blackbutt and red stringybark[2] across approximately 10,000 acres in two blocks at the upset royalty of nine pence per 100 super feet for satinay and brush box, and two shillings per 100 super feet for tallowwood, blackbutt and red stringybark. However, the only attendee at the auction was Wilson Hart, and no bids were made.

In July 1918, McKenzie finally secured the timber rights on Fraser Island he had eagerly pursued. He agreed to pay the original upset prices and held a ten-year contract that began on 1 April 1919.

Building a settlement at North White Cliffs

McKenzie quickly arranged for the construction of a curved jetty, tramline and settlement at the old quarantine site at North White Cliffs. The jetty was designed with an elliptical layout to take advantage of a stronger foundation for the piles, proving to be more stable than a traditional straight structure extending from the shore. It also allowed ships to be in deep water while berthed parallel to the shore.

---

[1] Memo by Jolly dated 18 August 1915. ITM 25184, QSA.
[2] Also known as red mahogany.

Felling a satinay tree, McKenzie's operation.
(Courtesy MWBBHS (Image_ID FR002))

Ned Armitage was hired to build the jetty and its loading facilities,[3] while Bill Seelke transported cypress and satinay logs for the piles.[4] The satinay trees were felled in the winter of 1918 when the bark was tight to help protect the logs from marine borers. A steam pile driver was used to position the logs. The curved jetty, approximately 600 feet long, extended over shoreline sand, mud and a sandstone ledge into deep water. During construction, the workers built temporary bark huts on the beach.

---

[3] This is reported in a couple of historical texts. However, according to Edward Armitage's great grandson Gavin Patterson, who had access to Armitage's reminiscences, Armitage made no mention of this contract or work.

[4] It is widely reported that satinay was used as piles for the wharf. Samples were taken from remnant piles in 2024 and 2025 for analysis to confirm the species. Results show the piles closest to the shore are cypress and the remaining piles are *Syncarpia* spp.

Temporary huts on beach at McKenzie's. (Charles McKenzie collection courtesy Ruth Jones and MWBBHS (Image_ID FR107))

Plans were made to build three small bush sawmills along the tramline to convert logs into flitches for shipment to Sydney for processing into boards for the southern timber market. This market preferred satinay and brush box for wharf and bridge decking despite the higher transport costs. Brush box also grew in New South Wales and had been used by sawmillers for many years without any drying issues. McKenzie believed that the Queensland variety of brush box was superior to its New South Wales counterpart.

Ultimately, McKenzie decided to build the sawmills near the jetty; these were the only sawmills ever to operate on the island. Bob Small managed the primary sawmill,[5] which was equipped with a breakdown frame saw and a 48-inch circular saw bench. Logs were processed into slabs or flitches, then cut into boards of various sizes. A second sawmill was later constructed and equipped, while a third mill was established but remained incomplete due to a lack of machinery. Both mills produced approximately 6,000 to 7,000

---

[5] Small fell seriously ill and went back to Sydney and was replaced by Keith Standford, after whom the Standford Logging Area is named.

super feet of sawn satinay, brush box, blackbutt, and tallowwood daily. A log siding was installed above the two mills, situated next to each other, providing ample storage. Logs were rolled down from the tram bogies directly onto the frame carriage of each mill with ease.

Primary sawmill in operation. (Charles McKenzie collection courtesy Ruth Jones and MWBBHS (Image_ID DR107))

Initially, McKenzie employed the teams of bullocks led by Albert Berthelsen, who pulled jinkers loaded with logs to loading points along the tramline. In 1924, two American engineers installed an American-designed steam winch, or log hauler, at the Seelke Terminus. This was primarily used to pull logs from a hollow to the south-east, up a steep hill to the terminus.

The large winch featured a double drum with two rolls of steel cable operated by Walter Jarvis. One cable was a heavy $^7/_8$-inch diameter wire, a third of a mile long, used for hauling logs, while a smaller ½-inch return cable was hooked into a snatch block to pull the heavier cable back, ready to attach to the next log.

Steam winch or log hauler with double drum at Seelke Terminus. (Charles McKenzie collection courtesy Ruth Jones and MWBBHS (Image_ID FR172))

The front end of each log was positioned on a hardwood fork slide to prevent it from sinking into the sand while being winched. A hook on the end of the steel cable was secured through a wire sling looped around the log's end and through ring bolts in the V-end of the slide. Although this method effectively moved logs up the steep sandhills, it left a deep, unattractive trench over six feet deep.

The tramway extended to the end of the jetty, where up to 60,000 super feet of sawn timber were stockpiled in slings. A winch loaded the slings into the hold of the *SS Glenreagh*, a shallow draught vessel chartered by McKenzie from a Sydney firm. This boat, specially designed for transporting timber, had a forward cargo hatch for quick loading and unloading and could carry about 40,000 super feet of timber. Loading took approximately ten hours and involved three employees – a rigger and two men inside the hold.

Sawn timber on the jetty awaiting shipment. (Charles McKenzie collection courtesy Ruth Jones and MWBBHS (Image_ID FR189))

McKenzie tried to sell sawn timber in Queensland, but local merchants refused to deal with him. As a result, he had to send the timber to Sydney for the local market.

McKenzie established a primitive frontier settlement around the old quarantine site. Services for the sawmills and jetty included a saw doctor's shop, a blacksmith, a pumping station, a store and about 30 houses for workers and their families. Most employees constructed their houses using slabs of bark along the southern side of the tramline between the jetty and the timber mills. One child who spent time there recalled that the living conditions were nearly intolerable because of the large number of fleas from the many dogs. Everyone had to go to bed covered in kerosene to ward off the fleas and sleep comfortably. On wet nights, large centipedes, unaffected by the kerosene, sought refuge in their bedclothes.

At its peak, the settlement supported 80 to 100 residents. A school was constructed on the southern hill, away from the noise of the sawmills, overlooking the jetty. It opened in 1921 with about 40 children enrolled but closed in April 1925.

McKenzie's school c1920. (Charles McKenzie collection courtesy Ruth Jones and MWBBHS (Image_ID FR145))

Despite the tough living conditions, fishing off the jetty was pretty good, with large whiting easily caught and plenty of prawns hauled in kerosene tins from the mangrove banks using a lantern in a dinghy. A regular dance on Saturday nights in a small hall became the social highlight everyone looked forward to, with an old chap playing the accordion and being fed glasses of beer all night to keep him going.[6]

McKenzie's operation required a significant amount of capital to establish. With McKenzie assuming full control, the company's directors sought an independent opinion from a timber expert in 1920 to ensure the venture was a sound proposition for the company and its shareholders. The expert provided a favourable report:

---

[6] The information about the fleas, fishing, and dances came from a letter by William Chappell, who lived as a young boy at McKenzie's from 1922 to 1925. The letter, written to survey overseer George Wex in June 1971, was supplied courtesy of Dennis Wex.

A considerable sum of money has been spent on the jetty, tramline, mills, log-haulers, cottages, locos and trucks, launches and other facilities which have been provided. I was greatly pleased with my inspection throughout and sincerely hope Mr. McKenzie will be successful. I have no doubt whatever in my mind that he is on an excellent basis so far as the raw materials for the mills is concerned, and that the investment will prove to be the most satisfactory one that he has engaged in for some years past.[7]

Financial struggles and union pressures

Shortly after launching his operations, McKenzie discovered that his business struggled to generate a profit after investing over £80,000. In 1921, he founded a company called H McKenzie (Queensland) Limited to separate the Fraser Island business from his valuable assets in Sydney. H McKenzie Limited, the parent company, owned most of the shares. However, due to the new company's lack of profitability, attracting capital or selling shares publicly proved to be difficult.

By 1925, McKenzie's financial losses were mounting. High transportation costs for shipping timber to Sydney and union disputes contributed to the financial strain. The jetty was technically part of the Maryborough Harbour Trust, and the Queensland wharfies insisted on handling the loading process, threatening to blacklist McKenzie's ship if he did not comply.

McKenzie had to pay for eight hours of work, even though only four hours were productive. Requests for better accommodation and overtime further raised costs.

Adverse weather and ineffective communication with the mainland caused delays and worsened the situation. Due to poor conditions, the *SS Glenreagh* could arrive up to three days late, and without proper communication, McKenzie was often unaware of its arrival time. Nonetheless, union workers still had to be paid. There

---

[7] Report attached to the Annual Report of H. McKenzie Limited for the year ending 31 March 1921.

were always delays in getting the waterside workers to the island; some even arrived intoxicated. They also divided the sling loads into smaller units, prolonging the loading process.

Due to ill health, McKenzie resigned from his company in March 1925 and died five months later. He was not alive to see the failure of his Fraser Island venture, although he sensed it was inevitable. The new company's shares were written down to a third of their original value due to accumulated losses, rumoured to be around £100,000. A few months later, operations on Fraser Island ceased, and in May 1926, the business was liquidated. The company offered all equipment to Forestry, but they refused to meet the requested price.

The following month, a massive auction was held on Fraser Island – one of the largest in the state. About 60 prospective buyers were ferried to the island, where assets worth tens of thousands of pounds were sold for a fraction of their value. After the auction, Forestry bought the tramway assets for £5,000.

Forestry then assumed responsibility for cutting timber, hauling and transport to the sawmills in Maryborough. This acquisition was part of a broader plan aligned with the government's state enterprise policy. Starting in 1915, several sawmills were progressively purchased, partly to prevent sawmillers from colluding to keep royalties low and retail prices high.

However, the operation experienced losses from the outset. Practices were frequently careless; for instance, workers rolled logs off rail trucks into the water at the jetty while waiting for a punt or log barge to take them to Maryborough.

By owning and directly controlling tree harvesting, Forestry convinced Maryborough sawmillers to accept the previously rejected underutilised satinay. Once fully air-dried, satinay proved to be an excellent timber.[8]

The Great Depression in the early 1930s, coupled with a change

---

[8] More details about the marketing of satinay is outlined in Chapter 12.

Loading logs at McKenzie Jetty, 1929. Note the logs in the water.
(Department of Forestry)

in government, resulted in the sale of government-owned sawmills and assets. The closure of the former McKenzie's operations on Fraser Island in 1935 marked the end of the experiment in state sawmilling.

Map of tramlines

10

TRAMLINES OF FRASER ISLAND:
A LEGACY ON RAILS

Before the introduction of internal combustion engines, horse and bullock power were essential to economically log timber on Fraser Island. As operations expanded and accessible stands were harvested, timber cutters had to travel further from the west coast to reach the higher dunes and access the highly productive forest stands. Consequently, bullocks and horse teams struggled to haul logs to the log dumps on the creek estuaries that were farther away. The lack of sufficient grass for feed made it challenging to work the teams daily, resulting in significantly increased logging costs. As a result tramlines became an important replacement.

Pettigrew and Sim's wooden tramway

Recognising the inefficiency of bullock teams on sandy terrain, Pettigrew and Sim pioneered the use of tramways for log transport. In 1873, they built Queensland's first private railway – a 9-mile wooden tramway – on the Cooloola sands, connecting their newly acquired licence to the water's edge at Tin Can Bay. Although not on Fraser Island, it was a pioneering line that paved the way for future tramlines on the island.

They commissioned Queensland's first steam locomotive, built by John Walker & Company in Maryborough and named *Mary Ann* after their daughters, to run the operation. The locomotive was launched in July 1873, just in time for the tramway's opening. This innovation enabled timber to be transported much more quickly and cheaply than using traditional bullock teams.

After the success of his relatively inexpensive wooden rail tramway, Pettigrew planned to build a tramline on Fraser Island in 1876 to access kauri pine stands for his sawmill at Dundathu. However, the idea was abandoned because he operated only under an annual licence and could not guarantee sufficient volumes of kauri pine to justify the capital needed to construct the line.

The tramway concept ultimately achieved considerable success in the similar sandy terrain of Fraser Island.[1] The timber industry operated light rail on the island from 1905 until approximately 1935. In total, three steam-operated and one horse-drawn tramlines were built. Two were developed jointly by Maryborough sawmillers Wilson Hart and Hyne & Son, terminating at log dumps on the western shore creeks. The third tramline concluded at a purpose-built jetty at North White Cliffs.

The Woongoolbver skipway

The first tramline built on Fraser Island remains somewhat mysterious. Constructed of timber, it ran from a loading ramp at Deep Creek to Woongoolbver Creek, near Central Station, following the forest's edge along the wallum swamp. Horses hauled bogey trucks along the track.

Ned Armitage is believed to have constructed the tramline, but its exact origins remain uncertain. The line ceased operations after Wilson Hart and Hyne & Son finished their second tramway in 1915.

Pioneers of Fraser Island rail

Maryborough sawmillers Wilson Hart and Hyne and Son recognised a significant resource of hardwood timber waiting to be exploited on Fraser Island. With Armitage's support, they sought government assurance of secure forest access to justify investing in a tramway.

In 1905, Armitage surveyed the tramline route with a manageable 1:16 grade, extending from Urang Creek to the Poyungan and Bogimbah Logging Areas as part of the auction won by the

---

[1] More details were provided in Chapter 8.

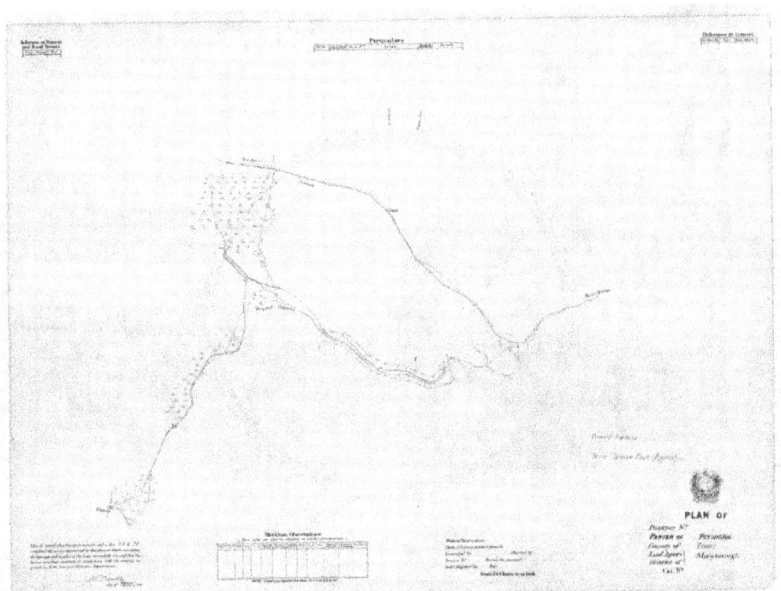

1921 survey plan by Assistant District Forester Merrotsy showing the approximate location of the horse tramway. (Queensland State Archives)

companies in the previous year. The sawmillers awarded him the contract to construct the tramline, utilising a team of six horses for hauling. Armitage employed Alf Jarvis and Peter Sorrensen to assist with the construction.

They built a three-foot-six-inch gauge line using 30-pound steel rails and tallowwood sleepers. By July 1906, seven miles of the tramline was completed.[2] For locomotive power, the companies acquired a former Queensland Railways 28-ton Class 2-4-4 side tank engine, which had previously been used for constructing the first jetty at Townsville. Affectionately known as *Doris*, it was operated by Alf Jarvis, with his brother Willy serving as the fireman.

Brothers Rudolf and Fred Wendt were responsible for loading and unloading logs, but they were later replaced by George and Owen Wells. In addition to these tasks, they also had to cut and

---

[2] According to Evelyn Gebbett, a forest trainee on the island between 1919 and 1921, the tramline was built from satinay, "probably because it was fire resistant". However, no information supports this. Source is Eckert, D. (2003) *Op. cit.*, p. 143.

Tramway surveyed and built by Ned Armitage in 1905.
(Armitage family collection, courtesy Tess Patterson)

stack fuel wood for the locomotive into easily accessible heaps along the tramline.

The tramway ultimately extended eight miles, including two branch lines, each approximately three miles long. The northern branch, known as the "blackbutt patch line," led into the Quandong Scrub and was added in early 1911 after securing approval to access a blackbutt forest. The southern branch was built first to reach a prime stand predominantly composed of tallowwood.

The blackbutt patch line into Quandong Scrub.
(Courtesy MWBBHS (Image_ID FR006))

When Wilson Hart and Hyne & Son finished harvesting the blocks related to their original line and successfully secured timber rights at the head of Woongoolbver Creek in 1915, they quickly lifted and relocated the rails to the new route. This line passed what later became Central Station and included a couple of branches. One ended just 2½ miles west of Eurong on the east coast, while the other, built in 1917, extended a mile east of Lake Birrabeen to access additional tallowwood.

The tramway kept running until 1923, when the steam locomotive was sold to the Fairymead Sugar Company in Bundaberg.

McKenzie's ambitious venture

In 1918, after Hepburn McKenzie contracted to purchase timber from a 10,000-acre area, he built a three-foot-six-inch gauge tramline from the forest to a jetty extending into deep water for loading ships.

Black Bess locomotive on McKenzie's tramway, 1920. (State Library of Queensland)

He hired railway engineer and surveyor Arthur Thorpe from New South Wales to survey and construct the tramline, with assistance from McKenzie's son Charles. A team cleared the route in preparation for laying the sleepers and rails. Sleepers were cut from satinay, and iron was used instead of steel for the rails to minimise noise. The line was well-sleepered to reduce maintenance costs, settling into the sand as if it were cemented. Due to the lack of rock or gravel, sand was utilised as ballast.

The tramline gradually rose from the sawmill site near the old quarantine station heading south-east to the "6-40" junction[3] at the head of Bennett Creek. Here, the line split into two directions: one artery ran northwards for about two miles to the Standford Terminus within the Standford Logging Area.

The southern branch continued directly to the "7-20" junction, which then forked into two lines, each approximately two miles long. The southern branch led to a logging camp known as The

---

[3] 6-40 was short for six miles and 40 chains from the jetty, which is about 10 kilometres.

Rat's camp, while the northern branch extended east towards Lake Wabby, ending at Bill Seelke's camp.

Following the Great Northern Timber Company's takeover of the sawmills and tramways from the British Australian Timber Company near Woolgoolga in northern New South Wales in 1916, McKenzie purchased two locomotives, 25 timber bogey trucks and six tram cars. The locomotives were 13-ton steam engines. The Murray and Paterson locomotive was named *Black Bess,* while the American-made Climax was called *Little Strug*. With its reduction gearbox, McKenzie intended to use the Climax to haul logs off the steeper inland branch lines and assemble loads for the faster Murray & Paterson to transport back to the sawmills. However, *Little Strug* saw limited use and required significant repairs because the sand on the island damaged its gears and caused them to wear out quickly.

Curly Cooper, Jackie Glendon and Bert Jarvis were the locomotive drivers, while Singer Pearce served as the fireman. Bert Herrenberg was the brake boy responsible for managing the brakes. While sitting on the back wagon, he would engage the brake when the locomotive driver blew one whistle, and if he heard two whistles, he would release the brake.

A fatality occurred on the tramline in April 1922. One of McKenzie's employees, John Harwood, was sitting on the buffers of the locomotive about eight miles from the sawmill. On reaching a steep incline, Pearce saw Harwood fall forward onto the rails and signalled the train to stop. Harwood's right arm was severed below the elbow, his right leg broken, he had a large cut on his forehead and many abrasions. He died as the train returned to the mill. A message was sent to McKenzie, who was then in Brisbane. The body was taken to Sydney by rail in a coffin accompanied by McKenzie. Apparently, there was blood on the train seat afterwards.

The Great Depression reduced timber demand, rendering full-scale production unfeasible. The tramline operated sporadically from 1930 until 1936, when all operations ceased.

* * * * *

Fraser Island's steam-powered transport era concluded with the closure of Wilson Hart and Hyne & Son's tramline in the 1920s, followed by McKenzie's in the 1930s. The hiss of locomotives and the scent of burning wood disappeared, replaced by the growl of internal combustion engines and the haze of exhaust fumes. The tramways had left their mark, but progress called for a new mode of transport.

11

SATINAY: FROM MISCONCEPTION TO MAJESTY

Fraser Island turpentine is absolutely useless for mill purposes.[1]
Forest giants with trunks so massive they could support the sky.[2]

Fraser Island, known for the unique satinay tree, has a history intertwined with timber exploitation and misconceptions. Found only in a few locations where it grows on sand, satinay was initially dismissed as unsuitable for milling, but later recognised for its exceptional timber qualities.

Satinay is the island's most renowned timber and a truly remarkable species. It stands tall and majestic among the island's flora, reaching heights of 165 feet, with the lower third devoid of branches. The largest trees have a girth measuring 16 feet, and their trunks are coated in thick, fissured, stringy-fibrous bark.

Aborigines called it "peebeen", while botanists recognise it as *Syncarpia hillii*. It was named in honour of Walter Hill, the first curator of the Brisbane Botanic Gardens.

Although tough and dense, satinay timber is surprisingly easy to work with. Being fine-grained, and close-textured it is ideal for furniture and structural applications. However, it is best known for its natural resistance to marine borers, which is attributed to its high silica content.

Magnificent examples of this majestic tree still exist on the island. Some were preserved in the 1930s as a beauty spot near Central Station known as Pile Valley.[3] Additionally, large trees can be found in the Valley of the Giants, where satinay and tallowwoods

---

[1] Land Agent telegram to Director of Forests, 2 June 1908. ITM 25784 Batch 193, QSA.
[2] Source unknown.
[3] Before the area became a beauty spot, it was known as the Turpentine Patch.

thrived. Many giants remained standing because they were too massive to fall and too large for the sawmills to manage.

Yet, despite its grandeur, satinay was not favoured when the island's hardwood forests were first logged. Sawmillers were discouraged by its tendency to warp and shrink after being cut into boards. Its reputation declined so much that early timber getters bypassed the trees, and many were ringbarked to encourage the regeneration of other native species and the planting of hoop and kauri pines.

Ringbarking satinay, 1922. (Department of Forestry)

In 1875, during a Select Committee inquiry designed to promote Queensland's timber industry, sawmiller Robert Hart admitted that his fallers overlooked satinay while logging but recognised its potential after cutting just one log:

> It is the easiest-cutting hardwood I know. You can get piles seventy and eighty feet with a little trouble, if you can

draw them in square; and you can get thousands of trees, six, eight, ten feet through – the larger the timber is better.[4]

Misconceptions persisted for years, partly due to confusion with the more common mainland turpentine, which had a wider range of applications, including marine piles.[5] Richard Dalrymple Hay praised the value of turpentine for wharf piles:

> ... its power of resistance to toredo [*marine borer*] appears to be due to the oleo-resin between the timber and bark, hence piles should always be driven in tidal waters with bark intact.[6]

Satinay was initially referred to as turpentine[7] or Fraser Island turpentine.

Some even credited satinay with roles it never fulfilled, such as lining the Suez Canal and being used as piles for the Urangan Pier. Most tourism outlets and individuals make these erroneous claims, probably originating from former technical officer Morris Lake, who wrote in his book:

> Satinay was used in the construction of the Suez Canal. The entire length of the canal walls was lined with satinay cut from Pile Valley on Fraser Island. The rainforest zone where most of the timber came from was one of the most important timber production areas for the Suez Canal project completed in 1869.[8]

Completed in 1869, the canal was not lined with timber. Instead,

---

[4] Queensland Legislative Assembly (1875) *Report from the Select Committee on Forest Conservancy – Minutes of Evidence*, p. 125. Accessed 24 July 2024.

[5] Mainland turpentine is from the same genus and was discovered and named earlier than satinay. It has a somewhat complex nomenclatural history but when *Syncarpia* was first described as a genus in 1839, it was known as *Syncarpia laurifolia*. It is now known as *S. glomulifera*. Baker, R. T. (1919) *The hardwoods of Australia and their economics*, Government Printer, Sydney, listed three *Syncarpia* species – *S. laurifolia* found in the Blue Mountains and coastal districts; *S. leptopetala* found in coastal forests of Queensland and New South Wales; and *S. hillii*.

[6] Dalrymple-Hay, R. (1905) *Suitability of New South Wales timbers for railway construction*. Government of New South Wales, Sydney, p. 6.

[7] To add to the confusion, early papers and reports also named tallowwood as turpentine.

[8] Lake, M. (2019) *Australian Forest Woods: Characteristics, uses and identification*. CSIRO Publishing, Canberra, p. 169.

the Suez engineers initially relied on sand embankments designed to have a 26-degree slope. However, these slopes proved unstable; water undermined the sand and clay, causing bank collapse and canal infilling. The solution was to let the banks slope naturally and deepen the canal rather than attempt to reinforce the sides with structural materials.

At the time of the canal's construction, satinay had not yet been recognised as a distinct timber species. More significantly, there was no practical way to harvest and export hardwoods like satinay from Fraser Island in the 1860s.

Logging on the island during this period focused exclusively on softwoods – primarily kauri pine, hoop pine, and white beech – which were easier to fell, raft, and float across the Great Sandy Strait to sawmills along the Mary River. The island's massive hardwoods were simply too difficult to transport using the available technology and infrastructure.

Despite these facts, a story later emerged from Evelyn Gebbett, who served in Gallipoli and then worked as a forestry cadet on Fraser Island in 1920–21. Gebbett claimed that following the Gallipoli campaign, he was posted to Egypt where, while travelling on the Sultan's powerboat along the Suez Canal, he noticed mooring posts placed at regular intervals – every three chains, or roughly 180 feet. The Sultan supposedly asked if the soldiers knew of Fraser Island, stating that's where the mooring posts came from. Gebbett recalled closely inspecting the posts and identifying them as satinay.

This anecdote, though colourful, is highly questionable. It is not corroborated by any Suez Canal records, and it seems improbable that a 16-year-old with no formal forestry training could have confidently distinguished satinay from turpentine or other dense hardwoods, especially with timber submerged or weathered by marine exposure.[9]

---

[9] Gebbett has an interesting war service record. He enlisted at age 15 and 3 months, making him most likely Australia's youngest recruit in WWI. He served in Gallipoli in its final days and was wounded three times on the Western Front. After being reported killed in action, he read his obituary while travelling on a London train.

In the 1880s and 90s, as well as during World War I, jarrah – the Western Australian hardwood known for its resistance to marine borers – was commonly used. It served as a sheet pile on both sides of the canal sections widened enough to allow two vessels to pass, helping to prevent backwash that could erode the sand embankments and thus avoiding the need for a second canal.

Another story shared by Gebbett suggests that when the London Docks were rebuilt at the turn of the 20th century, satinay piles were used. Once again, there is no official corroborating evidence to support this claim. However, according to Dick Eckert, for many years, a centre spread, said to be from the *London Illustrated News*, was displayed on the wall of the Central Station office, depicting hundreds of satinay piles stacked on the Thames Docks.[10]

The assertion that satinay piles were used for the Urangan Pier, constructed in 1917, is also a myth. Percy Hansen, the superintendent responsible for the pier's construction, meticulously recorded that all piles were locally sourced grey ironbark. This myth originated from John Sinclair, who recounted that his grandmother told him his grand uncle, Arthur Smith, cut and hauled satinay piles from Fraser Island.[11]

The first recorded use of satinay as a pile was in 1918 at McKenzie's jetty on Fraser Island.[12]

Discovering the redeeming features of satinay

The rise of satinay, earning it a reputation as the aristocrat of timbers, unfolded over several years and tells a fascinating story.

The timber's ability to resist the cobra or marine borers was first recognised as early as the late 1870s. Hart's testimony mentioned this, and Pettigrew, in a speech at the Queensland Philosophical Society, cautiously stated that the timber:

---

[10] This story came from Eckert, D. (2003) Op. cit., p. 146. I searched the internet, including British newspaper archives, and could not find this story in any of the British newspapers, nor could I confirm its date.

[11] Sinclair's claim is published in the beautiful book produced by the Hervey Bay Historic Village and Museum (2017) *The Urangan Pier Hervey Bay: Celebrating 100 years*. Hervey Bay Historic Village and Museum, Hervey Bay, p. 41.

[12] Williams, F. (1982) Op. cit. p. 114. Samples of the remaining piles were collected in May 2025 and sent to Gary Hopewell who identified them as *Syncarpia* spp.

Was said to be capable of resisting cobra, and thereby a great value was set on it by the government. Yet, when tested by the Harbor Master here, it has been found that such is not the case, as the specimens on the table will show, one of which is peebeen, another turpentine, and the third swamp mahogany. The latter is not touched; the other two are both eaten into. They were in the water ten months, nailed to piles.[13]

In 1904, when Forest Ranger Gilbert Burnett marked the earlier logging blocks for Wilson Hart and Hyne & Son, he discovered numerous satinay trees growing at the head of Bogimbah Creek, and later wrote:

These trees make excellent piles as they last a long time in water.[14]

In another letter, he described satinay:

Is an unknown timber ... it may therefore prove to be a useful milling timber ... There are many hundreds of these trees which, as regards length, size and straightness could not be surpassed of piles, but the question arises – is the timber suitable as regards durableness for such purposes?[15]

Burnett compared the features to those of turpentine, as they were similar species. At that time, turpentine was not a favoured milling timber in New South Wales, although it was a preferred sleeper species exported to South Africa. It was assumed that satinay would also be a good sleeper option for the proposed tramline. However, there was no reference to Fraser Island turpentine (satinay) in the 1905 book by the Director of Forests, Philip Mac Mahon.[16]

---

[13] Queensland Philosophical Society, *The Queenslander*, 3 November 1877, p. 26. (Trove). Accessed 24 July 2024.

[14] Undated report by Gilbert Burnett on Fraser Island Timber (believed to be 1904). ITM LAN/AK23, QSA.

[15] Gilbert Burnett (1904) Letter to Forestry Board, 12 December. ITM LAN/AK23, QSA.

[16] Mac Mahon, P. (1905) *The Merchantable Timbers of Queensland (Australia) with special reference to their uses for railway sleepers, railway carriage and wagon building, and engineering works*. Government Printer, Brisbane.

In 1906, Wilson Hart reported that while they were sawing tallowwood, blackbutt, red stringybark and brush box on the island, they had not yet worked with satinay:

> Many say [*Fraser Island*] turpentine in the island scrubs is a better timber than the turpentine on the mainland, but we have not yet had an opportunity of testing this.[17]

Even after intensive logging began on the island in 1905, satinay remained largely unappreciated and was frequently overlooked.

In 1908, a request was made to purchase satinay logs of any size for use as piles; however, this fell through when it became evident that satinay had a poor reputation in the sawmilling market, leading the Railways Department to brand it as a sleeper species.

Mac Mahon believed that satinay would eventually be used widely, especially for piles, sleepers and specialised engineering purposes. He inspected the island in August 1910 and estimated that 80 per cent of the hardwood volume was found in the often overlooked satinay–brush box forests.

The building boom following World War I, coupled with a shortage of building materials and new kiln drying technology, prompted a re-evaluation of previous prejudices against logging satinay and brush box. Until then, there was no market for blackbutt, satinay, or brush box in Queensland, even though a strong market had developed for these timbers, except satinay, in New South Wales over the previous 20 years. Queensland was more focused on land settlement, lagging behind its southern neighbour. They selected the timbers most suitable for building purposes, excluding those for secondary manufacturing, which meant the Queensland timber industry used only about 25 per cent of the state's available timbers.

Gradually, satinay's redeeming features became apparent. Mac Mahon's successor, Norman Jolly, wrote to the Director of Forests

---

[17] Wilson Hart (1906) Letter to Director of Forests, 12 June. LAN/AK40 Batch 113, QSA.

for the 1913 Annual Report, acknowledging that while the value of satinay for sawmilling had not yet been established "its value for sleepers and piles has been proved".[18]

Although this didn't immediately result in commercial sales, Forestry played a crucial role in changing perceptions about satinay. Between 1918 and 1924, under Edward Swain's leadership,[19] the service launched a comprehensive timber research program, establishing Australia's first Forest Products Laboratory. One of its officers, Tom McLean, was sent to Fraser Island to experiment with different timbers, testing their grain and sap. He lived in a tent at the Old Petrie camp on Bogimbah Creek.

In 1922, Swain visited Fraser Island to explore silviculture options and develop a logging plan. He expressed frustration over the "millions of super feet" of satinay and brush box that had yet to be cut. He hoped to find a market for satinay as an affordable hardwood suitable for flooring and panelling. The following year, a Timber Investigations Branch was formed within Forestry to examine the properties and uses of Queensland timbers, including satinay. The results were enlightening; after sawing satinay into boards, it was soon discovered that the timber seasoned well when dried patiently undercover.

This marked a significant breakthrough, as it enabled the sawmillers in Maryborough to begin accepting satinay at their mills when Forestry took control of McKenzie's operation in 1926. By then, McKenzie had already successfully introduced satinay logs to southern markets, securing an order for 250,000 super feet of sawlogs in 1924.

Through further studies and experimental applications, Forestry discovered that satinay wood closely resembled one of the finest

---

[18] Jolly, N. W. (1914) *Report to the Director of Forests*, in Annual Report of the Director of Forests for the Year 1913, 16 July, Department of Public Lands, Brisbane, p 3.

[19] Edward Harold Fulcher Swain was an Australian-educated forester, succeeding Norman Jolly as Director of Forests in 1918.

tropical timbers, the French Guiana cabinet wood known as satine. To enhance its marketability, it was renamed satinay, effectively shedding its previous reputation as unmerchantable. In 1929, during a Forestry exhibit at the Brisbane Show, a mock-up of the Valley of the Giants on Fraser Island, built on satinay flooring, ultimately led visitors to a display of furniture made from satinay.

The utilisation of satinay

Satinay is a stunning timber used for a variety of purposes. Its remarkable resistance to marine borers and exceptionally straight trunks makes it well-known as a marine pile for major projects worldwide.

The first confirmed cutting of satinay for piles was reported in 1918 when satinay trees were felled to build McKenzie's jetty. The first confirmed sale of satinay piles occurred in 1924, when the Wilschefski brothers and Albert Berthelsen cut down 51 "exceptionally sound and flawless" 60-foot logs that were "as straight as a die" near Yankee Jack Creek. These logs were sent to the Rockhampton Harbour Board for use at Port Alma, showcasing the quality of timber from Fraser Island.

In July 1924, Forestry displayed a satinay duchess chest at the Brisbane Showgrounds, featuring beautiful figuring that resembled maple. This exhibit further enhanced satinay's reputation as a premium cabinet and furniture timber. Additionally, its resistance to marine and lyctid borers, as well as termites, quickly earned it worldwide recognition.

In 1926, satinay piles were used in the construction of the Granville Bridge in Maryborough. McKenzie & Company's annual report confirmed satinay's introduction to the market as a preferred sawn timber, which contributed to establishing a robust timber market in the southern states.

In 1929, Forestry engaged the renowned Brisbane cabinet maker Ed Rosenstengahl to craft a suite of period furniture from satinay,

Curly Cooper, Keith Standford and Hepburn McKenzie sitting on satinay piles in 1924. The trees were felled in winter when the bark was firm as the bark was an inhibitor to marine borers. These piles were sold to Sydney pile experts, E. D. Pike. (Charles McKenzie collection courtesy Ruth Jones and MWBBHS (Image_ID FR184))

which was displayed at Sydney's Royal Easter Show, further strengthening satinay's role in the southern timber markets.

By the late 1920s, satinay had gained international recognition in the pile export market. Following failures in the Panama Canal due to weak timber structures, engineers and builders sought alternatives, testing samples of turpentine, satinay and brush box piles. Word soon spread about the high quality of the satinay piles from Fraser Island, reaching engineers working on the new Empire Wharf at the Falmouth Dock in London.[20]

By 1931, an initial order was placed for 18 satinay piles, although Forestry was initially hesitant to handle such a large order.

---

[20] The Empire Wharf was built between 1931-33. The decking on the wharf was brush box, also from Fraser Island. Seventy-five years later, it was demolished, not because of the deterioration of the timber, but because deep water around the derelict wharf (and neighbouring King's Wharf) could not be used. The wharves were replaced with a marina.

However, with the collaboration of teamsters, fallers on the island, barge contractors, shipping companies, and waterside workers, 167 piles were delivered to Brisbane in just five weeks. They were so long that if laid end to end, they would stretch 2½ miles.

Transporting these massive logs from the forest to McKenzie's jetty posed a significant challenge. Each log was 75 feet long and weighed around eight tons. Puntman Frank "Bendy" Webber devised a clever solution: he dismantled the engine on his punt and connected it to the railway trucks, remnants from McKenzie's era. Using a friction clutch and chain drive to the axle, he successfully towed the logs along the railway to the jetty.

Satinay piles await shipment at Brisbane wharf for Falmouth Dock, London, 1931. (Photo JA Lunn, Department of Forestry)

Satinay's reputation grew as other suppliers struggled to meet the demand for long piles, measuring up to 120 feet and more.

Forestry promptly emphasised the unlimited availability of long satinay piles on the island to secure future large-scale orders.

Demand for satinay piles continued to rise, with ongoing orders for piers and jetties in Sydney, Bowen, and Townsville, as well as additional piles for the Falmouth Dock.

Beyond its applications in high-end furniture and piles, satinay was also valued for making excellent pipes for smokers, runways for cattle at abattoirs, stumps, joists, flooring in thousands of homes, plumber's dressers, mallet heads, cask headings, chisel handles, fishing rod handles and walking sticks. It was also a favoured species for plywood production.

By the outbreak of World War II, satinay was recognised as a premium timber, known for its use in high-profile projects. It became a favourite for marine piles and a valued material for fine furniture and cabinetry. This transformation from a previously dismissed, unmerchantable timber to a respected product highlights the importance of proper research and market positioning.

The satinay forests on Fraser Island were once vital sources of timber. Today, they stand as symbols of the island's ecological and economic history, representing a tree that was once overlooked and undervalued but is now recognised for its unique qualities. However, the harvesting of satinay and all other timber on the island ceased over 30 years ago, and the public can no longer utilise its high-quality timber.

12

THE JOURNEY TO THE SAWMILLS

The log dumps

In the early days of logging on Fraser Island, transporting logs from the bush to the sawmills or loading facilities was a complex and carefully orchestrated operation that evolved out of necessity. Initially, softwood logs were floated down the island's creeks, tied into rafts, and towed by steamers to the sawmill at Dundathu, near Maryborough. The return trip could take up to a week, highlighting the island's isolation and the difficulty of navigating the Great Sandy Strait.

However, everything changed when the focus shifted to hardwood logging in the 1870s. Unlike softwood logs, hardwood logs do not float, rendering the original transport methods obsolete. This shift led to the construction of log dumps, where logs were collected and loaded onto barges. These dumps were strategically positioned along the tidal estuaries of creeks on the western side of the island, spanning from Woralie Creek in the north to Figtree Creek in the south, with a total of 19 separate sites.

The log dumps served as storage depots for sawlogs, awaiting the arrival of the barges that carried them across the waters to the mainland. Barges used the tides to manoeuvre into position. At high tide, they could navigate the creeks, while at low tide, they rested on the creek bed, making it easier to load logs. Transferring logs from the shore to the flat-bottomed barges was accomplished by rolling the logs on skids using a parbuckle system.

Some of the earliest log dumps were located at Yankee Jack and Bogimbah Creeks. These sites were positioned further upstream and sheltered from the winds, making it easier for the barges to rest close to the bed logs. In contrast, other log dumps exposed at the creek mouths required stabilisation with piles driven into the creek bed, such as the Urang Creek log dump, which was established in 1902 when Bill Seelke transported the first tallowwood logs to the site.

Rafting logs towed by Charlie Mathison.
(Photo Ruby Jensen courtesy MWBBHS (Image_ID FR011))

Remnants of the Bogimbah log dump, 2024. Now encroached by the return of mangroves. (Photo Shane Bradbury)

THE JOURNEY TO THE SAWMILLS

LOG DUMPS ON FRASER ISLAND

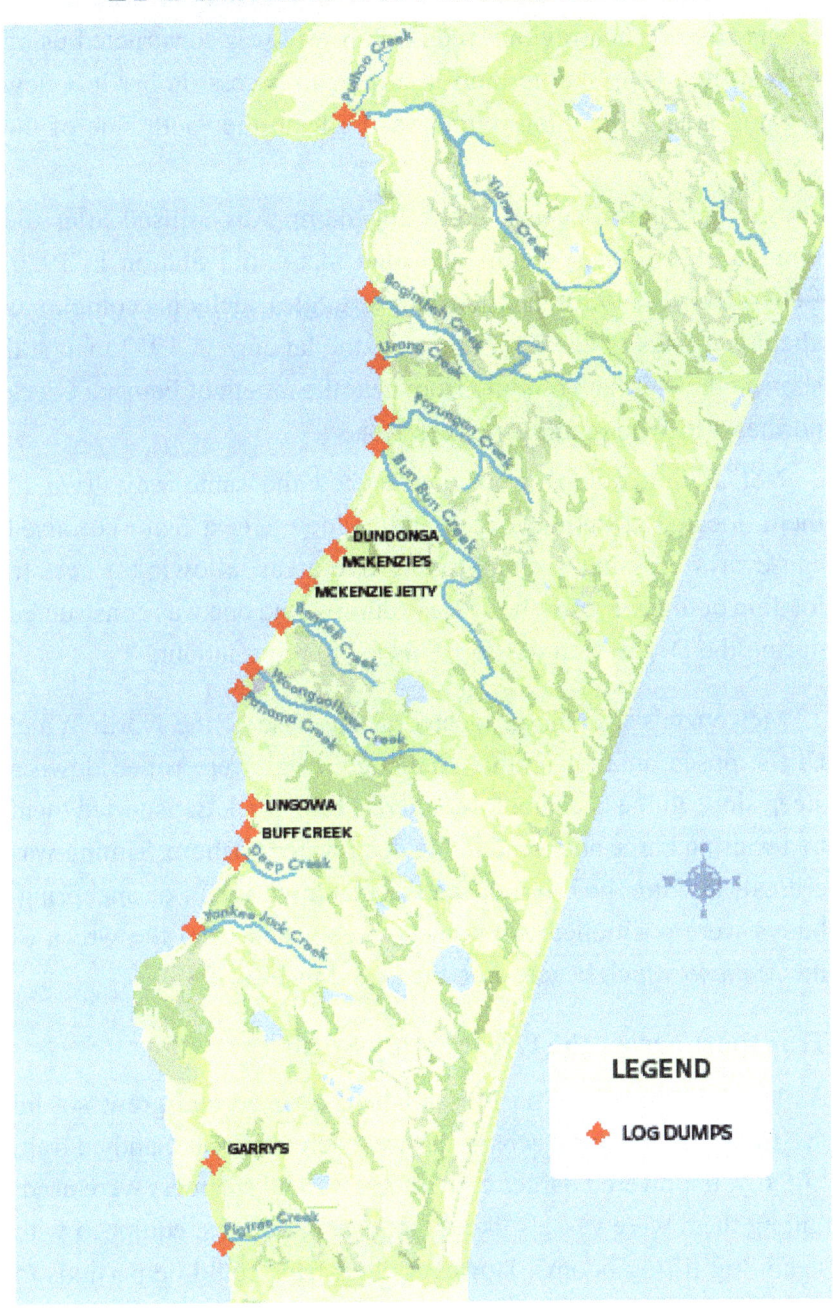

Woongoolbver Creek became another important site in 1916 when Walter Petrie established a forestry camp nearby called Orange Tree. The previous year, a tramway was constructed using rails shifted from the northern tramway to access timber in a new logging area. A new log dump was built on the south side of the creek.

Similarly, the Panama Creek log dump was utilised after the Orange Tree forestry camp relocated to Central Station in 1920. Letters from the 1930s mention daily struggles, including complaints about wet bags of chaff for horses at the landing. A 1952 map still showed the old track running from near the mouth of Panama Creek northeast to Woongoolbver Creek Road.

Not all log dumps were constructed the same way. Two of them, located at Puthoo Creek and Yidney Creek, featured raised causeways crossing swampy mangrove areas, allowing access to loading points. Forestry built these dumps, and one was constructed during the Depression of the 1930s using relief labour.

McKenzie's log dump, located at the base of the North White Cliffs, posed another unique challenge. Logs were rolled down a steep slope to the beach below, where a blitz truck transported them to a waiting barge anchored in the deep water offshore. Timing was critical; the blitz had to outpace the incoming tide. For anchoring, buoys were positioned using anchors salvaged from the wreck of the *Maheno* which beached on the island in July 1935.

Transport across the Great Sandy Strait

As logging operations on Fraser Island evolved and grew, so did the transport methods across the treacherous Great Sandy Strait. Initially, unpowered barges converted from old steamers were used; among them were vessels like the *Muriel* and *Essex*, equipped with steam log-lifting booms. However, their trips could be perilous in rough weather, making anchorages like Garry's Anchorage in the south safe havens for the barges.

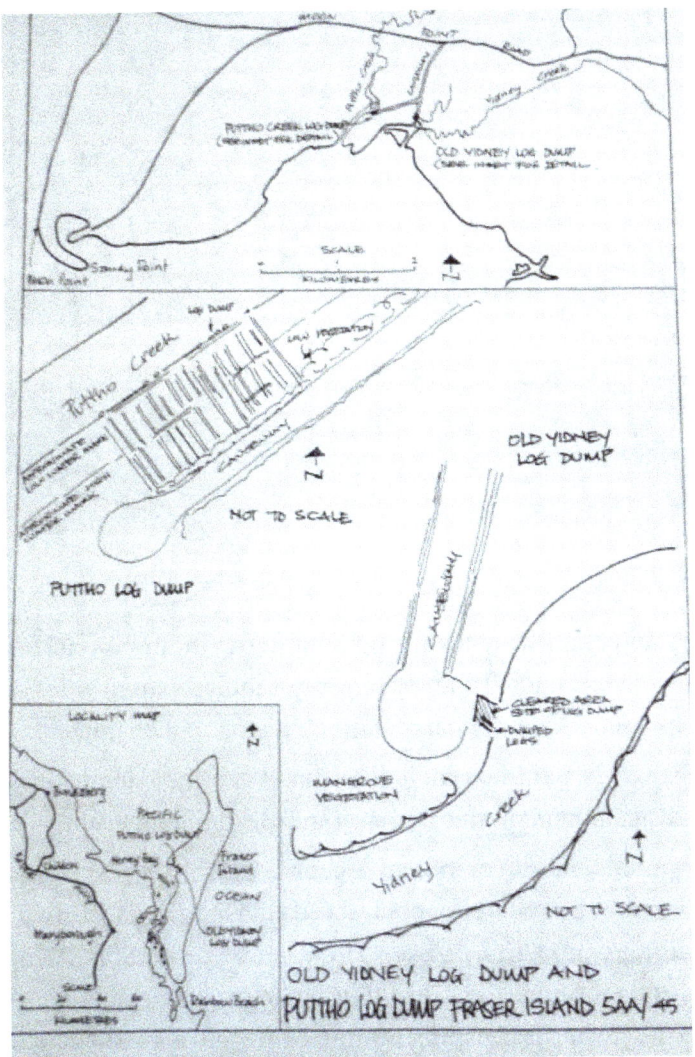

Plan of Puthoo Creek and Yidney Creek log dumps.
(Courtesy of Queensland Government)

By the 1870s, the demand for Fraser Island's prized timber had increased sufficiently to warrant the use of paddle steamers. The *Culgoa*, mastered by Captain Goodall and owned by Pettigrew, became a staple, transporting millions of super feet of timber annually. In 1884, the Mathison brothers, Christie and Matthias, pioneered regular punting operations. They utilised flat-bottomed wooden punts like the 24-foot *Slave*, which had two long oars called

Lass O'Gowrie being loaded at McKenzies log dump. (Photo David Postan)

sweeps and hand winches for loading logs. Another punt, formerly a sailing ketch named the *Wave*, only required small tides to float and was used to mainly carry bullock teams to the island.

Other early puntmen included Hans Hansen, Captain Jack Blue and his steam launch, the *Dagmar* and Bertle Sundstrupt.

A significant development occurred in 1904 when Edward "Ned" Armitage secured a contract to transport logs for two major sawmilling companies, Wilson Hart and Hyne & Son. Armitage's steam-powered tug, the *Geraldine*, made weekly runs, delivering logs to the sawmills. Despite its limitations, and because its V-shaped hull could only navigate creeks at the highest tides, the *Geraldine* became a vital link between Fraser Island and the mainland. Each week, the whistle announced its arrival, carrying not only logs but also letters, messages and supplies, helping workers stay connected to the world beyond the island.

The *Geraldine II* replaced its predecessor in 1911 after the original vessel was wrecked near North White Cliffs. Frank "Bendy" Webber took over operations following Armitage's retirement in the early 1920s, continuing the vital service.

THE JOURNEY TO THE SAWMILLS

Edward "Ned" Armitage.
(Armitage family collection, courtesy Tess Patterson)

In the 1920s, Christie Mathison's son, Charlie, inherited his father's passion for water transportation and expanded the fleet of tugs and barges. From 1938 to 1960, Charlie operated the *Watoomba,* towing barges laden with logs. He also owned the *Palmer*, a former twin-screw steamer with a steel hull, which carried logs from Fraser Island and gravel from Woody Island. Today, the wreck of the *Palmer* can be seen among the mangroves of Deep Creek.

The transition from manual to mechanised loading systems marked a significant turning point for the timber industry. Motorised winches significantly accelerated the loading process, and vessels like the *Hopewell,* a self-propelled barge equipped with slewing cranes, represented the pinnacle of this technological evolution, enabling faster and more efficient loading and unloading.

Log punt on Bogimbah Creek, c1911. (State Library Queensland)

The fleet, which included vessels owned by Wilson Hart and Hyne & Son, such as the *Pelican, Otter, K'gari, Lass O'Gowrie, Goori* and *Kundu,* became essential to the success of the island's timber operations. All except for the *Kundu* were scuttled on the eastern side of Woody Island at the Roy Rufus artificial reef.

Allan Shillig was a puntman from 1965 for 27 years, only finishing with the cessation of logging on the island. He worked on *K'gari* until 1976 and then skippered the *Hopewell* for 16 years.

Even friendly rivalry contributed to the industry's competitive spirit. Puntmen like Neil Simpson of Wilson Hart and Des Shillig of Hyne & Son epitomised that spirit during its heyday. According to Joe Cunningham, one day, while they were moored next to each other at a landing:

> Here they both were one day; Neil was sitting in the wheelhouse and Des was sitting on the bollard. Des was having a bit of a whinge and Neil placed a bucket between Des' legs, and he said, 'What's that for?' and Neil said, "that's to catch the tears".[1]

---

[1] Fred Williams' interview with Joe Cunningham, 1998 from Williams, F. R. (2002) *Princess K'gari's Fraser Island*. Self-published, p. 123.

THE JOURNEY TO THE SAWMILLS

Loading *Hopewell* at Poyungan Creek, 1978. (Photo Peter Lear)

Loading blackbutt logs on *K'gari* at Bennett Creek, 1957.
(Photo E. Suchting, Department of Forestry)

Forestry transport

Forestry also played a crucial role in transporting workers, supplies and equipment to and from the island. After staff were stationed to live and work on the island in 1913, it became necessary to establish a reliable transport service. In 1917, they acquired their first boat, the *Heather*, a wooden vessel with a kerosene engine. Piloted and maintained by mechanic Tom Weaver and later by Wally Barton, the *Heather* became a lifeline for those on the island, making fortnightly trips between Fraser Island and Maryborough. Without a jetty at the time, the boat was tied to two trees in Urang Creek until a jetty was built sometime after 1920.

As operations on the island expanded, so did the infrastructure. By 1920, Ungowa, also known as South White Cliffs, was designated as a deep-water port area for the southern part of the island, reducing dependence on tides for flat-bottomed barges. The construction of a jetty at Ungowa provided a stable docking point for forestry vessels, eliminating the need to rely on high tides, although this jetty was not designed to load logs onto boats.

Completed in February 1940, the jetty was constructed using Johnny Hansen's barge *Muriel* on short cypress pine piles near the bank. The remaining piles supporting an equipment shed were satinay. In the late 1970s, when the outer row of jetty piles became too weak, their removal resulted in a shorter jetty.

Over the years, more modern boats replaced the *Heather*. A small 20-foot vessel named the *Satinay* was briefly utilised, followed by the *Adventure* in 1941, which was a wooden launch powered by a Thornycroft petrol engine and could carry 20 passengers. One of its advantages was the much shorter travel time to Ungowa – about three hours. The Harbours and Marine pilot steamer *Relief* was used when the *Adventure* was in for repairs or maintenance.

However, the *Adventure* was considered too small and was replaced by the 55-foot launch *Korawinga* in 1961, followed by

Cec Neilson at helm of *Korawinga*, July 1964.
(Department of Forestry)

its successor, the *Korawinga II*, which was introduced in 1979. These vessels kept the island connected to the mainland, effectively transporting workers, equipment, and supplies.

The *Korawinga* was built in Bundaberg with decking made from white beech timber sourced from trees on HH Road, east of Pile Valley. It could carry a four-wheel drive vehicle on its deck. The *Korawinga II* was a fast, twin-hulled fibreglass shark-cat launch, powered by twin 175 horsepower Johnson outboard motors, and operated until around 1983.

The launch masters were former timber contractors George Gossner and Fred Josefski. Gossner lived aboard while moored at the jetty and maintained the boat. Josefski worked as a storeman during the week and handled minor engine repairs and vehicle maintenance, despite not being a mechanic. He was a jack of all trades and proved to be quite handy.

Cec Neilson began his forestry career as Josefski's assistant launch master in 1969. When Josefski retired in 1974, Neilson took over and managed the *Korawinga* as if it were his own. He set his own rules, and no one dared to overstep them. Neilson earned the nickname "Sandbank Cec" because of his frequent encounters with sandbanks.

* * * * *

Relying on sea transport to move logs to the sawmills has left a lasting mark on Fraser Island. Many log dumps, jetties, and other structures still stand as historic sites, silently bearing witness to the island's past. The journey of these logs from the dense forests of Fraser Island to the bustling sawmills of Maryborough encapsulates a fascinating chapter in the history of Queensland's timber industry.

Even today, the remnants of the logging era and the stories of those who worked on the barges stand as a testament to the determination and ingenuity that fuelled the industry's growth. Though now silent, these vessels once played a crucial role in transporting the island's valuable resources.

PART 3
MAKING AND MANAGING NEW FORESTS

13

ROOTS OF QUEENSLAND'S FORESTRY:
EARLY SILVICULTURE AND REFORESTATION

Fraser Island is a key historic site and the focal point for Queensland's early trials in planting and silviculture. Here, pioneering foresters laid the foundation for softwood and hardwood silviculture in the state, despite facing numerous challenges.

When silvicultural operations began in the early 1900s, the primary focus was on increasing native softwood production, particularly species such as hoop pine and kauri pine. Although both species of pines were already cultivated in plantations, by 1920, the depletion of kauri pines had become so severe that simply planting thousands of them wasn't enough.

Challenges of kauri reforestation

Unlike hardwood species, kauri trees did not form dense forests. Instead, they were scattered across limited rainforest areas and wet sclerophyll forests, standing as giants highly sought after by timber cutters.

In 1879, during his visit to the island, Walter Hill proposed selecting, clearing and planting an acre or more of land with young kauri trees under the watchful eye of a resident caretaker. He suggested:

> This would test the growing powers of the trees under favourable circumstances and prove the desirability of clearing the ground.[1]

In 1882, Archibald McDowell reported on the wasteful destruction of native timbers, using kauri pine on Fraser Island as an exam-

---
[1] Hill, W. (1879) Op. cit., p. 3.

ple. By 1883, it was noted that hardly any kauri trees exceeding the regulation size remained on the island. It soon became evident that measures needed to be put in place to prevent their disappearance.

As a result, early efforts focused on growing kauri pine seedlings for planting, in line with the government's initiative to experiment with "renewing timber scrubs using the indigenous pine." Fraser Island was chosen for the trials because of its favourable rainfall.

McDowall employed several workers, including Ronald Mitchell, a timber getter on the island, his son Alexander, and John Ingham, an Englishman who had established the public gardens in Maryborough. A nursery was set up in a 90-foot-wide clearing near the head of Bogimbah Creek. Starting in January 1882, around 10,000 seedlings were planted in nursery beds, gathered from various locations near the stumps of trees cut roughly ten years earlier.

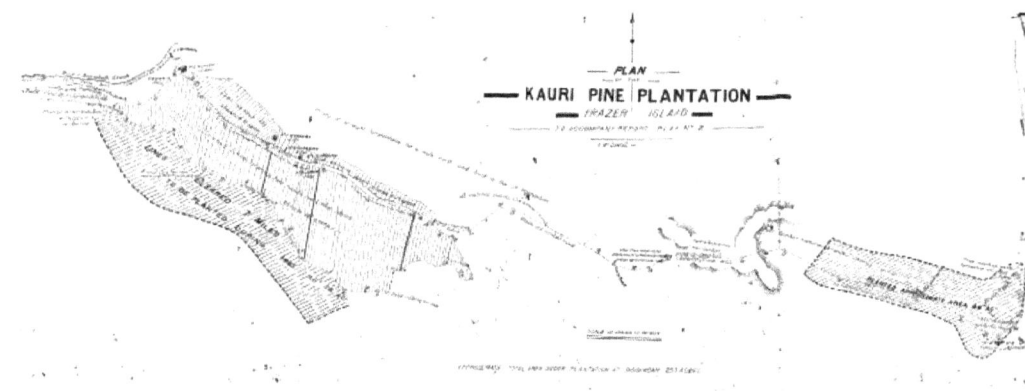

Plan showing the location kauri plantations at Bogimbah, planted between 1882-84. (Queensland State Archives)

A strip of recently logged forest was cleared of undergrowth to a width of one chain on either side of the road for a quarter of a mile, and 26,100 kauri seedlings were planted. The following summer, an additional 20,000 seedlings were planted five feet apart under dense scrub. Another 3,000 seedlings were planted in two old logging clearings, spaced about 10 feet apart. Rows of seedlings were also planted on each side of the old timber track, and the undergrowth was cleared around young saplings that had naturally regenerated. In total, over 230 acres were planted.

Another area at Yankee Jack Creek was cleared for a kauri plantation, where a small nursery was set up to grow about 5,000 seedlings for planting on 82 acres.

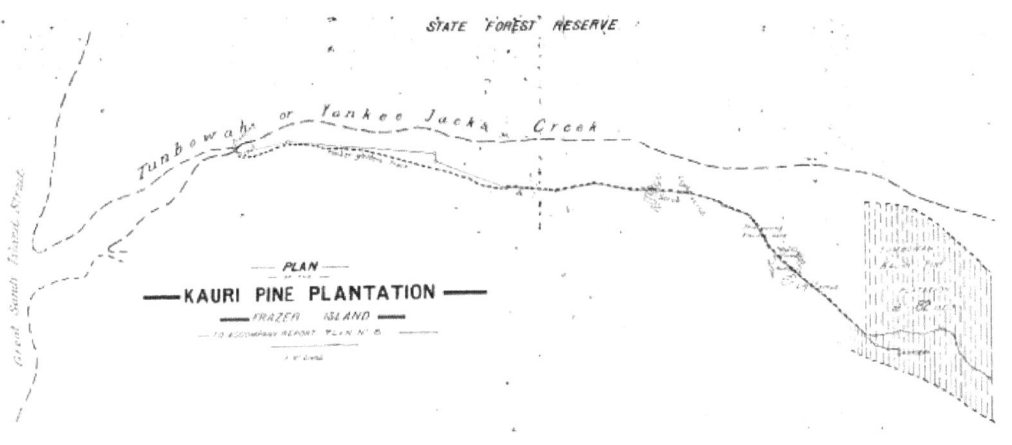

Plan showing location of kauri plantation at Yankee Jack Creek, 1882-84. (Queensland State Archives)

Some re-clearing and refilling of gaps in failed sections occurred in 1884. The strategy shifted to cutting lanes a chain apart and planting kauri seedlings six feet apart. A report on the plantation scheme indicated some of the better seedlings:

> ...now average a foot and a half in height and have all the appearance of sturdy but slow-growing plants. The two seasons since their planting have been very dry and the growth in consequence abnormally slow.[2]

In January 1890, Leonard Board, serving as Land Commissioner at Maryborough, inspected the kauri plantations, which had expanded to 600 acres. He provided a positive report, stating that the saplings were healthy and thriving, with less than ten per cent

---

[2] Hooper, E. D. M. (1885) *Arboriculture Queensland*, Report of Deputy Conservator of Forests, Madras Presidency. 1884 Annual Report of the Department of Public Lands, 29 January, p. 3.

failing. However, he recognised the slower growth, which he attributed to transplanting seedlings too small from the nursery. He also observed that the plants had been neglected. Mitchell and his son, based at Bogimbah, struggled to keep up with the maintenance needed to clear vines and undergrowth around the bases of the seedlings at both plantations.

Although McDowell initially reported that the kauri plantings were successful and that "pine scrubs" could be reforested with little trouble or expense, this proved to be an overly optimistic assessment. Kauri pine is not shade-tolerant, and the plantings were established under a canopy of satinay and brush box trees. An inspection in 1899 revealed that the plantings had largely failed:

> Here and there a young kauri sapling has shot up to a height of 15ft or 20ft; but in a vast majority of cases, they are not more than 5ft or 6ft high, and, what is worse, the leading shoot at the top is dead or dying, from some cause not apparent. The trees also have been planted too close together, and will require to be again transplanted if they live, which does not now appear likely with many of them.[3]

Around 1905, the Department of Agriculture became interested in growing trees using methods from Fraser Island with kauri pine seedlings. However, they preferred natural regeneration over the more expensive approach of enrichment planting.

In 1940, relieving forester Jules Tardent, working on the island, observed that many of the original kauri plantings at Bogimbah were still alive, but struggling:

> ... A goodly number of these trees can still be seen today, but few are even of sapling size and many are stunted, spindly runts 20 feet tall due to the suppression by the very tall and

---

[3] The Poor Blacks: Aboriginal station at Fraser's Island. *The Brisbane Courier*, 22 April 1899, p. 4 (Trove). Accessed 17 December 2024.

gigantic scrub trees ... Had clear falling and burning prior to planting been tried, it is interesting to conjecture how the future of reforestation in Queensland might have been fundamentally influenced and accelerated.[4]

Although the planting of kauri pine on the island was largely unsuccessful, a small but effective plantation program was established on the mainland in the 1930s. However, insect attacks hindered any opportunity for a more commercial and large-scale effort.

The genesis of Queensland's hoop pine plantations

Despite a gradual shift towards hardwood, hoop pine remained Queensland's premier timber species. It was widely used for indoor woodwork and was an excellent choice for joinery, cabinetry, staves and weatherboards. Additionally, it was the primary timber used in railway workshops for sheeting, flooring, panelling, framing and finishing carriages. Hoop pine also became the preferred timber for the emerging plywood industry.

In 1911, approximately 500 acres of young hoop pine stands underwent "improvement felling" or regeneration treatment, mostly in the Bowarrady Scrub in the northern part of the state forest. All undesirable scrub undergrowth and small trees were cleared, while larger trees, excluding hoop pines or commercial eucalypts, were ringbarked.

The goal was to create a nearly pure stand of hoop pine, which was seen as more cost-effective than starting new plantations. Because young hoop pine seedlings grow slowly after logging, the strategy sought to enhance seedling growth by removing unproductive and competing trees since the initial open-root plantings of hoop pine seedlings were largely unsuccessful.

In 1919, Forestry began to develop better methods for planting hoop pine seedlings. The first experiment was conducted on the

---

[4] Tardent, J. L. (1948) Fraser Island. Address to the Royal Geographical Society of Australia (Queensland), 7 May. *Queensland Geographical Journal*, 52:75-98.

island using bamboo tubes, but the cost of sowing and cutting bamboo on the mainland was considered too high. Early trials dismissed the use of heavy paper tubes. Ultimately, it was found that two-year-old open-root planting stock yielded much better results.

Motivated by the success of this project and the favourable outcomes from mainland plantings at Imbil in the Mary Valley, Forestry initiated the first commercial hoop pine plantations across the state in 1920–21, including on Fraser Island.

Experimental plantings and early forestry failures

In the first decade of the twentieth century, Forestry, led by Mac Mahon, concentrated on small-scale experimental plantings rather than large-scale plantations. They believed that funding was better spent on developing techniques for regenerating native forests, particularly in hardwood regions.

While the initial silvicultural efforts on Fraser Island faced several challenges, a few individual successes sparked a sense of optimism. Ned Armitage shared a passionate account of the earliest eucalypt silvicultural activities on the island:

> After a lifetime spent in timber and forestry work myself, I could not have believed it – it seems incredible – but I am forced to believe it because I was on the island at the time and saw it done. In 1912 a 12-acre patch of scrub was cleared and burnt off. In January 1913, it was planted with seed or a crude variety of eucalyptus, tallowwood, blackbutt, redwood, etc. In exactly three years from the sowing of the seed, measurements were taken ... The average height of the young trees was 43 feet, diameter of trunks four to five inches ... Three years later another trial measurement was made – height 7 feet, diameter nine to ten inches. Two years later again another test measurement was made – height 84 feet, diameter 2 to 14 inches.[5]

---

[5] Nature's bounty. Op. cit., p. 14 (Trove). Accessed 3 September 2024.

Additionally, a story published in the *Sydney Mail* in 1918 included a photo of three-year-old blackbutt regeneration growing to a height of 40 feet.[6]

In 1913, Director of Forests Norman Jolly relocated forest management from Maryborough to Fraser Island by sending Forest Ranger Walter Petrie, grandson of Andrew Petrie, along with his family to establish a new camp on Bogimbah Creek, approximately 2½ miles upstream from the creek's mouth, near the site of Mitchell's camp. This area was selected for its proximity to the existing Wilson Hart and Hyne & Son tramway logging operation.

Petrie was tasked with investigating the natural regeneration of eucalypts, establishing suitable treatments for hoop and kauri pines, and initiating experimental plantings of exotic conifers. Along with his assistants, cadets Fred Epps and Buck Geoghan, he cleared areas of carrol scrub near the new camp to create a nursery for raising seedlings for planting.

In 1914, approximately 21 acres of scrub were cleared, burnt and sown with blackbutt and tallowwood seeds. However, the cost of this treatment was significant, and its success depended on effectively managing the satinay–brush box forests. The economic regeneration of hardwood areas remained uncertain until those trees could be harvested commercially.

Another 14 acres were cleared and planted with exotic pines such as loblolly pine, Roxburgh pine, Norfolk Island pine and longleaf pine, alongside native bunya and cypress pines. Due to a lack of rainfall, most of these plantings suffered, except for the bunya pines, which thrived surprisingly well, considering their natural occurrence in richer soils on the mainland. The cypress pines performed particularly well at the old Bogimbah Mission site. Other species, such as red cedar, Queensland maple and Monterey pine, were planted over the next five years; however, all were unsuccessful for various reasons.

---

[6] Forestry in Queensland. *Sydney Mail*, 9 October 1918, p. 16 (Trove). Accessed 3 September 2024.

During his time on the island, Petrie undertook an ambitious program of trial plantings, most of which ultimately failed. Unfortunately, the records of these experiments are either missing or no longer exist. Consequently, they hold little practical interest today, aside from being a historical curiosity.

Exactly what specific forestry experience or knowledge Petrie had when he started working with the Forests Branch in 1913 remains unclear. His abilities were questioned, as he was described as:

> Something of a greenhorn. He knew very little about the species and quality of timber, and the timbermen found they had to act as his advisors.[7]

His trial work on the island was quite basic, primarily involving the raising of seedlings, clearing patches of brush, and planting various species to see which thrived best. There was little focus on understanding specific silvicultural requirements of different native species. Even as late as 1925, Petrie argued against using fire to promote regeneration.

After leaving the island, he tried to claim all the credit for the initial success of the ringbarking program, much to the annoyance of the foresters who succeeded him.

> I wish at the outset to query Mr Petrie's oft repeated claim to be the main instigator of ringbarking on a large scale as a means to achieve natural regeneration of eucalypts ... I cannot, however, concede to Mr Petrie, the right to claim either the stimulus which has lately been given to ringbarking on Fraser Island, nor of the prescription which is at present in operation – particularly when Mr Petrie ... advocates quite a different method to that now adopted.[8]

---

[7] Williams, F. (1982) Op. cit., p. 113.
[8] Mocatta, A. W. (1924) Letter to Grenning – Eucalyptus Regeneration: Ringbarking Prescriptions, 25 June. ITM 843639, QSA.

Emerging silvicultural practices in the 1920s

In the 1920s, Forestry began new silvicultural trials on Fraser Island to investigate how native species regenerated naturally and assess the performance of exotic species. These trials involved planting various species, and about 24 per cent of the state's reforestation budget was spent on Fraser Island at that time.

In 1922, under the Director of Forests, Edward Swain, Victor Grenning developed a management plan for the island that stipulated:

> ... the liberation, regeneration and fire protection of eucalypt areas; the improvement of the satinay and brush box stands by ringbarking of useless trees and the planting of poorly stocked areas with conifers. In the hoop, kauri and cypress pine areas, the regeneration treatment was planting of understocked areas with more valuable softwoods and fire protection for all treated areas.[9]

By the mid-1920s, nearly 1,200 acres of plantations had been established on Fraser Island, achieving varying degrees of success. These plantations included new species such as spotted gum, lemon-scented gum, Gympie messmate, camphor laurel, crows ash, blue quandong, white cedar and northern silky oak. Unfortunately, very little information is available regarding the locations of these early plantations and experimental areas.

Between 1923 and 1930, larger, more intensive plantations near Central Station replaced smaller trial plantings. These were located in a strip near the McKenzie tramway railhead on the high dunes behind Eurong. From 1933 to 1940, additional planting occurred on the southern side of Central Station, near Pile Valley.

The primary species planted included hoop, kauri, bunya and cypress pines, white teak, along with exotic varieties such as loblolly, Caribbean, weeping Mexican, and maritime pines. These trees were planted across approximately 217 acres and can still be seen today.

---

[9] Tardent, J. L. (1948) Op. cit., p. 18.

Beautiful plantation of spotted gum 1925. (Department of Forestry)

The overall conclusions from the exotic pine plantings indicated that slash pine could thrive in most locations, provided they were not excessively dry. This includes lower slopes and creek flats, with phosphorus applied to all sites every 20 years.

Table 2

Area of plantation established in the 1920s

Logging Area	Compartment	Year	Species	Area	Total Area (acres)
McKenzie	1	1925-26	Kauri	41.7	50.7
			Hoop	9.0	
	22	1925-26	Kauri	3.2	8.3
			Hoop	2.9	
			P. caribaea	2.2	
	12	1925-26	Hoop	2.1	2.1
Eurong	1	1926-27	Kauri	7.0	54.0
			Hoop	33.2	
			P. caribaea	3.2	
			P. taeda	2.4	
			P. patula	2.6	
			P. maritima	5.6	
	2	1927-28	Hoop	3.9	4.7
			P. patula	0.8	
	3	1927-28	Hoop	0.8	0.8
	9	1926-27	Kauri	3.9	3.9
Woolan	2	1925-26	Kauri	5.5	5.5
	6	1926-27	Hoop	38.5	38.5
	7	1929-30	Hoop	40.9	42.9
			P. caribaea	1.0	
			P. maritima	1.0	
Tahwan	9a	1924-25	Hoop	2.2	4.4
			Kauri	2.2	
	9b	1925-26	Kauri	1.0	1.0
	9c	1922-23	Kauri	0.5	1.4
			Bunya	0.7	
			Cypress	0.2	
	3	1926-27	Kauri	4.0	4.0
	7	1924-25	Kauri	0.7	2.6
			Hoop	0.7	
			P. caribaea	0.2	
			Cypress	0.4	
			P. maritima	0.2	
			Gmelina arborea	0.4	

Part of 80-acre block with two-year-old blackbutt and tallowwood regeneration, 1922. (State Library of Queensland)

By the end of 1923, basic silvicultural prescriptions for Fraser Island's forests emerged from their initial experimental phases and began to form part of developing working plans. However, the ongoing unsaleability of satinay and brush box, which constituted the predominant merchantable forest communities on the island, continued to pose a significant challenge, obstructing effective large-scale silvicultural efforts.

In 1924, there was a shift in silvicultural policies, moving from scattered activities across different parts of the island to more concentrated operations. This change was made possible by dividing the forest into logging areas and compartments. Clearfelling had been practised in heavily timbered areas set aside for replanting, but it was very costly. As a result, ringbarking and brushing were introduced as more affordable alternatives for preparing sites for planting.

Developing specific silvicultural practices to promote natural regeneration remained challenging. The diversity of vegetation types, sandy soil, rapid vine growth that crowded cleared areas, and the presence of large, rotten trees that were too costly to remove and difficult to burn all posed significant hurdles for foresters.

However, there were glimpses of success and optimism. Certain silvicultural practices, including advanced felling techniques, showed potential. What was most appealing was the improved growth seen after post-logging burning, particularly when using seeds from blackbutt, tallowwood and red stringybark.

* * * * *

Although many early plantations and experiments on Fraser Island faced challenges, these foundational efforts significantly influenced silvicultural practices and ultimately sparked widespread reforestation endeavours across Queensland. Notably, the introduction of controlled burning after logging generated new insights into forest regeneration, which, over time, greatly enhanced the structure and productivity of the forests on Fraser Island.

14

THE BLACKBUTT STORY: A LEGACY OF INNOVATION AND SUSTAINABILITY

One of the most successful and enduring examples of native forestry management in Australia is the stewardship of blackbutt forests on Fraser Island.

Thanks to innovative regeneration techniques developed by foresters, blackbutt emerged as the island's most valuable hardwood. This transformation of less productive, mature, and overharvested areas into thriving, resilient and beautiful forests helped establish a new standard for forestry practices nationwide.

The journey to achieve this is a captivating tale of perseverance and dedication, involving extensive and repeated experimental work conducted on Fraser Island over many years.

The rise of blackbutt on Fraser Island

The initial phase of forest exploitation on Fraser Island was far from sustainable. Timber cutters focused on removing the finest trees, neglecting inferior species and unproductive timber. A major challenge in managing these forests was ensuring sufficient regeneration following harvesting.

Foresters were originally responsible for managing extensive stands of mixed hardwoods, where the sought-after blackbutt grew alongside other less valuable species. However, change arrived, sparked by innovative thinking and a series of practical experiments that aimed at improving forestry practices on Fraser Island and throughout the state.

In the 1920s, Fraser Island emerged as a proving ground for early silvicultural trials, showcasing its unique ecosystems and hardwood forests. Forestry practices started to adopt more structured methods to improve forest regeneration. The main issue was ensuring that valuable species, such as blackbutt, could regenerate effectively after logging.

Initial efforts involved burning the forest floor during seedfall to create optimal conditions for regeneration. This strategy, along with targeted planting in gaps, marked a transition to a more intentional approach to forest silviculture.

These early methods laid the foundation for sustainable forestry in Queensland. By the mid-20th century, even-aged blackbutt regrowth stands on Fraser Island – many originating from regeneration burns in the 1930s – demonstrated the effectiveness of these techniques. As forest management evolved, so did the understanding of how to balance timber production with forest health.

The silvicultural requirements of the satinay–brush box forest differed considerably. This forest type has matured over a longer period than blackbutt, resulting in a broader range of age and size classes. These stands are substantially denser, supporting a greater number of trees and an increased volume of wood per unit area compared to blackbutt. They also sustained adequate advanced growth suitable for retention over two or more cutting cycles, making further regeneration a lower priority in these stands. This meant that the satinay–brush box maintained an acceptable stocking of younger trees to replace those removed during logging.

Swain's vision

One of the key figures in this transformation was Edward Harold Fulcher Swain, a forester who understood that merely harvesting mature trees was insufficient; forests required careful management to regenerate properly. Swain championed a more holistic approach, viewing logging as the initial step in the regenerative cycle rather than the final act. Through his vision, forests could be restored naturally by selectively choosing seed trees, using fire to create fertile ground for blackbutt seedlings, and removing unproductive trees.

A pivotal moment occurred in 1920 when a significant experiment demonstrated the effectiveness of this concept. A trial regeneration burn in the blackbutt and tallowwood forest at Bogimbah Scrub established optimal conditions for seedfall. After ten inches of rain in January 1920, the blackbutt seeds germinated, resulting in 60 acres of dense, healthy regrowth within months where the logged and burned forest once stood. This success reinforced the idea that, when managed properly, sufficient natural regeneration could be achieved.

Swain's methods in blackbutt silviculture gained further validation following a massive fire in 1923 at Mapleton State Forest on the Conondale Ranges. His response to this disaster was truly revolutionary. Instead of seeing the destruction as a loss, Swain viewed it as an opportunity for renewal. His plan involved removing fire-damaged trees and managing the natural regrowth that followed. This led to a flourishing blackbutt forest with as many as 2,430 trees per acre. Over the years, these stands were thinned, managed and sustainably harvested, setting a benchmark for forest recovery after a wildfire.

From degradation to productivity

Initially, unregulated logging practices tended to "cherry-pick" the largest, straightest, and most defect-free trees. This approach resulted in the retention of a mix of older, defective trees, those with marginal sawlog potential, and a high amount of non-commercial growing stock, making it difficult to adequately regenerate commercially desirable species.

The blackbutt forests, along with certain areas of the satinay–brush box forests, lacked sufficient advanced growth under suitable conditions to qualify as future growing stock. They depended heavily on the early establishment of a regenerating crop to ensure future productivity.

In 1924, Swain introduced a more intensive approach, beginning with the ringbarking of non-valuable trees, primarily satinay and brush box, several years prior to logging. This strategy allowed debris to be consumed in a regeneration burn. Logging then took place, adhering to girth limits while leaving seed trees on compartment edges and in scattered clumps. This logging operation, which approached clearfelling in intensity, gradually boosted forest productivity.

Petrie enthusiastically reported to Swain about the ringbarking operations on Fraser Island:

> This is the time of the year that the other ringing was done on those areas which you saw gave such excellent results. The local Fraser Island control is to be congratulated, as under these prescriptions, thousands of acres will become rapidly and cheaply filled with vigorous young eucalypts, and the credit of achieving the largest economically successful silvicultural undertaking in Queensland is within Fraser Island's grasp.[1]

Aerial view of Blackbutt coupe showing retained seed trees, 1968.
(Department of Forestry)

In 1938, new tree marking rules were introduced to enable foresters to selectively remove marketable timber while safeguarding

---

[1] Petrie, W. R. (1924) Memo – Eucalypt Regeneration: Ringbarking Prescriptions, 9 March. ITM55213/1/1349, QSA.

younger growth for future harvests in forests with more advanced growth resulting from previous logging or burning.

By the time World War II broke out, significant progress had been made in transforming highly degraded forests into productive stands. Ringbarking was replaced by chemical treatment of stems that were not needed as seed trees, and the use of logging machinery to disturb the soil further advanced the process.

By the 1960s, it became evident that selective logging needed to be more sophisticated to suit different forest structures. New rules were introduced to protect future timber crops while allowing periodic harvests. The focus shifted from marking trees based on diameter to marking them according to tree quality. This change allowed for the harvesting of poor or slow-growing trees that had reached their maximum usable size.

Flowering and fruiting patterns of blackbutt

Understanding blackbutt's flowering and fruiting cycles is crucial for successful regeneration, as natural regeneration depends on the availability of adequate seeds. Extensive studies conducted between 1913 and 1960 revealed that blackbutt trees generally flower every three years, on average, from mid-March to the end of April, with the flowering period typically lasting about three months.

The capsules mature five months after flowering ends and are usually fully mature 13 months later. Seedfall lasts for about 11 months after seeds reach maturity and can happen in any month of the year, as long as the conditions are sufficiently dry enough and accompanied by fire.

In what is regarded as one of the most intensive phenological studies of eucalypts, detailed observations were carried out each month from 1929 to 1948. This involved collecting capsules, or woody fruits, from specific trees during particular seed crops. Comprehensive notes on the seed crop's condition were recorded, and monthly germination tests were performed on the collected seeds.

At any given time, a single tree may have up to three capsule crops, each originating from distinct flowering events. Typically, only one crop will contain fertile seeds, since the first-year crop may be immature, and the third-year crop might have already released all its seeds.

The age of each crop is determined by its position on the branches. The crop from the first year is located among the leaves at the end of the branch, and the older third year crop being further along the branch closest to the tree's main stem. During natural seedfall, the second crop is usually the most fertile and serves as the primary seed source for a regeneration burn.

The challenges of regeneration burning

The main reasons for conducting burns after logging are to reduce competition from undergrowth, create a suitable seedbed and remove litter that hinders the regeneration of blackbutt seedlings.

Areas designated for regeneration burns often contain a high density of large, old trees, along with a low stocking of smaller, commercially desirable trees.

While regeneration burns effectively promote the growth of blackbutt, they also encourage the spread of "fireweed" species such as wattles, common hop bush, and vigorous climbers and creepers. The intensity of the burn affects the prevalence of these species after the burn. For instance, a very hot burn can create a cleaner seedbed that limits the germination of fireweeds. If not properly managed, these plants could inhibit blackbutt seedlings.

Despite the challenges, burns carried out before 1957 were largely successful, resulting in well-stocked, even-aged blackbutt stands. Long-time Maryborough District Forester Andy Anderson noted that the "hills were white with flowers" in those days, as the blackbutt trees flowered heavily and produced abundant seeds consistently. This was evident in the well-stocked, even-aged stands from that period, which were thinned several times to an average stocking of 60 to 110 stems per acre, as can be seen today. A good example is the blackbutt forests along the road from Poyungan Valley to Bogimbah.

Until 1957, a total of 6,538 acres were subjected to regeneration burns, averaging 385 acres each year.

Blackbutt regeneration burn at Compartment 6 Lake McKenzie. Logging Area, 1940. (Queensland State Archives)

The first regeneration burns after WWII did not begin until 1957. Anderson directed his senior ranger on the island to initiate a series of regeneration burns during the cooler winter months. The areas chosen had been logged previously and carried numerous trees with dead tops. A dozer line was established around the designated compartments to control the burn. These areas were surveyed and marked on maps for future inspections.

By 1975, 4,059 acres had been burnt at an average of 224 acres per year. The burns after 1957 generally occurred in the Type 1 and Type 2 blackbutt stands following selective logging. This accounted for the difference in outcomes, as there was significantly less flowering due to the lack of burning for over a decade, resulting in lower nutrient turnover in the soil.[2]

Season of regeneration burning

While understanding the flowering and fruiting patterns of blackbutt trees helped inform the development of a regeneration burning program, the optimal time to conduct the burn remained unknown. Between 1931 and 1941, a series of experimental regeneration burns, each covering approximately five acres, were carried out annually to determine the most suitable months for successful regeneration establishment burns.

Observations of flowering and fruiting showed that the seeds were fertile in capsules during December and January, with most falling between February and April. Before each burn, the tree seed crop was routinely inspected.

Results from the experimental burns indicated that optimal regeneration occurred when burns took place between February and March, when conditions remained favourable for a successful burn. The exact timing depended on the maturity of the available seed crop and the prevailing weather conditions.

Burning in November and December resulted in excessive sun exposure, which led to the death of subsequent regeneration. Furthermore, obtaining a satisfactory burn from April onwards often proved difficult.

The burns resulted in a range of stocking levels, from 3,480 to

---

[2] The blackbutt forests on Fraser Island were divided into three site quality classes characterised by the predominant top height of the original stand. Type 1 forests had trees more than 100 feet; Type 2 – 78-100 feet; and Type 3 – less than 78 feet.

110,000 seedlings per acre. An initial stocking of 4,850 seedlings per acre was considered the minimum needed for full stocking. Given that the average survival rate for germinating seedlings was 32 per cent, a target of 1,550 established seedlings per acre by September following a burn was essential to achieve full stocking.

From this research, Forestry developed detailed prescriptions for conducting regeneration burns, scheduled to coincide with the availability of a reliable, mature seed crop and suitable climatic conditions for a sufficiently hot, uniform burn.

Similar studies were conducted on a much smaller scale for tallowwood and satinay, but they were mainly discontinued because of the dense understorey and unsatisfactory conditions for a controlled burn.

Tending blackbutt regeneration

Following the burns, rapid regeneration of various species, including satinay, brush box and fireweeds, was evident. Between 1936 and 1938, a series of experiments were carried out to manage the regeneration pool and promote the dominance of blackbutt.

Two years after experimental burns in 1934, two plots were established to test whether blackbutt could recover from suppression by other species. In one plot, competing species, such as fireweeds were removed, while the other plot was left untouched as a control. Three years later, results showed that blackbutt seedlings in the brushed plot had a diameter 40 per cent greater and were 14 per cent taller than those in the control plot. These limited trials demonstrated that blackbutt could recover from suppression when competing seedlings were eliminated.

Additional trials were conducted to identify the optimal season for brushing fireweeds in young blackbutt regeneration. Visual observations taken three years after brushing and five years following the regeneration burn indicated that brushing in winter or early spring was most effective at controlling wattle regrowth.

In 1940, two experiments were carried out to determine the best timing for the first and second tending treatments. It was concluded that the first treatment was most effective two years after the burn, when unwanted regeneration was rigid and could be easily brushed away, while desirable blackbutt regeneration was more recognisable. The second treatment was also considered effective if performed two years after the first.

However, these treatments were rarely implemented after 1957 due to high costs. It became clear that the expense was not justified by the growth advantages. Research indicated that if a satisfactory stocking of blackbutt stems was achieved after a burn, they would naturally become dominant. In dense, unthinned stands at least ten years old, there were enough dominant blackbutt stems to ensure an optimal stocking of 120 to 160 stems per acre.

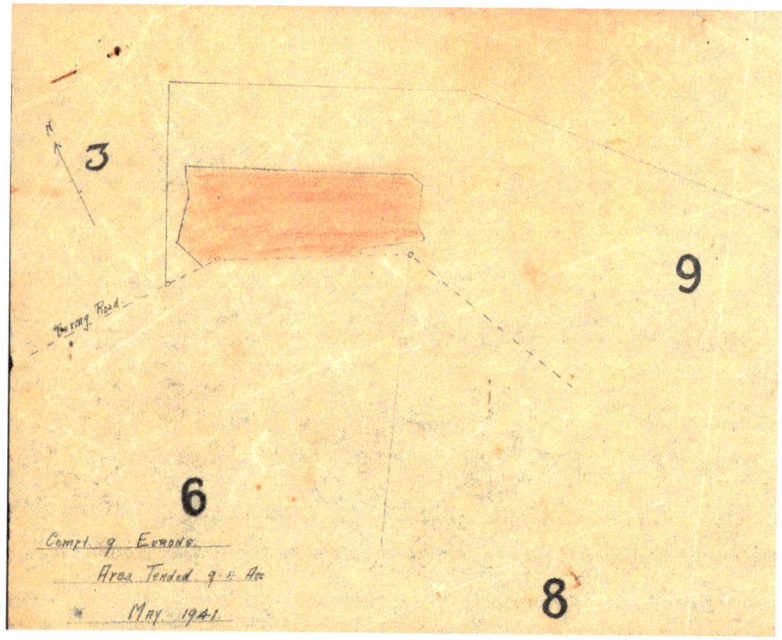

Hand-drawn silviculture map of compartment 9, Eurong Logging Area, 1941. (Queensland State Archives)

The evolution of thinning practices

Thinning is a forestry practice that redistributes growth from many stems to a select few by removing unwanted stems. It is essential for managing even-aged stands, providing necessary growing space. Early thinning programs tended to be conservative and often failed to adequately space the trees. Additionally, there were very few studies on thinning even-aged blackbutt to guide foresters.

A significant ten-year experiment that began in 1943 was conducted in a forest that had regenerated after a burn in 1938. The study assessed the effects of routine thinning and the liberation of blackbutt regeneration, determining the optimal spacing after ten years. It showed that wider spacing was necessary to achieve reasonable growth rates. When a fully stocked stand (1,070 stems per acre) was thinned non-commercially to a spacing of 20 feet (110 stems per acre) at age six, it resulted in at least a one-inch diameter growth advantage.

Despite the benefits, periodic non-commercial thinning was found to be costly. The study concluded that thinning could be postponed until trees reach 10 to 15 years of age while targeting a 25-foot spacing (70 stems per acre) and still achieve satisfactory growth rates. Since commercial thinning could begin around 40 to 45 years of age, no further non-commercial thinning was required.

Eventually, three key principles of blackbutt thinning were adopted: removing unproductive and non-commercial trees through harvesting or felling; selecting the retained stand based on preferred species and future log potential; and spacing the remaining trees to ensure adequate growing space.

Enrichment planting

Foresters used enrichment planting in areas where natural regeneration was insufficient or difficult to achieve. This approach was common in parts of the blackbutt forests and the satinay–brush box transition forests, which were characterised by a dense, shrubby understorey that was hard to burn. Enrichment planting involved adding blackbutt seedlings to promote a satisfactory level of regeneration.

Research was carried out to identify the best methods for raising seedlings, selecting appropriate containers for potting or tubing, and optimising the use of raised stock in enrichment planting when natural regeneration was inadequate.

Seed provenance from Fraser Island was found to be superior for enrichment plantings. Experiments indicated that tube stock yielded better results than square peat pots, which were favoured for their lower cost.

Enrichment planting peaked in the 1970s and '80s, primarily on high-quality blackbutt sites, especially where regeneration burns failed, mainly due to poor weather conditions or inadequate seedfall. It was also used on snig tracks and log dumps in selectively logged forests, replacing the seed tree system. Although enrichment planting was more expensive than regeneration burning, it was less susceptible to unpredictable factors and delivered more consistent results.

Planting occurred promptly after logging to take advantage of the ground disturbance. No burning was performed, and the required level of ground disturbance ranged from 40 to 60 per cent. Any remaining overwood trees considered unnecessary were removed by ringbarking, with or without herbicide application.

By 1978, about 790 acres had been subjected to enrichment planting. In cases where enrichment planting was conducted on lower quality blackbutt sites, fertilisation became necessary due to low soil fertility.

Measuring the forests and sustained yield

Sustainable timber cutting was vital for the long-term success of forestry operations on Fraser Island. Although a yield analysis was first conducted in 1921, the initial permanent yield plots were established in 1952, and measurements were taken. By utilising volume tables and increment data from the plots, foresters estimated the volume of timber that could be harvested annually without depleting the forest.

A sustainable yield of seven million super feet was determined based on a 20-year cutting cycle, with the plots remeasured in 1954.

In 1958, a detailed ground inventory and aerial photo interpretation, utilising cartographer Jack Craig's 1952 vegetation maps, assessed the island's commercial forest types to determine sustainable timber yields. Approximately 330 random one-acre plots were established and thoroughly evaluated across a complete range of size classes, including regeneration. The sustained yield figure remained consistent with the 1952 analysis.

A less extensive survey in 1965 and a subsequent yield interpretation analysis in 1978 confirmed that the standing volume was similar to the 1958 survey. This demonstrated that careful forest management maintained sustainable cutting levels for decades, with yields remaining below the forest's natural growth rate.

Forestry concluded that this sustainable yield could be sourced exclusively from the higher quality blackbutt forests (Types 1 and 2) and the satinay–brush box forests, based on established yields from native hardwood forests of similar productivity on the mainland.

Following the 1978 analysis, the two sawmills in Maryborough could harvest up to 24,000 cubic metres each year, equivalent to 8 million super feet.

Before 1 October 1976, hardwood timber availability was managed through an auction system. After that date, this system was replaced with an allocation method. Under the new system, each sawmill licensed to harvest crown hardwood timber received an annual allocation based on the sustained yield. Since both Wilson Hart and Hyne & Son had previously shared production from Fraser Island under the auction system, the sustainable timber yield was allocated to these firms in equal portions.

Regrowth blackbutt in the Poyungan Valley, 2024. (Photo the author)

A cabinet decision on 5 July 1977 granted Wilson Hart and Hyne & Son long-term timber rights on Fraser Island. These rights were awarded for an initial period of 20 years, with the option for a further 20-year extension. This action followed the Commonwealth's inclusion of the island in the National Estate Register. It was aimed at safeguarding the firms' long-term supply from any future adverse actions by the Commonwealth.

In 1986, the approved cut was decreased to 7.8 million super feet per year to accommodate the reduction in total available commercial forest area, caused by the extension of buffer strips around beauty spots and the expansion of the national park estate.

*****

By the time logging ended on Fraser Island in 1992, the blackbutt forests had become symbols of sustainable forestry. They served as a testament to Swain's vision and the pioneering efforts of early foresters and forest workers. Their careful stewardship left a legacy that continues to influence modern silvicultural practices. Once devastated by fire and inappropriate harvesting, these forests were transformed into resilient ecosystems capable of supporting biodiversity and timber production for generations.

These efforts are so significant and enduring that magnificent blackbutt trees now stand as sentinels preserved in a national park. Their sheer beauty and grandeur are so impressive that they have earned a place in a World Heritage Area.

15

FIRE MANAGEMENT: A LEGACY OF MISMANAGEMENT AND LESSONS UNLEARNED

Before European settlement, Fraser Island's forests and wallum country appeared more open than they do now, reflecting centuries of Aboriginal land stewardship. Aboriginal people used fire to sustain an anthropogenically influenced ecological balance, encourage grass growth, and control scrub species.

Area of mature satinay forest in the 1920s. Note the much more open understorey compared to the same forests today.
(Department of Forestry courtesy MWBBHS. (Image_ID TS049))

However, after their displacement, many of these practices stopped. This caused the island's ecosystem to shift towards a less open structure, despite early bullock drivers burning areas to promote grass growth for feed.

The early foresters often noted that they could ride horses through the tall forests from Central Station to Bogimbah Scrub without obstruction. However, over the decades, the forests became thicker, and open grassy areas gradually disappeared. A map from 1926, for example, depicted a grassy horse paddock southwest of Lake McKenzie, but by 1960, it had vanished, replaced by dense shrubs with no sign of grass.

The early fire exclusion policies

In August 1910, Director of Forests Philip Mac Mahon reported that scrub species were spreading unchecked, highlighting the escalating issue of fire exclusion. Early European-trained foresters believed fire was incompatible with forests, a view rooted in their education abroad. As a result, forestry policies on Fraser Island, similar to those in other regions, sought to eliminate fire from the forests based on the misconception that all fires would damage young regrowth. This decision negatively impacted fire management strategies for decades that followed.

Under this policy, efforts were made to protect the forests from fire. Firebreaks were established, and detection methods were promoted. However, the lack of controlled burns resulted in the very issue foresters feared: an excessive build-up of fuels – leaves, twigs and other organic matter – which increased the intensity of future wildfires.

The island's first formal Working Plan, created in 1922, further reinforced the fire exclusion approach by recommending a ban on any fire in the forests. The plan advocated the construction of green firebreaks, two chains wide, which were maintained clear of vegetation through regular brushing. By the end of that year, 15 miles of firebreaks had been built, designed to prevent uncontrolled fires from spreading. However, firebreaks alone were not enough.

As the 1920s progressed, small fires – many which were ignited by teamsters burning areas to improve pasture for their bullocks – continued to flare up during a hot, dry spring. In 1919, sparks from the McKenzie locomotive caused premature burns that jeopardised regeneration efforts. By 1923, a fire had grown so large that it risked destroying new plantations and a prized blackbutt area north of Central Station. Forestry workers and labourers from McKenzie's operations toiled long hours over two days to contain these blazes. It became clear that simply excluding fire from the forest was not an effective strategy.

Hard lessons learned and forgotten

The island's loose sand made it possible to construct and maintain firebreaks using a sledge or delver, which was pulled by horses. The delver scraped aside the sand and undergrowth forming a shallow furrow approximately six feet wide. The value of the firebreaks lay not in their ability to halt a major fire, but to create the opportunities for back burning towards a wildfire. Later on, the delver was replaced by a drott, a machine that sat between a bobcat and a front-end loader.

However, a serious fire season in 1926 highlighted the difficulties of excluding controlled burns in the forests. Further extensive damage occurred during infrequent but severe fire seasons, including in 1935, when a large fire in the Poyungan Valley area threatened the forests further south. With few firebreaks in place, forestry workers found it hard to bring the fire under control. When strong northerly winds pushed the fire southward, fire crews were apprehensive about the threat. Fortunately, a change in the wind enabled the fire to be managed a couple of days later, but it wasn't a long-term solution.

By the early 1950s, a series of parallel or double firebreaks – the western and eastern firebreaks along Northern Road and Campbell's firebreak – were constructed to protect the main commercial timber areas on the island, including the 22,000 acres of silviculturally treated land. They were regarded as a seemingly innovative solution at the time. The western firebreak consisted of two parallel breaks, each 12 feet wide, which were cleared, grubbed and harrowed. The one-chain strip between them was brushed and burned. It ran along the western side of the island through some cypress pine areas from Ungowa to Figtree Creek in the south.

Section of the 1951 SFR 12 Parish of Talboor map sheet showing the western firebreak from Big Aldridge Creek to Gowrie camp. (Queensland State Archives)

However, the severe state-wide fire seasons in 1952, 1957 and 1964 prompted a reappraisal of the fire-exclusion policy. One of the largest fires happened in February 1952, when the island was ablaze from stem to stern. The fire approached Central Station from both the north and south. The northern fire was halted on the old

FIRE MANAGEMENT

Section of Northern Road north of Lake McKenzie, 1970. Shows area cleared and treated on either side of the track. (Queensland State Archives)

McKenzie tramline, while the southern fire was extinguished by rain at Lake Birrabeen.

Controlling fires was particularly challenging in the blackbutt forests, where flames charred the bark high on the trees, and strong northerly winds carried sparks. Wildfires originating from campsites along the eastern beach also caused periodic major issues when blown inland. During the cooler months, small-scale, strategic control burns were regularly carried out, mainly in the wallum and scrubland behind the foredunes. Maintaining firebreaks and tracks clear in case of a fire remained essential.

It was not until 1965, when a small, prescribed burn got out of control, that Fraser Island's fire management began to change significantly. This fire, which started north of Bowarrady Scrub, was whipped into a frenzy by a sudden change in wind direction. Fire crews fought tirelessly for three days as flames jumped from firebreak to firebreak, driven by strong northerly winds. The fire was finally extinguished only after heavy rains arrived, but the damage had already been done by then.

This blaze starkly revealed the shortcomings of relying solely on firebreaks and fire exclusion, particularly under the influence of hot, strong northerly winds that roared up the sand dunes, igniting the heavy vegetation in their path.

A shift towards broad-scale prescribed burning

Lessons learned from the fires of the 1950s and early 1960s led to the approval of regular small-scale prescribed burning. The 1968 fire season highlighted issues related to edge lighting and limited penetration into burn blocks. A different approach emerged after the appointment of a new Conservator of Forests at the end of 1969, who supported large-scale prescribed burning over the fire-exclusion policy.

Initially, prescribed burns were conducted using continuous strip lighting around the perimeter. However, this method proved too aggressive and was quickly replaced by a more measured approach. In this new method, fires were ignited in a grid pattern, allowing small blazes to burn slowly and consume limited amounts of fuel before extinguishing themselves. This controlled burning technique not only reduced fuel loads but also mirrored traditional Aboriginal fire practices. The burns left a mosaic of burnt and unburnt patches, ultimately resulting in a healthier forest.

To help control wildfires and create separate burning blocks, two east-west roads – Awinya and Moon Point Roads – were built as control lines to halt fires advancing southward under strong northerly winds. These roads proved effective during the 1968 wildfire in the north, where back burning from Awinya Road aided in containing the blaze.

Meanwhile, Dick Pegg, a hardwood research forester, set up a series of prescribed burning plots in blackbutt stands within the Deep Creek Logging Area. Later, in 1970, as the State Fire Protection Officer, he expanded the prescribed burning program while continuing his research into fire behaviour.

Queensland was one of the last states to adopt aerial burning. After several small trial burns on the mainland, the state's first operational aerial burn took place on Fraser Island, south of the Figtree Logging Area, in July 1972. The following year, another burn was conducted north of Awinya Road. These burns mainly targeted the central wallum vegetation surrounding the valuable commercial forests.

As tourism grew and settlements like Eurong and Happy Valley developed, they contributed to fire management challenges. Forestry used its TD18A bulldozer, supplemented by wheeled log skidders from logging contractors, to fight fires. A small, tracked machine kept roads and firebreaks clear and maintained.

From the 1970s onwards, a fuel reduction program primarily relying on aerial ignition became the main method for forest protection. The medium-to-low, open, and drier forests adjacent to the tall and valuable forest types were divided into several zones and intentionally burned in a planned rotation every three to four years.

Extensive research was conducted in mainland coastal wallum country to determine the optimal frequency for prescribed burning. Monitoring the regrowth of species after each burn revealed that when the fire consumed both ground litter and flammable shrub species, the area typically would not sustain another fire for three years. This research guided the management strategy for burning the wallum and coastal scrubs surrounding the commercial forests on Fraser Island, aiming to protect them from threats posed by intense fires.

During the cooler winter months, low-intensity burns were conducted in the highly flammable wallum country along the eastern and western coastal strips every three to four years. Burning took place under mild atmospheric conditions with relatively high fuel moisture content, aiming to partially reduce rather than eliminate ground fuels.

In the 1980s, the senior ranger on the island collaborated with the rural brigades to carry out regular burns every three years to protect communities and their assets. These burns were carefully timed to balance community protection with preserving the island's ecosystems.

The struggles continued

Despite these advances in fire management, challenges have persisted on Fraser Island. The strategically placed east-west roads and tracks have proven invaluable in halting the southerly spread of fires through controlled backburning. Routine maintenance of these tracks involved removing dead trees, tea trees, and banksias from the edges, as they could readily spark fires across the track.

The importance of having contractors with machinery available for wildfire response was emphasised by the outbreak of two fires ignited by lightning strikes just ten days after forestry workers had left the island in 1992. Logging contractor Andy Postan and his son Andrew have made significant contributions to combating fires over the years, often being the first called upon for their machinery to create new firebreaks.

The two fires – one at the northern end and the other near Dilli Village – were challenging to contain with the limited resources available on the island. Consequently, they engulfed a vast area, producing a cloud of smoke that hung over the island, Hervey Bay, and Maryborough for several days. The coast guard had to issue a hazard warning to passing ships.

Volunteer firefighters were left to pick up the pieces, and

Murray Reid from the Eurong Bush Fire Brigade summarised the sentiments of those who laboured 15 hours straight without relief:

> It's pretty damn annoying when the greenies, who spent so much time on the island to save the forests from logging couldn't even send one person to help us save them from fire.[1]

* * * * *

Fire stands as an ever-present force in Fraser Island's narrative, demanding respect and a nuanced understanding. The island's history of fire management is marked by trial and error, along with occasional successes. Most importantly, it reminds us that nature is always in control, and we must learn to work with it rather than against it.

---

[1] Burger, A. (2008) *Last of the barefoot tycoons: the story of Fraser Island's Sid Melksham and the $1,000,000 debacle*, M & B Publishing, Southport, p. 301.

16

PEOPLE AND SETTLEMENTS

Fraser Island has long been recognised for its abundant timber resources, which has been a big part in the island's history and affected the lives of those who lived and worked there. The timber history of Fraser Island is intertwined with the stories of its people, from Aboriginal timber workers who contributed to the island's early development to foresters, forestry workers, and logging contractors who established settlements amidst the forest and worked beneath its canopy.

Aboriginal contributions to the island's early forestry history

The Badjala Aboriginal people played an important part in Fraser Island's forestry history. Some found stable jobs in the timber industry, escaping the hardships of mission life while also helping the island's economy and community.

Roger Bennett was one such individual. Born at the Bogimbah Mission, he was raised by a European timber cutter and his wife. His life reflects the intersection of cultures on Fraser Island as he integrated into the island's forestry community from a young age. He worked as a timber cutter for the Wilschefski and Berthelsen brothers at Deep and Yankee Jack Creeks, as well as at the Dundathu sawmill. His athletic prowess earned him local fame, and Bennett Creek is named in his honour.

Roger's son, Elliott "Elly" Bennett, followed in his father's footsteps and briefly worked as a bullock driver for Stan Jennings. However, Elly became famous beyond forestry as a boxer. At just 16 years old, he won the Australian bantamweight title in 1940, and defended it twice. His talents extended further, allowing him to claim the featherweight championship during a golden era of Australian boxing.

Elly Bennett, Bantamweight Champion of Australia.
(National Library of Australia)

Despite his success, societal barriers prevented Elly from reaching the world championship level, depriving him of the opportunity to become Australia's first Aboriginal boxing world champion.

Other Aboriginal men, including Freddy Ross, Henry "Banjo" Owens, and Isaac "Ike" Owens, were also involved in the island's forestry operations. Freddy Ross was well known for his tree-climbing skills and, like Roger Bennett, was a champion runner, winning the Queensland 880-yard sprint in the 1920s.

Banjo and his younger brother Ike worked in various roles, from guiding tourists at Warry's Happy Valley Resort to bullock driving and mustering across the island's expansive open saltwater couch grasslands. Ike started out as a bullocky for McWatters, hauling logs near Lake Wabby to the tramline, before moving on to mustering horses and cattle for George McLiver and Wyn Bagnell. Hundreds of horses grazed between Wathumba Creek and Sandy Cape in the open grasslands, taking part in extensive horse drives. Their father, Garry Owens, was the namesake of Garry's camp and Anchorage.

Aboriginal workers on Fraser Island 1908. Fred Wondunna is on the left.
(Department of Forestry)

Fred Wondunna was born on Fraser Island and belonged to the Wondunna clan. He spent many years as a timber cutter. While training to be a preacher, he married Ethel Reeves, the sister of Bogimbah Mission leader Ernest Gribble. This marriage forced him to leave Queensland because, at the time, laws banned marriages between Europeans and Aboriginal people.

However, Fred eventually went back to the island, where he resumed his work as a timber cutter, settling at Wondunna camp near North White Cliffs. His return to Fraser Island was a quiet act of defiance, a way of reclaiming his place on his homeland.

Forestry settlements

Fraser Island's first formal forestry settlement, Old Petrie camp, was established at Bogimbah Creek, as detailed in Chapter 13. Once the logging operations associated with the tramline at the Bogimbah Scrub were completed, the tramline was moved south to the Woongoolbver Creek area. In 1916, Forestry instructed Walter Petrie to relocate further south, where he selected a site about two miles above the tidal mark on Woongoolbver Creek, known as Orange Tree camp. Old Petrie camp remained operational until its closure in 1922, when overseers Fred Epps and Elten Sharman were transferred to Orange Tree camp.

Orange Tree camp, named after the trees planted by the workers, was a remote and uncomfortable place to live. Residents had to contend with sandflies, mosquitoes, and fleas, making daily life a constant struggle against the elements. Despite these challenges, the camp expanded, and by 1917, workers had constructed a house for Petrie and his family, along with several huts for themselves.

They also established a shade nursery, where George Holmes worked full-time as the nurseryman, assisted by 11 other employees, primarily cadets. Two of them could not work on the mainland due to excessive drinking. Under Petrie, alcohol was banned. The workers had to organise their own accommodation, horses, and food. In 1960, Forestry surveyor Dick Eckert found the remains of the nursery, which still contained rows of stunted bunya pines about a foot tall.

Nursery at Orange Tree camp showing the overhead shades, 1922.
(Photo JA Lunn, Department of Forestry)

In 1920, the settlement was moved inland, near the tramline, to escape the relentless insects. A flat area of about six acres on the southern side of Woongoolbver Creek was cleared, and large rectangular tents with wooden floors were erected. The tents included a galvanised iron fly for shade and protection. Bill Jarvis dismantled the house at Orange Tree and transported it to the new site.

The new camp was initially named the new Woongoolbver Creek camp, later becoming Scrub camp and eventually Old Station. According to Eckert, his assistant and eventual replacement, George Wex, insisted on calling the camp Central, a name he used on maps, and it is now known as Central Station.[1]

---

[1] Rollo Petrie, Walter's son, wrote in his book that the camp was shifted in 1917-18. See Petrie, R. (1995) *Early Days on Fraser Island 1913-22*. Go Bush Safaris, Gladesville, p. 18. Other reports, such as Eckert, D. (2003) Op. cit. say 1920. It is most likely the shift of the settlement took a couple of years to complete.

By 1927, Central Station housed approximately 50 forestry employees and their families, creating a community that resembled a small town. The settlement comprised 16 wooden houses, including the forester's house with large verandahs, a school, stables, truck sheds, vegetable gardens, and ferneries.

One notable character of Central Station was Lawrence "Sandy" Luck, who was born on the mainland in 1930. In the late 1930s, he attended Central Station School and later worked as a plant operator with logging contractors and Forestry, providing long and valuable service to the industry. He was known for his extensive knowledge of every road and firebreak on the island.

Sandy's father, Allan, also worked for Forestry on the island. The family lived in a bark house under the mango tree near the current barracks before moving to a smaller home that would later function as an interpretive centre.

In the late 1950s, a survey camp consisting of tents at the western end housed four workers and a cook. Two workers' barracks and three demountable units were also built at the eastern end. By this time, Forestry had acquired two blitz buggies and several short-wheel-base Land Rovers for its staff.

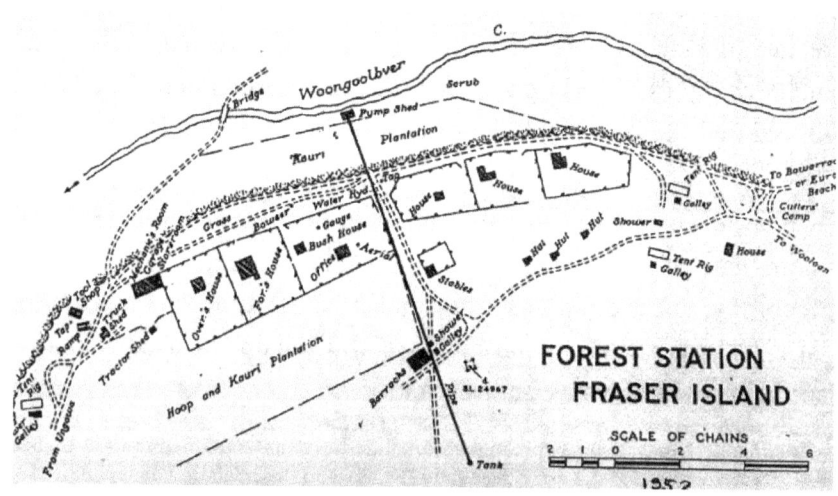

Plan of Central Station, 1952. (From D. Eckert, 2003)

Chapter 13 details the plantings in and around Central Station, including the beautiful hoop and kauri pines on its eastern edge, established in the 1920s. Just above Woongoolbver Creek is a fine patch of about a dozen rose gum trees mixed with rainforest. Trainee John Rudder planted them in 1950.[2] There is a lovely, pure stand of blackbutt on the hill behind the barracks, providing a splendid backdrop for the settlement. Many tour operators mention the magnificent stand of hoop pine at Central Station, but they overlook the fact that it was all planted during forestry's halcyon days under their stewardship.

Rose gum trees planted at Central Station, 1950. (Photo the author)

---

[2] This information was provided to me by Dick Pegg, who worked on the island in 1958. However, Sandy Luck claims his father Allan planted them in 1950, along with the row of pine trees parallel to the old through road near the creek. Rudder may have planted the row of exotic pine instead.

Hoop pine plantation near Central Station. (Photo Sam Van Holsbeeck)

Row of loblolly pine planted at Central Station 1926-7. (Photo the author)

During the 1940s, '50s, and '60s, many long-term forestry employees lived on the island, including George "Choker" Wex, Harold Saint, Jim Morgan,[3] Bob Barbeler, truck driver Toby Fletcher, Herbie Tanner, delver operator Jack Gardiner, Jack Gilchrist, and brothers Bill, Sandy, and Ivan Luck. These men were remarkable bushmen.

Ivan and Sandy Luck. (Photo Narelle Evans)

After the *Korawinga* ceased operations and Forestry no longer required a vessel, they appointed former launch master Cec Neilson to manage the campgrounds. While his main focus was at Central Station, Lake McKenzie, and Lake Boemingen, he was also responsible for delivering recreational services throughout the entire state forest. His duties included signage and maintenance from Lake Bowarrady Forest Drive to Hook Point Road via Garry's

---

[3] It is not definite, but Jim Morgan was either the older brother, half-brother or cousin of Chad Morgan, the famous Australian country music singer and guitarist known for his comic country and western and folk songs, his prominent teeth and goofy stage persona. Chad was known as "the Sheik of Scrubby Creek".

Anchorage. Cec's dedication was unmatched. He and his team built and maintained toilets and picnic tables, provided tap water, and meticulously looked after the camp areas for many years under Forestry's stewardship.

The introduction of radio communications after the war period raised concerns about the effectiveness of Central Station due to its inadequate radio reception. In 1959, Forestry relocated its headquarters to a cleared sandhill near the Ungowa jetty. The lack of vegetation and the higher elevation of the settlement above the tidal swamps made for a more pleasant environment, with fewer midges and mosquitoes compared to other sites on the west coast.

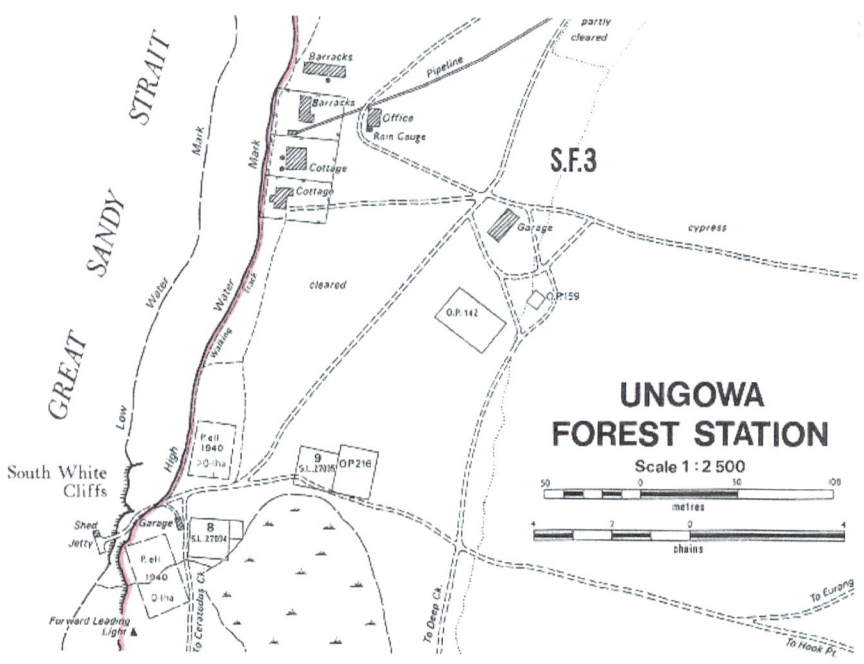

Plan of buildings at Ungowa settlement, based on aerial photos from 1970. (Department of Forestry Map Sheet 3, Fraser Island, 1977)

Carpenter Eddie "Wonga" Pidgeon dismantled one of the forester's houses at Central Station and moved it to Ungowa, where it was rebuilt. Forestry also built a house for the ranger, along with barracks, visitor quarters, an office, a garage, and a workshop. A residence for the sawmill's representative was also constructed on a special lease. In 1971, a boat shed and a wooden ramp were built near the jetty to house the speedboat *Werriga*, used for emergencies and short visits by forestry officers to the island. In 1980, the shed was extended to accommodate the 23-foot shark-cat, *Korawinga II*, which was used intermittently.

Ungowa became the island's administrative centre, also housing harvesting and marketing staff, and a clerk. Two long-serving employees from the Harvesting and Marketing Branch, Bill Duke and Snowy Buffy, lived at Ungowa for many years and were responsible for carrying out their duties across the island.

A small nursery was set up north of the workshop to raise blackbutt seedlings; however, it only lasted 12 months due to issues with phytophthora. After the nursery closed, overseer Ken Cochran moved on to harvesting and marketing, supervising the harvesting activities alongside senior overseer Doug Gordon for many years. Following his retirement, the nursery area was named Ken Cochran Memorial Park in recognition of his contribution to the effective management of the timber resource over a long period. Cochran was one of many dedicated forestry workers on Fraser Island.

Aerial view of Ungowa settlement, October 1968. (Department of Forestry)

During Forestry's occupation, the high-quality weatherboard buildings with commanding views across the Great Sandy Strait were well-maintained and painted regularly. Each house featured a wooden fence and lawns, while the workers transformed the entire settlement into a grassy area they mowed periodically, replacing wattle, old stumps and logs with a smooth, grassy slope. They even developed a small golf course. After 1971, each building was fitted with its own 32-volt generator and battery bank.

Forestry camps

A series of permanent and temporary camps supported logging operations on Fraser Island. These camps accommodated workers and provided the essential necessities for life in the island's remote areas.

One of the earliest camps was Ding Donga, also known as Dundonga camp, located just south of Bun Bun Creek on the Northern Road. It was originally used by the roading gang, a group of eight men who felled small trees with axes and crosscut saws. They utilised tree pullers – devices fitted with geared winches and wire ropes – to bring down larger trees after they had grubbed out as much sandy soil as possible from the roots using a mattock. Massive tree trunks with stump roots still lie along the road just north of Bun Bun Creek, serving as a testament to their hard work. In the late 1940s and '50s, the camp was taken over by silvicultural gangs, who used brush hooks to thin out the blackbutt regeneration in nearby compartments.

The teams then moved north along the same road to Aqua camp. The old campsite is marked by a small patch of regrowth forest and a hand-planted rose gum located where Aqua Road intersects Poyungan Creek. It is close to the survey blaze L24 on a tree.

There was a camp for the maintenance crew near Pile Valley on HH Road, now part of the Great Walk, called "Rat's camp" because of the swarms of rats that invaded the area and ate the provisions. In the early 1930s, the men cared for the young hoop pine plantations in the vicinity.

Other camps were established during the 1950s at Yankee Jack Creek, Poyungan, Coomboo Lakes, Red Lagoon and McKenzies. The first three were permanent, with Yankee Jack being the largest, housing four single men, an office, and a garage. Poyungan camp accommodated six men in two fibro huts with a central kitchen galley. The Coomboo Lakes camp was built in the mid-1960s to house workers in the far northern extremities of the state forest and included two prefabricated huts that could sleep four men. The intention was to fly the workers in and out to avoid the long, slow daily trip from Ungowa.

In 1985, a camp was built just south of AB Lake (now called Lake Allom). It housed groups of workers primarily engaged in post-logging silvicultural work. The lake is worth visiting because it is surrounded by natural stands of hoop pine and is home to many turtles.

Another camp, known as AC8, was situated along the AC traverse, previously Garry's Road, on the southern shores of Woocoonba Lagoons.

In later years, during the 1960s, two six-man barracks were built at Yankee Jack. Like the barracks at Ungowa and other parts of the state, each room was designed to accommodate two men and included an attached kitchen, galley, shower and an outside dry toilet. Water was pumped from the lake. These barracks housed silvicultural crews who carried out forest treatments in the southern part of the island.

Although the camps for all the workers – logging contractors and forestry personnel – were theoretically dry camps, the men gained a reputation for enjoying a few beers when the opportunity arose. Provisions allowed anywhere from one to six cartons of beer during the workers' fortnightly stint on the island. Many stories circulated about their attempts to acquire grog for their days off while on the island. John Kitt, who first worked on the island as a 19-year-old forest trainee in 1964, remarked:

> I was not on the island for long before it hit me that there were some very hard, heavy and seasoned drinkers over there![4]

George Luke, who worked on the island as a forester in the mid-1960s, recalls feeling particularly upset with Jack Gardiner one Sunday afternoon. After returning to the island from his weekend off with a sack of pumpkins, Gardiner fell between the boat and the jetty while disembarking, severely cutting himself on the oysters lining the jetty piles. Luke's wife had to tend to his wounds. However, Luke initially refused to approve his compensation claim because Gardiner was drunk and had travelled on private transport via Sid Melksham's boat outside of work hours. Ultimately, Luke had to approve the compensation claim because it was Gardiner's usual means of transport, and he was known to be intoxicated when travelling back to the island![5]

Living conditions on Fraser Island were quite basic. For those who valued a social life and the finer things, and disliked solitude and isolation, Fraser Island simply wasn't for them. Because of these challenges, some workers didn't stay for long.

There was no power, so the men had to rely on unpleasant carbide lights. These lights produced a foul odour and highly flammable gas but, when used correctly, provided a powerful yet soft, bright light. Each worker was issued one carbide lamp, although some chose the Tilley light, which used methylated spirits for priming and kerosene for fuel. They were much safer but also more expensive.

---

[4] Kitt, J. (2024) *The Big Timberland – my life as a Queensland Forestry Trainee: Part Two*. John Huth Publishing, Little Mountain, p. 10.

[5] There are many similar stories. Some have been published such as the fight between staff from Ungowa and Central Station after a few drinks at a Christmas break up party in 1968 – see forester John Alcock's version of what happened in Huth, J. (2023) *As We Were*. Self-published, Brisbane. p. 9.

Hot water for showers, washing clothes and dishes was supplied by a copper tub heated by a fire that required a significant amount of firewood each evening. Fortunately, there was plenty of firewood available on the island. Each camp's woodpile was stacked with dead hardwood logs, and workers took turns chopping them into suitable lengths and splitting them with an axe.

Communication with the mainland was rudimentary and limited. A telephone line connected Central Station, Poyungan, Bogimbah and Yankee Jack camps to Ungowa, then to the mainland. This line operated through an exchange in one of the forester's houses at Ungowa. It consisted of a single earth return line supported by small, dilapidated, leaning poles along the road, which needed regular maintenance. Vehicles were equipped with two-way radios, with the base station at Ungowa; however, communication was unreliable and had a limited range.

The tragic death of logging contractor Laurie Postans in 1963, along with the severe leg injury suffered by faller Vernon Ward, prompted Lambert Hyne to lobby for improved communications on Fraser Island. Eventually, a telephone cable was laid from Boonooroo across the Great Sandy Strait to a point just south of Figtree Creek and then north on the island to Ungowa using poles.

In the mid-1960s, Luke organised the installation of new telephone lines between Ungowa and Central Station, as well as from Ungowa to Yankee Jack camp. A better alignment with a wider clearing path was selected, using cypress pine poles and double wires, which improved service between the three forestry stations. Logging contractors Postan and Cunningham extended the lines to Poyungan and Bogimbah camps to the north.

Logging contractors

The logging contractors on the island were a tough and innovative bunch, constantly adapting to the island's challenging environment. In the early days of logging, bullock teams were predominant, and tramways were constructed during the early 20th century. However, by the 1930s, internal combustion engines started to replace them.

Albert Berthelsen first arrived on the island around 1905 and began after working with his father in the Bennett Creek area. By about 1910, he moved to Deep Creek and teamed up with the Wilschefski brothers, operating six bullock teams at Figtree, Garry's and Yankee Jack.

Figtree camp 1920s. Believed to be Berthelsen and Wilschefski camp.
(Photo courtesy MWBBHS (Image_ID FR067))

During the 1920s and '30s, Stan Jennings and Edmond "Ezzy" Sengstock were the main logging contractors on the island and the last known operators to use bullocks for snigging logs. Vic Hope was another timber contractor who brought an International T20 crawler tractor to the island in 1935. He also owned a rear-wheel drive timber truck that transported people around the island. While hauling logs, he had to navigate spider bridges – simple structures made of two logs spanning a creek without decking boards. As he approached the bridge, Vic always positioned himself with one foot on the brake and the other on the running board, ready to jump out if he missed the bridge log. If the truck suddenly stopped, the log load could shift forward and crush him in the cabin.

In 1935, Andy Postans from Western Australia arrived on the island as an employee of logging contractors Richard and Neville

Smith for Wilson Hart. He met the Smiths while cutting cane and timber near Cairns. The Smiths owned a small, 35-horsepower Caterpillar crawler tractor used to snig the logs to landings and haul them to Urang Creek, where John Hansen would barge them to Maryborough. The Caterpillar towed a bobtail to lift the front of the logs, and the Smiths had various models over the years. In 1964, an International TD9 with a blade and winch replaced it. The Smith-Poyungan Road is named after the Smiths.

In 1940, Andy[6] bought the logging business and equipment from the Smiths. They moved their camp from near a swamp on the Smith-Poyungan Road to a higher base camp above the Poyungan Creek log landing to escape the biting midges that thrived near the mangroves. The secret to keeping the pesky insects at bay was to clear the area to encourage a breeze and maintain short grass.

Initially, he worked in various areas but ultimately became the northernmost contractor on the island. His son, Andrew, joined him in 1954, and they established a partnership in 1964, naming the business A. R. Postan and Son.

Jacob Lack was Andy Postan's earliest and most prominent tree faller. He lived alone in a small shack in Compartment 6, Poyungan, and retired in 1962. He also conducted tours on a part-time basis.[7]

Frustrated with relying on tides to transport himself, his family and his workers to and from the island, Andrew decided to learn to fly and obtained his pilot's licence in the late 1960s. He eventually replaced their launch, *Maralon*, with a Cessna 185, enabling him to travel more efficiently between Fraser Island and Maryborough, where his wife Helen had moved to secure better educational opportunities for their children.

Andy's older brother, Laurie Postans, arrived on the island in 1944. He purchased the contract and machinery from the Berthelsen brothers to start his own logging business at the eastern end of

---

[6] Andy changed his name to Postan by deed poll after setting up his business name inadvertently as Postan. It was easier than changing the business name.
[7] For more details see Chapter 20.

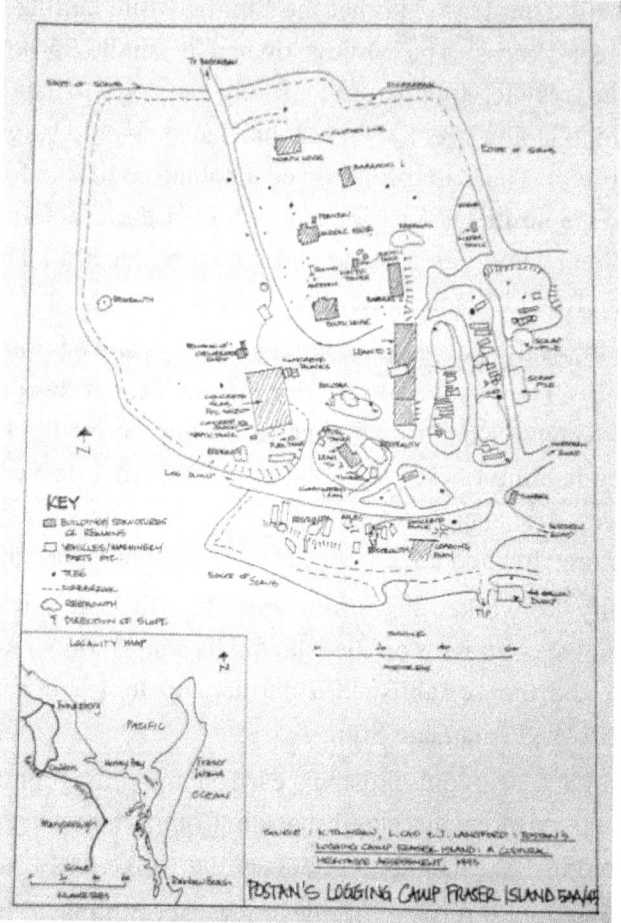

This plan shows in detail the layout of Postan's camp when it was operational. (Courtesy Queensland Government)

Central Station. Laurie was a champion woodchopper, winning titles in Western Australia, Victoria, New South Wales and Tasmania. He was also an accomplished heavyweight boxer. He and his crew camped at Central Station, using high stumps as springboards for his training.

Laurie's crew famously cut down what was reputed to be the largest tree ever on the island in October 1951 at the Woolan Logging Area, not far from Lake Birrabeen. It was a tallowwood measuring 98 feet to the first limb, with a diameter of 198 inches, and contained approximately 14,000 super feet of timber after being cut into two massive logs.

Sadly, Laurie's life was tragically cut short on 26 January 1963, in a logging accident when a log rolled over him from a truck, serving as a stark reminder of the dangers associated with the trade. Nearly a year later, Andrew narrowly escaped losing his life in a similar incident.

In 1945, 17-year-old Thomas Errol "Joe" Cunningham travelled to the island to work for Andy Postan, camping at the head of Yankee Jack Creek. He later cut piles for the Department of Mines and installed lights in the Great Sandy Strait for over two years. Afterwards, he worked for Laurie Postans for six months before a 12-month stint with Cliff Sanderson, transporting logs on Wilson Hart's barge, the *Lass O'Gowrie*.

Cunningham left the island to work in Maryborough and then Papua New Guinea, returning in 1958 to establish his own logging contract business cutting for Hyne & Son, taking over from Bill Short. Short lived on the island with his partner Pat, a barmaid he met at the Royal in Maryborough. The Wilson brothers, John and Jim, were his cutters, along with George Wilson, who was not related.

Initially, Cunningham lived full-time on the island with his family at their bush camp then later, at Deep Creek for many years. As most of his work shifted further north, the camp was relocated to the mouth of Bogimbah Creek in 1962, marked by a few coconut trees and some debris. His boat, the *Joycey-Q*, ferried family members and workers to and from the island.

After obtaining his pilot's licence in 1967, he bought a Cessna 182, which greatly reduced travel time to and from Hervey Bay. Along with Andrew Postan, he constructed the Bogimbah airstrip behind Poyungan Creek in the late 1960s.

Before switching to rubber-tyred skidders, Cunningham purchased two GMC trucks, a Caterpillar D6 and International TD9 bulldozers. He kept experimenting with machinery to enhance the efficiency and safety of his operations, especially after a serious incident where one of his employees, Clarrie Sullivan, lost both legs in a bridle accident while loading a truck. Cunningham modified the bucket of an old LD7 Scoopmobile with log forks to further improve how logs were loaded, making it safer and more efficient. His son, Tom, started working for him from the age of 14, snigging timber, driving trucks, and maintaining machinery.

In 1958, Codford "Taffy" Lewis arrived on the island from Landsborough as a logging contractor for Wilson Hart, taking over from Jennings. He established his camp at Lake Jennings and logged in various areas, including Ungowa, Central Station, Lake Birrabeen and Lake Jennings. He harvested satinay, brush box, red stringybark, and tallowwood, utilising a TD9 bulldozer alongside a rubber-tired bobtail. His tree fallers were Roy Fish, Bob Cook and John Swanson.

Claude Cornwall, who logged for Wilson Hart on the mainland in the Cooloola Sands, travelled to the island in 1959 with his son Warwick. They set up a camp at McKenzie's with their families and departed in 1969.

Eddie Kopp was stationed at Garry's camp in the Forestry barracks but also had a camp at Bogimbah, where he lived with his wife and crew. His brother-in-law, Col Barker, who had an artificial leg, worked for him along with truck driver Bevan Fleming and tree fallers Jack Krogh, Bill Freeman, and Kopp's son Max. Freeman brought along a lady friend, who was formerly a barmaid at the Royal Hotel in Maryborough, and was rumoured to be skilled at handling one end of the cross-cut saw.

Little is known about the other contractors, Mel Backhouse and the Shum brothers, who lived in a rough camp behind the log dump at Deep Creek.

Mel "Sleepy" Wilson left school early to work in timber cutting and as a bullock driver in the Conondale Ranges. After getting married, he moved to Maryborough to work at the Hyne & Son sawmill. Later, he moved to the Kilkivan area and returned in 1954 to start a logging business on Fraser Island when an opportunity arose. Wilson and his brother John began their work in the Dundonga Scrub, staying at a nearby camp in bark huts at both ends of the clearing. Wilson's family – his wife and two young boys – lived on the island with him for a time. Wilson owned a Caterpillar D4 bulldozer, which lacked a cabin or blade, but it towed a jinker to lift the front part of the log, making snigging easier. He also had a GMC truck for transporting logs.

"Mel "Sleepy" Wilson on tractor assisting a loaded truck up a steep incline, 1959. (Department of Forestry)

In the 1960s, the logging industry experienced some consolidation among contractors. Andy Postan had the opportunity to buy out Kopp in 1961, but he turned it down, despite Andrew's enthusiasm. However, over time, they gradually acquired other contractors or took over their contracts as those contractors departed: Laurie Postans in 1964, Taffy Lewis in 1965, and Claude and Warwick Cornwall in 1969. By then, the Postans were cutting timber for both Wilson Hart and Hyne & Son.

In 1962, Cunningham bought Eddie Kopp's operation, which included an Allis Chalmers HD10 bulldozer and several trucks. He then purchased Wilson's operation in 1968 and acquired Backhouse and the Shum brothers in 1970.

In 1974, Cunningham decided to leave the island, and Andy Postan purchased his machinery, securing the cutting rights, and becoming the sole logging contractor on the island. Andy Postan retired in February 1977, and Andrew took over with his wife, Helen, while retaining the business name. They remained the only logging contractor until logging ceased at the end of 1991.

Andrew Postan was the last man standing, largely due to his resourcefulness and success as an operator – skills essential for anyone dealing with heavy machinery logging in the tough environment of Fraser Island. His foresight and practical mindset drove him to continuously improve his machinery and operations. He developed impressive mechanical and engineering skills despite leaving school and heading straight to the island without any formal training.

In May 1979, a devastating fire in his workshop nearly cost him everything. Although he was tempted to leave the island, he persevered and reinstated both the workshop and his business.

Andrew provided more sophisticated accommodation for his family and workers than most timber contractors. Instead of simple bush timber huts with galvanised iron roofs and walls, he constructed proper houses with septic tanks. However, one notable exception was an old Brisbane bus he used in remote areas to minimise the need for daily trips back to the base camp.

Before World War II, various types of trucks were used on the island to haul logs, including a two-wheel drive Commer, a Karrier, a Leyland, and an International C50 truck. Postan converted the International to tandem drive, transforming it into a 6 x 4. They also purchased a Ford Marmon Herrington and GMC 6 x 6 trucks by the end of the war. In 1964, they bought an ex-Army six-wheel drive

Postan's camp in the 1980s. (Photo courtesy David Postan)

International, and in August 1967, they added a new Associated Equipment Company (AEC) six-wheel drive truck.

Cunningham owned second-hand Diamond T, AEC, Matador, GMC and Studebaker trucks, all of which were in use until around 1967.

Andrew acquired three AEC trucks when he bought Cunningham's business. In the late 1970s, he owned a Mack 6x6 truck, but its suspension was inadequate for the island. In the 1980s, he purchased two eight-wheel-drive MAN trucks.

The dangers of tree felling

Felling trees was a very dangerous occupation. Unfortunately, several fallers died or sustained serious injuries while working on the island over the years. While working alone in the forest in the early 1950s, Laurie Postans was pinned against a tractor by a falling tree. Although he broke his back in two places, he managed to free himself and drove the tractor back to his camp for help. He was in plaster for several months but returned to work on the island as soon as he was declared fit.

One Saturday in 1958, John Swanson was injured by a widow-maker while felling a blackbutt tree, sustaining severe damage to the side of his skull. He was taken to the emergency boat, the *Satinay,* at Deep Creek, where an ambulance was organised via the radio system to meet them at River Heads. Bill Luck started the motor, but it cut out soon after. With a stiff north-west wind blowing directly at them, they faced a rough journey. The *Satinay* was taking on water, and Dick Pegg was above the forward hatch, tossing buckets of water overboard while George Wilson passed the buckets to him through the hatch, all the while feeling seasick. They were almost at River Heads when Laurie Postans caught up with them in his boat, bringing relief as they spotted the ambulance awaiting them. Postans then escorted the stricken vessel back to Deep Creek.

George Davison died in February 1964 after a tree-felling accident. Sandy Luck and Andrew Postan's younger brother, Rob, spent the night guarding Davison's body from the dingoes until it could be transferred to Maryborough.

Syd "Danny" Jones worked alongside the legendary faller Graham Brady in June 1974. Tragically, he was killed when a tree he was felling struck a nearby stump and swung back, striking him in the chest. Jones had been working on the island for three years. His last words to Brady before he died were, "I think I'm gone this time."

Brady, who spent many years working on the island for Cunningham and Postan, suffered several injuries throughout his career, with the most severe being a fractured blood vessel in his scrotum, as he describes:

> One time, I finished with the biggest personal private parts of anyone ever to cut timber on the island, but sadly, some might say it was not a permanent feature ... I was using a Stihl 090 chainsaw with a 25-inch cutter bar. It jammed and kicked back and hit me in my delicate area, and unlike

cricket players who wear protection, I had none ... I bet those nurses at Gympie Hospital had some laughs and probably drew straws to see who was going to dress my greatly increased in size personal parts.[8]

George White was employed for only a week and narrowly escaped a fatal injury when a limb fell, breaking his neck in 1978. Meanwhile, Ernest Ward broke his back in 1980 after a tree fell on him.

* * * * *

By the late 20th century, the forestry activities that had defined Fraser Island for over a century were ending. After logging stopped in 1991, many of the once-thriving settlements and camps fell into disrepair.

Once a thriving community, Central Station has become a day-use and camping site with limited facilities. The grand forestry houses and other structures at Ungowa have been allowed to deteriorate. The manicured grassy areas are completely neglected, further contributing to the site's decline. These facilities suffer from neglect and government indifference towards this important cultural heritage.

The decline of the logging industry on Fraser Island mirrors broader shifts in Australian forestry policy, as environmental concerns increasingly overshadow timber production. Nevertheless, the forestry legacy remains a source of pride for those who lived and worked on the island, highlighting their hard work and dedication.

As visitors wander through the forests of Central Station or stand on the shores of Lake McKenzie, they can witness the effects of a century of human ingenuity and labour. The trees planted by forestry workers, the roads carved through dense scrub, the remnants of camps, and the visitor facilities all form part of the island's history – a history that deserves recognition and respect.

---

[8] Williams, F. R. (2002) Op. cit., p. 132.

PART 4
FROM PROSPERITY TO CONTROVERSY

17

SAND MINING AND THE BEGINNING OF THE END FOR LOGGING ON THE ISLAND

Before the sand mining controversy emerged in the mid-1970s, Fraser Island was largely unknown, except to those who relied on it for their livelihood – timber workers and a few local fishermen. These individuals lived and worked on the island, maintaining its natural balance while extracting its resources for over a century.

Nevertheless, environmental issues brought the island out of obscurity and captured global attention. Sand mining sparked a battle over Fraser Island's future and marked the beginning of the decline of forestry; an industry deeply tied to the island's identity.

For decades, timber was the island's main industry, but its vast dunes held untapped value. Heavy minerals, primarily titanium, magnesium, zircon, rutile, and ilmenite, were found in greater abundance in Australian coastal sands than anywhere else in the world. In 1948, sand mining commenced with the granting of mineral leases at Teewah, located between Double Island Point and Noosa's North Shore. Additional leases were also issued in some eastern beach areas on Fraser Island in 1950.

The Cooloola back down: a prelude to a larger battle

Enhanced extraction techniques and rising demand for aerospace technologies in the 1950s and '60s resulted in an exploration surge in the coastal sand masses of south-east Queensland, primarily by two companies.

In 1952, Titanium Alloy Manufacturing Company Pty Ltd, a wholly owned subsidiary of the National Lead Company of New York, was granted an authority to prospect over 170,000 acres on

Fraser Island, Tin Can Bay, and Bribie Island.[1] After an extensive drilling program that revealed moderate-sized, low-grade rutile reserves in selected areas, the company applied for two mineral leases – one at Inskip Point and another on Fraser Island.

The company's mineral reserves in northern New South Wales were nearly depleted at that time. They planned to establish a long-term, large-scale mining and processing operation in the Cooloola sands, aiming to produce 20,000 tonnes of rutile and zircon annually over approximately a 20-year period. Additionally, they obtained a mineral lease for Fraser Island on 5 September 1968, with no objections raised. On 20 May 1966, Murphyores, an Australian company, applied for sand mining leases covering 19,000 acres on Fraser Island. Both companies aimed to extract rutile, zircon, and ilmenite for shipment to the USA.

Rutile was used in the flux coating of arc welding electrodes and smelted into titanium for use in space vehicles and high-speed aircraft because it was more heat and corrosion resistant than aluminium. It was also processed into titanium oxide pigments, which provided the whiteness in paint, paper, and textiles. Zircon has an exceptionally high melting point and is valuable as moulding sand in foundries. It is also used to produce opacity and glazes in the ceramic industry and creates high-temperature fire bricks for furnaces as well as in cosmetics and chemicals in the paint, textile, tanning and pharmaceutical industries. Although ilmenite along the east coast was not used commercially due to chromite contamination, it was found in greater proportions than other heavy minerals in sands north of Brisbane, and both companies were eager to extract it. Ilmenite was used as a metallurgical alloy and to produce paint pigments through a process that was distinctly different from that of rutile.

Before the environmental struggle reached Fraser Island, the

---

[1] Interest in the lease was transferred to Queensland Titanium Mines Pty Ltd (QTM) on 21 April 1965.

first significant confrontation over sand mining occurred on the Cooloola Sand Mass, located on the mainland. When QTM renewed its mineral lease applications in 1970, a coalition of various environmental groups, known as the Cooloola Committee, launched the "Save Cooloola" campaign, which gained traction in Brisbane. They aimed to have the entire sand mass from the Noosa River to Double Island Point designated as a national park and argued that the land's restoration after mining was inadequate, threatening the area's natural values.

The activists' modus operandi was all or nothing, with no intention of compromising between preservation and development. They heavily lobbied and convinced the anxious city-based Liberal Party backbenchers to abandon any idea of mining. Queensland's Mines Minister Ron Camm, viewed as a rival to Premier Joh Bjelke-Petersen, both members of the National Party, sensed a growing momentum against the sand mining proposal and tried to broker a compromise in cabinet to permit mining over a significantly reduced area, leaving 48,000 acres for a national park.

The party room held a secret vote, and although Camm's compromise was never tested, the government ultimately rejected all new mineral leases for Cooloola.

The mineral sands that helped put astronauts on the moon remained in situ, and the residents of Tin Can Bay were furious that their dreams of jobs and local investment had suddenly disappeared. The mining companies threatened legal action to seek compensation. One executive described the decision as:

> The greatest example of mob psychology since Julius Caesar.[2]

Following this backdown, the Premier wrote to the cabinet in September 1970, warning them that the Cooloola decision had raised expectations for similar campaigns against new sand mining

---

[2] Conservationists battle to save Cooloola, *The Canberra Times*, 17 September 1970, p. 16 (Trove). Accessed 24 September 2024.

proposals elsewhere. He sought to evaluate potential future mining sites along the coast and classify them for optimal use to prevent future conflicts. To achieve this, the government established an Inter-Departmental Committee to undertake the task.

A defiant new voice

Fraser Island differed from Cooloola because of previous sand mining activities and the issuance of multiple mineral leases. However, after the successful campaign at Cooloola, environmentalists aimed to oppose any attempts to expand sand mining on Fraser Island. They gathered public support and raised funds. Following public notices about new mineral claims on the island, the Fraser Island Defenders Organisation (FIDO), led by John Sinclair, emerged as a significant opponent in the battle against further mineral extraction.[3]

Sinclair's strategy involved postponing mining by requiring a comprehensive land use study of the entire island. He aimed to illustrate that Fraser Island's environmental and recreational values far outweighed its mining potential. While his approach appeared sensible, he had no intention of permitting mining to proceed, even if some areas of the island were deemed suitable.

Through relentless lobbying, letter-writing campaigns and public speeches, Sinclair garnered support from various groups, including the state Labor Party. As FIDO's influence grew, so did the effort to save Fraser Island from what Sinclair called the "indiscriminate granting of mineral leases".

Sand mining meets the courts

In January 1971, DM Minerals lodged new claims for two mineral leases. Three objections were filed: one from the Labor Party, another from the Wildlife Preservation Society of Queensland, and 1,375 objections from individuals on behalf of FIDO, which, at the

---

[3] More details about John Sinclair are provided in the next chapter.

time, was an unincorporated organisation and could not lodge an objection. The only objector to present evidence was Sinclair during a 14-day hearing – a record for Queensland. Despite the attention, the Mining Warden recommended that DM Minerals' applications be granted.

According to Sinclair, he was determined to pressure the government never to treat:

> Major environmental issues with such casual indifference and with such a bias favouring exploitation of resources.[4]

Over the following two years, he took every opportunity to raise public awareness about Fraser Island, including appeals to the Queensland Supreme Court and, ultimately, the High Court of Australia. In a landmark decision, the High Court unanimously upheld Sinclair's appeal in June 1974 against the successful sand mining applications granted to QTM. This victory was not merely a personal victory; it was the first time Australia's highest court ruled on an environmental matter, setting a legal precedent for future cases.

Whitlam's vision

While Sinclair was engaged in legal battles, political winds shifted in Canberra. The election of a Labor Government and the appointment of Gough Whitlam as Prime Minister in late 1972 heralded a new agenda for preserving Australia's natural heritage. Whitlam's ministers announced plans for a National Estate Inquiry to identify and protect areas of significant environmental and cultural value. Fraser Island was a top priority, with FIDO leading the efforts for these preservation initiatives. The National Estate Committee spent four days on Fraser Island, hosted by Sinclair during one of his FIDO tours. His direct influence helped elevate the profile of their campaign.

---

[4] Sinclair, J. (1982) A brief history of the fight for Fraser Island. Supplement to *Moonbi* 54.

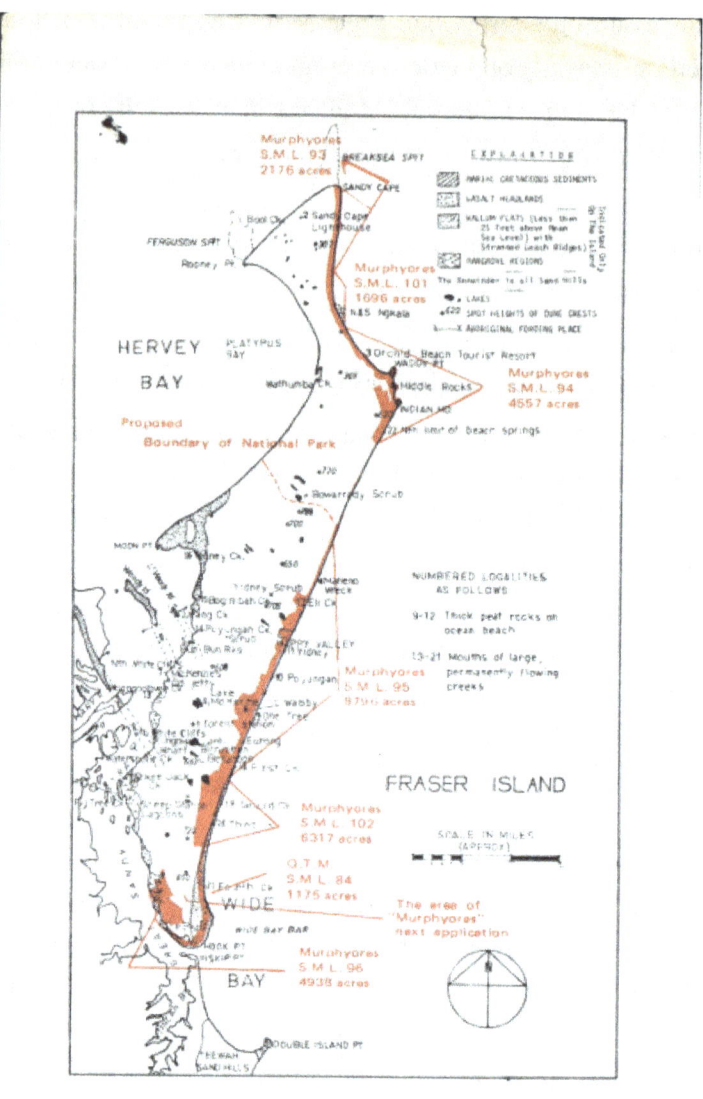

Sand mining leases on Fraser Island c1975.
(Queensland State Archives)

QTM began sand mining on the southern end of Fraser Island in January 1972, investing $900,000 in roads, wharves, and related facilities. By mid-May 1975, the total area disturbed by mining amounted to 390 acres, with 44,292 tonnes of rutile and 32,793 tonnes of zircon extracted.

DM Minerals sand mining operation on Fraser Island, 1976.
(Photo Peter Rutherford)

In April 1973, QTM and DM Minerals lodged two new mineral lease applications. FIDO opposed QTM's application, which had the support of 3,500 petitioners, but their objections did not persuade the Mining Warden. A few months later, DM Minerals' court application produced a similar outcome.

Considering the legal challenges surrounding the granting of mineral leases, the Federal Government recognised the growing environmental pressures and showed sympathy for their cause. They quickly established an environmental inquiry into land use on Fraser Island, even after issuing export permits just months earlier. However, following a legal challenge from DM Minerals, the government suspended the inquiry.

A second inquiry began in April 1975, just months after the Federal Government enacted the *Environmental Protection (Impact of Proposals) Act 1974*.

Federal intervention, the inquiry and science versus sovereignty

Under the Constitution, the Federal Government has no jurisdiction over state matters. However, it believed that its new environmental act allowed it to refuse to issue export licences if a project was deemed harmful to the environment. This interpretation caused significant concern among the state government, the sand miners, and the local community, who viewed it as a threat to sovereign risk.

Unsurprisingly, the Queensland Government believed there was some uncertainty about the legality of the inquiry and sought Crown law advice, which stated:

> The Commonwealth has no direct power to step in, in the name of conservation, to stop mining, even if it has the power to take into consideration in its great power concerning export … it follows, in my opinion, that the Commonwealth has no power to stop mining by any lawful or legitimate means.[5]

The Federal Government requested that DM Minerals halt its sand mining operations while awaiting the outcome of the inquiry. However, they declined, and the government caucus nearly voted to defer the export licences that had already been issued during the inquiry's findings.

DM Minerals subsequently launched another legal challenge, seeking a High Court writ to contest the validity of the inquiry and the new act. They requested an injunction to prevent the inquiry from proceeding and to declare that the minister was not authorised to make decisions regarding environmental protection under the Constitution. The High Court unanimously dismissed their case, ruling that the Commonwealth was legitimately exercising its trade and commerce power.

---

[5] Arnold Bennett (1976) Memorandum of Advice, 12 November. ITM 963213, QSA.

The inquiry lasted for seven weeks, during which it received 658 exhibits and evidence from over 100 witnesses. It became a flashpoint in the escalating conflict, as the sand mining companies declined to participate, and the Queensland Government opted not to cooperate or assist. Despite this, they submitted a comprehensive report.

After a year of deliberation, the inquiry released its final report in October 1976. It recommended sand mining cease on Fraser Island and that the island be included in the National Estate.

This was a significant victory for environmentalists; however, the recommendations ignited a fierce backlash from mining interests and local communities. Besides losing $750 million in export income, the Commonwealth Government's intervention in state matters threatened Australia's credibility as a reliable source of high-grade sand minerals and resources.

Used as political pawns

There was a broad consensus that the inquiry's findings were exaggerated and biased in favour of preservation. Unfortunately, because the mining companies and the Queensland Government declined to participate in the inquiry, they never provided substantial evidence to counter the suspected environmental impacts.

In November 1976, Bjelke-Petersen wrote to Prime Minister Malcolm Fraser to refute the inquiry's findings of "probable" damage to critical environmental features, such as lakes and creeks, caused by sand mining. He based his argument on evidence from a year of mining on the high dunes.

In contrast to the environmental assumptions presented by experts during the inquiry, the consultants' hydrological studies found no immediate or long-term effects on surface or groundwater. These studies also showed that rehabilitated dunes reacted to fluctuations in plant nutrient levels at the same rate as the unmined control areas. Bjelke-Petersen stated that the mined dunes retained nutrients and water similarly to the unmined regions.

However, this effort was in vain, as the decision had already been made and would not be reversed. On 10 November 1976, Fraser announced that his government would fully adopt the inquiry's recommendations. On 31 December 1976, the export of mineral sand mined from Fraser Island was restricted to minerals extracted from designated areas. Despite the thorough report and intense inquiry, Parliament spent only 25 minutes debating the report before reaching a decision. The political nature of the decision was highlighted when the Federal Government issued additional export licences just three weeks after assessing rehabilitation efforts on the island.

In a double blow, Fraser Island was the first place added to the Interim Register of the National Estate by the Australian Heritage Commission (AHC), following the inquiry's recommendations.

It was a momentous occasion in Australian political history, coming soon after the Governor-General's dramatic dismissal of a Prime Minister. It was concerning that the Commonwealth Government was prepared to use powers initially granted to regulate trade to enforce environmental policies.

Most sand miners received only six weeks' notice, faced an uncertain future, and spent Christmas without work. They were also unsure how to meet their financial obligations. This was a harsh political decision for an activity that impacted only a small part of the island, shattering the hopes and aspirations of many. The Maryborough community was already struggling due to a decline in the dairy industry and the closure of Walker's shipyards. They saw sand mining as a crucial boost to their struggling economy.

Political fallout: jobs, compensation and community anger

The decision to ban sand mining had far-reaching consequences, particularly for the communities of Maryborough and Hervey Bay. These towns had long relied on Fraser Island's natural resources to support their economies, and the sand mining industry was regarded as a vital source of employment.

Tensions flared as local leaders, led by Maryborough's Mayor Jock Anderson, convened a public meeting to discuss the sand mining issue on Fraser Island. This was the first time those affected were invited to voice their opinions. Activists, particularly Sinclair, had dominated the discussion. Over 1,500 people attended and overwhelmingly voted in favour of regulated sand mining, arguing that industries on the island, including sand mining, forestry, and tourism, were crucial for the economic future of the Maryborough and Hervey Bay area.

They believed they had a much greater interest in and dependence on the future and welfare of Fraser Island than any other community. Many were upset with outside organisations and the Federal Government, which they felt disregarded their interests and sacrificed them in favour of distant environmental ideals.

They directed their frustrations at FIDO and Sinclair:

> We deplore the methods and extent to which a minority group of people in this area with extreme views on conservation have strived to have their own ideas forced onto the vast majority of local people.[6]

Bjelke-Petersen sought compensation for displaced workers and the economic losses experienced by the region. He requested a commitment of $78 million over a ten-year period to fund various projects. However, the Commonwealth's assistance package fell well short, offering only a "generous" amount of up to $10 million over 3½ years, contingent upon the state agreeing not to pursue legal action. This undertaking was never accepted, even though the state government surprisingly decided against pursuing any legal challenges regarding the decision to cease mining.

The Commonwealth offered an ex-gratia payment of $5 million to DM Minerals and QTM. However, DM Minerals rejected the offer, insisting on $23.9 million as compensation for what they

---

[6] Baventon, G. M. (1975) Maryborough City Council letter to Premier, 27 May. ITM 842336, Queensland State Archives.

considered an expropriated asset. In response, the government extended the offer for another 12 months, anticipating that DM Minerals would seek recourse in an International Court after exhausting options in the High Court. DM Minerals sought leave in the High Court but was ultimately unsuccessful. Following this setback, DM Minerals finally accepted the ex-gratia payment in June 1984.

* * * * *

The battle over sand mining on Fraser Island marked a pivotal moment in Australia's environmental history. It set a precedent for future conservation efforts in Queensland and across the nation. The triumph for environmentalists, led by John Sinclair and the Fraser Island Defender's Organisation (FIDO), fundamentally altered the island's future. However, it also signified the dawn of the decline of the island's forestry industry, which had coexisted with nature for a century.

Although Fraser Island's forestry practices had long been praised for their sustainability, the ban on sand mining represented a significant turning point in the island's management. Following the inquiry's recommendations, Fraser Island's identity began to change. As tourism replaced mining, forestry became increasingly marginalised.

In the short term, forestry operations continued, and the inquiry even praised the sector's careful management. However, the long-term pressures from rapidly growing tourism meant that the balance between economic development and environmental preservation could no longer be sustained. By the late 1980s, after a relentless campaign, it was evident that forestry on Fraser Island was nearing its end.

18

THE PIED PIPER OF ENVIRONMENTAL DECEIT

Let's give credit where it's due. Through his organisation, FIDO, John Sinclair played a pivotal role in shaping public opinion on environmental issues concerning Fraser Island, becoming a leading figure in environmental activism.

His relentless campaigns against sand mining and the forestry industries earned him considerable recognition, including being named Australian of the Year in 1976.

He was outspoken and skilled at leveraging the media to promote his cause, earning a loyal following. However, despite his successes, Sinclair's crusade was riddled with misinformation, half-truths, and a reluctance to compromise.

This chapter reveals Sinclair's tactics, the misleading narratives he promoted, and the personal hypocrisies that ultimately undermined his cause.

Fraser Island's false saviour

Sinclair was born and raised in Maryborough, a city with an industrial heritage. After earning a Diploma in Agriculture from Gatton Agricultural College in 1960, he worked with the Rural Youth Program, an organisation dedicated to addressing the challenges faced by rural youth in remote areas.

Longing to return to Maryborough, he studied at night school to qualify as a teacher. In 1967, he was employed by the Maryborough Adult Education office, a role established and previously held by Jack Pizzey, the leader of the Australian Country Party in Queensland, who briefly served as Premier. Sinclair was a member of the Country Party until his resignation in 1971, and his connections within the party undoubtedly helped him secure his position in Adult Education.

Sinclair's connection to Fraser Island was deeply personal, with family ties dating back to the 1930s. His experiences on the island, combined with his passion for the environment, led him to establish the Maryborough Field Naturalist Club in 1967 with Bart Cavanagh. Eventually, they became a branch of the Wildlife Preservation Society of Queensland. In 1969, Sinclair learned of the campaign to stop sand mining at Cooloola, which was led by Dr. Arthur Harrold, a medical practitioner from Noosa. The campaign's success was significant for Sinclair as he prepared for future battles over Fraser Island.

However, his role as the self-appointed guardian of the island revealed his true character. Environmental concerns alone did not drive his efforts to stop sand mining and forestry. He sought to impose his own vision on the island, often disregarding expert opinions, including those of ecologists who had validated the success of rehabilitation efforts following mining activities.

His criticism of the forestry industry was just as unwarranted. Even as he condemned the impacts of logging, Sinclair privately assured the timber industry that he was not seeking an immediate halt to activities. This contradiction raised questions about the sincerity of his motives.

A campaign of half-truths and misinformation

Sinclair built his public persona on a shaky foundation of questionable truths. His campaigns often twisted facts to fit his agenda, depicting legitimate industries like sand mining and forestry as environmental villains. His talent for swaying public opinion and charming politicians was undeniable, yet the stories he spun were rarely grounded in scientific or environmental facts. Instead, they were calculated moves meant to stir public sympathy, regardless of whether they were true.

Sinclair was a remarkable campaigner during the peak of the sand mining fight in the 1970s and continued his advocacy through the forestry battles of the 1980s. One of his main strategies was a relentless letter-writing campaign directed at politicians and the media. It's intriguing to consider how he balanced his regular teaching duties while seeking resources to support his claims.

His letters to Premier Joh Bjelke-Petersen and others started politely but quickly turned accusatory and often defamatory. Sinclair wielded his pen as a weapon, frequently making unsubstantiated claims meant to provoke a response in his favour. His confrontational tone alienated potential allies and undermined his credibility, especially when he exaggerated or fabricated environmental risks. Nevertheless, his sensational accusations gained traction in the media, which often accepted them without question.

Contradictions exposed in his war on sand mining and forestry

One of the clearest examples of Sinclair's distortion of facts occurred during his campaign to get Fraser Island listed as a World Heritage site in 1976. After the Whitlam Government ratified the Convention for the Protection of World Cultural and Natural Heritage in late 1975, Sinclair spread false fears by claiming that World Heritage status would empower the Australian Government to override state authority. In his newsletter, *Moonbi*, he wrote:

> It is worth noting that because it is an International Treaty, the Australian government gains the constitutional powers to overrule a state government, if necessary, in the management of the parts of the world heritage. Therefore, if Fraser Island is included in the World Heritage List, the Australian government would have an inescapable obligation which would override the decisions of the Queensland government.[1]

This constituted a deliberate misrepresentation. The Commonwealth Department of the Environment had to intervene, assuring

---

[1] Sinclair, J. (1976) Where does FIDO go now? Overseas!!!, *Moonbi* 31, p. 4.

PARADISE PRESERVED

the Queensland Government that the World Heritage listing did not give the Federal Government the authority to override state sovereignty. The state's solicitor-general also refuted Sinclair's claim, dismissing his notion that the Federal Government could leverage the World Heritage status to take control from the Queensland Government.

Such tactics were typical of Sinclair. Throughout his ongoing sand mining campaign, he consistently pressured Queensland's Mines Minister, Ron Camm, for meetings, and showed outrage at any rejections. His accusations often seemed more driven by personal frustration than genuine concerns for the public interest.

This obsessive pursuit for access, combined with his tendency for hyperbole, highlighted Sinclair's steadfast commitment to promoting his agenda, regardless of how much the facts were distorted.

He reinforced his opposition to sand mining by rejecting the evidence that rehabilitation efforts were successful. Ecologists, such as Dr. John Lewis, argued that the revegetation of mined areas was effective, and government inspections supported those findings.

Federal Minister Ray Groom addressed Parliament about the issue:

> Rehabilitation work has been very well done so far and is progressing very satisfactorily. The areas concerned are now quite stable and there is no present cause for concern that any area may become unstable or susceptible to wind or water erosion. Despite adverse weather conditions in the area, the growth of trees and shrubs is very encouraging.[2]

Yet Sinclair kept spreading fear regarding the island's alleged long-term damage, ignoring genuine efforts to restore its natural environment.

Even the editorial in the Australian Conservation Foundation's

---

[2] Groom, R. (1978) Questions without notice – Rehabilitation of Fraser Island. *Commonwealth House of Representatives Hansard*, 15 November, p. 2506.

(ACF) September 1978 newsletter recognised the exceptional rehabilitation work:

> It would be wise for conservationists not to even debate the success or otherwise of revegetation work on Fraser Island. Such debate only plays into the hands of the miners.[3]

Sinclair's campaign against forestry reflected a widespread trend of exaggeration and misinformation. Although forestry operations on the island were heavily regulated, meticulously managed, and aimed at minimising environmental impacts, Sinclair emphasised inflated claims of deforestation and habitat destruction.

His ignorance of practical realities was glaringly apparent when he told an encouraging audience:

> After sandmining, the most pernicious form of land misuse is the aggressive forestry operations, particularly clearfelling areas for blackbutt regeneration.[4]

However, amid the sand mining controversy, Sinclair regarded forestry operations on the island as harmless. In a letter to the Premier, Sinclair recognised the importance of forestry for Fraser Island and its role in supporting the local economy:

> Despite the ecology of seemingly sterile sand, the island is rich in forest resources, and it is currently producing an annual harvest of 7 million super feet of timber supplying 55 per cent of the timber used by Wilson Hart and Hyne & Son, Maryborough sawmills. As these two sawmills employ approximately one third of Maryborough's male workforce between them, Fraser Island plays a significant part in the Maryborough economy.[5]

In private correspondence with timber industry representatives, Sinclair acknowledged that he wasn't entirely opposed to forestry.

---

[3] Mosley, G. J. (1980) The revegetation debate: a trap for conservationists. *ACF Newsletter*:12(8):1.

[4] Sinclair, J. (1991) Priceless pearl or political pawn, *Moonbi*, 77 Educational Supplement.

[5] Sinclair, J. (1971) Letter to Premier, 29 March. ITM 540821, QSA. In the letter, Sinclair also wrote, "We are not totally opposed to sand mining".

Yet, in *Moonbi*, he criticised the timber industry, raising concerns among its workers by suggesting that the end of sand mining signalled the start of the decline for forestry. Although he gave assurances in *Moonbi* that there was no threat to the timber industry on Fraser Island until at least 2000, when the pine plantation resource would mature, Sinclair maintained that this fear was being deliberately stoked against him and FIDO by timber industry executives and politicians as a scare tactic to alarm 800 men in Maryborough, 45 per cent of whom relied on the Fraser Island resource for their jobs.

By 1990, however, he portrayed forestry and its workers as environmental vandals and as a minor industry on the island that should be stopped:

> Civilised society should not allow one of the natural wonders of the world, which has taken thousands of years in development, to be needlessly desecrated because a very small industry has been operating irresponsibly there for more than a hundred years.[6]

This contradiction between public outrage and private concession revealed the duplicity at the core of his campaign.

Tourism hypocrisy: from advocate to opponent

One of the most glaring examples of Sinclair's hypocrisy was his shifting stance on tourism. In the 1970s, he praised tourism as a viable alternative to sand mining on Fraser Island, arguing that the island's future depended on tourism. He even organised guided tours through FIDO, asserting that increased tourism would be a crucial source of revenue, compensating for the loss of sand mining.

While he strongly advocated for the island's natural values, he expressed criticism of Forestry's perceived neglect:

> Tourist services have been the least of Forestry considerations, otherwise there would have been a public

---

[6] Loggers to cut greens down to size, *Sunday Sun*, 11 February 1990, p. 19.

jetty at McKenzie's rather than Ungowa, and roads would have been sited to suit tourists rather than loggers.[7]

However, by the 1980s, his perspective shifted markedly. After witnessing the surge in tourism from 5,000 to 150,000 annual visitors, he condemned the very industry he once supported, complaining about the heavy and intolerable impact on Fraser Island and asserting that it was harming the environment. He had previously promised that increased tourism would offset the economic losses from sand mining and forestry, but in 1990, he called for restrictions on visitors to the island, seeking to curb that revenue. The irony of the situation escaped Sinclair, as the influx of tourists damaging the island was a direct result of the preservation controversies he had initiated.

Sinclair's glaring hypocrisy was evident in a submission to the Federal Government's Inquiry into the Register of Environmental Organisations in 2015, where he proudly stated:

> During FIDO's 44-year history we have seen Fraser Island become Queensland's most popular National Park (according to the Queensland Parks and Wildlife Service) attracting more than 400,000 visitors annually ... these outcomes would not have been possible without vigorous environmental advocacy.[8]

His contradictory stance on tourism reveals a man more focused on promoting his singular vision of preserving Fraser Island for himself than genuinely protecting its natural beauty. Sinclair revealed his duplicity regarding resource use in an honest admission to colleagues in the early 1970s when he outlined a calculated plan to systematically eliminate the island's key industries, stating:

---

[7] Sinclair, J. (1977) The sawmill scene. *Moonbi*, 34, p. 8.
[8] Sinclair, J. (2015) Fraser Island Defenders Organisation submission to the Inquiry into the register of Environmental Organisations. Submission 281, 19 May, pp. 1-2.<https://www.aph.gov.au/DocumentStore.ashx> Accessed 19 November 2024.

> We would stop sand mining, then get rid of forestry, then stop tourism, and we'll have the island to ourselves – we'll be the only ones allowed to go there.[9]

This candid admission, made early in his crusade, stripped away any pretence of altruism. It exposed Sinclair's true agenda: not preserving Fraser Island for public benefit but creating a private sanctuary for his select circle to enjoy its beauty. His willingness to dismantle livelihoods and industries underscored the self-serving nature of his campaign.

Arrogance and different rules for himself

One of the most troubling aspects of Sinclair's activism was his apparent belief that he was above the rules. In his dealings concerning the island, he maintained an air of arrogance and untouchability, genuinely believing himself to be the self-appointed guardian of Fraser Island.

In the 1980s, he carried out unauthorised tourist infrastructure works over four days at Eli Creek without conducting the necessary environmental studies or obtaining the necessary approvals. The area was under a mineral lease. He relied on the support of the Hervey Bay Town Council, even though it was outside their jurisdiction. They advised that he would need to liaise with other government departments.

A delayed response from the mineral leaseholders came as a surprise to him. They emphasised that their lease did not permit interference within three chains of land on either side of the creek. Interestingly, he asserted it was the state government's responsibility to "resolve" the issue, not his, despite the work proceeding without any authority.

If a mining company or government department had taken such actions, Sinclair would have been the first to demand their prosecution. However, he believed there was no need for accountability for his own actions. In 1982, Sinclair also planned to build a campground at Chard Rocks without obtaining a lease.

---

[9] Interview with Geoff McWilliam, Hervey Bay, 17 August 2024. Geoff said that Sinclair made this boast to a group including himself.

At the same time, he lost a tender to develop a campground at Cathedral Rocks to Geoff and Norma Hannant, who had already built the Fraser Sands Holiday Units at Happy Valley. Sinclair, through FIDO, planned to finance their scheme as part of a cooperative proposal involving 150 people, but it was a less favourable option. He was bitter about the rejection and disagreed with the Hannants' proposal. He issued several media releases to spread rumours and make allegations that the Hannants obtained their "scandalous land deal" purely through political patronage. He wrote in *Moonbi*:

> In 1978, after boasting in advance that they would secure land to push the Happy Valley store out of business, the Hannants, with the help of their local MLA and frequent guest, Lin Powell, eventually secured a lease to 22 acres of land which they had personally selected (who said the years of squatting were finished?).[10]

Sinclair never missed an opportunity for self-promotion, frequently declaring himself Australia's most experienced eco-tour guide and the foremost authority on Fraser Island. However, he misled the Hervey Bay Historical Village and Museum in their centenary publication about the Urangan Pier. He crafted a story about his grandfather, a former logger on the island, hauling satinay piles to the pier. Yet, the work diaries of the supervising engineer reveal that the piles used for the jetty were grey ironbark, most likely sourced from the forests around Maryborough.

During the 1975 Inquiry into the Environmental Aspects of Sandmining on Fraser Island, a witness gave evidence supporting forest management. Sinclair, eager to assert his dominance, stood up and verbally attacked their testimony. However, before he could proceed further, one of the Commissioners abruptly interrupted him, reminding him that he was not there to cross-examine the witness. This rebuke highlighted Sinclair's arrogance and his belief that he was the ultimate authority on all matters related to Fraser Island.

---

[10] Sinclair, J. (1983) The long drawn out Hannant saga, *Moonbi* 56, p. 6.

A similar confrontation occurred during the same inquiry when Sinclair attempted to question Olga Miller. Unfazed by his presumptuous questions, she dismissed some of his references, stating that those mentioned had no knowledge of the island. Her sharp rebuke publicly humiliated Sinclair.

Legal battles and a tarnished legacy

Unsurprisingly, Sinclair's confrontational attitude often landed him in court, mainly for defamation. He was quick to claim judicial bias toward the government whenever he lost, yet offered no such critique when the rulings favoured him. Although he sometimes garnered public sympathy, his legal defeats and eventual bankruptcy exposed the fragility of his crusade.

In his submission to the Commonwealth Commission of Inquiry into sand mining, Sinclair accused Murphyores of corruptly obtaining its leases and licences. While parliamentary privilege allowed him to make those defamatory claims without them being tested, that protection did not extend to publicly reporting the inquiry findings.

After Sinclair published his submission in *Moonbi*, Murphyores sued him, demanding an apology and damages for what they claimed was a baseless attack. Although Sinclair considered it was a heavy burden to prepare for and defend the lawsuit, he remained silent about the time he found to write all his newsletter stories and letters to politicians, companies, and newspapers.

Murphyores also sued the small Hervey Bay company that printed the newsletter at a low cost. Although he was willing to defend himself in court, Sinclair was worried that his small supporter might go bankrupt. Three days before the case, he backed down and accepted an out-of-court settlement that included an apology, a substantial yet undisclosed sum for Murphyores, and coverage of legal fees.

In June 1977, Sinclair found himself in court again, this time suing Premier Joh Bjelke-Petersen for defamation. After being named as Australian of the Year in 1976, Sinclair felt he had to respond after the Premier questioned his capacity to fulfil his role at the State Education Department citing his extensive involvement in environmental activism as a potential conflict with his role as a public servant.

By the following month, Sinclair's position in Maryborough was abolished, and he was reassigned to Brisbane. He portrayed himself as a victim of political persecution, asserting that a departmental investigation, that was initiated by the Premier, had been intentionally launched to target him. According to Sinclair, a senior officer told him that the department wanted to get rid of the "political monkey on its back".

Sinclair overlooked the fact that his position wasn't the only one eliminated; adult education services in the region were no longer in demand. Sinclair looked for sympathy over losing his job without showing empathy for the hundreds of sand miners whose livelihoods he had helped ruin during his crusade against sand mining.

Sinclair's writ against the Premier seeking $100,000 in damages turned into a lengthy legal battle. When the judge finally heard the case in 1981, the court awarded Sinclair only $500 in damages, with costs estimated at $30,000. Embarrassingly for Sinclair, Bjelke-Petersen appealed the ruling, and the Full Court overturned the decision, leaving Sinclair with a $50,000 bill for the Premier's legal fees.

Not one to miss an opportunity for self-pity, Sinclair utilised his platform on the ABC's *7:30 Report* to garner sympathy, receiving donations and letters of support. This surge of public sentiment enabled him to settle his debt and even establish the John Sinclair Trust for Fraser Island, funded by his devoted supporters.

In the early 1980s, Sid Melksham, the owner of Eurong Resort and a prominent tourist operator on the island, planned to invest in a new vehicular ferry to provide a regular service to the west coast. This required dredging a deep channel wide enough for a barge to navigate Woongoolbver Creek at all tides.

Sinclair opposed Melksham's proposal, fabricating tales about the demise of fisheries. He then launched an exceptionally slanderous attack, calling him a criminal and claiming he was involved in illegal activities.

Melksham demanded a written apology, but Sinclair refused, leading to another defamation case against him. The case was not heard until July 1991 in the Brisbane District Court. By that time, Sinclair had relinquished legal support and had not attempted to defend himself. The judge found Sinclair's accusations to be baseless, severe, and damaging, and ruled in favour of Melksham, awarding the highest defamation damages in Queensland's history at that time – $20,000 – plus costs and interest. Sinclair went bankrupt and never paid the amount awarded against him.

Many members of FIDO resigned, worried about the scale of the bill and its effect on the volunteer organisation. Nevertheless, Melksham never pursued them for damages, recognising that they were innocent victims of Sinclair's reckless outbursts and lies.

In the 1980s, Sinclair opposed the Hervey Bay Town Council's attempt to rezone land for development. To stop the project, he sought an interim injunction to prevent the minister from proceeding with the rezoning. However, the court ruled against him, ordering Sinclair to pay costs of approximately $4,500. When confronted with the financial penalty, Sinclair claimed he couldn't afford to pay and maintained that his actions, taken through FIDO, were entirely in the public interest without any intent for personal gain.

However, this narrative conveniently overlooked a crucial detail: FIDO's constitution explicitly authorised it to conduct tours, giving the organisation a clear financial interest. FIDO had previously attempted to establish a campground on Fraser Island for its tour participants. Sinclair's portrayal of his actions as altruistic was a deliberate misrepresentation, as he was acting in FIDO's financial interest rather than that of the broader public.

Vilification or just consequences?

Sinclair frequently portrayed himself as a victim, claiming that National Party politicians and others were waging a witch hunt against him. However, much of the animosity he encountered was a result of his own actions. His combative tactics, refusal to compromise, and relentless vilification of anyone who disagreed with him earned him few allies on Fraser Island and in Maryborough.

In 1973, after FIDO began collecting data on logging on Fraser Island, Sinclair claimed that Forestry was targeting him and his organisation. Suggesting personal grievances, he indicated that his father, Charlie Sinclair, a Forestry employee on the island, had become collateral damage:

> There is an issue of principle in which we believe that there are people being placed at unnecessary and unwarranted hardships because of their connection with FIDO.[11]

Years later, Sinclair intensified the accusation, stating in *Moonbi* that his father was dismissed from his role as a storeman in 1973 only because he was the father of FIDO's leader. He further claimed that when Forestry's attempts to have him censured through his employers in the Education Department failed, they shifted their attention to his father, despite what Sinclair described as "five years of exceptionally satisfactory service."

But Sinclair's version of events quickly unravelled. In the following month's edition of *Moonbi*, he was forced to issue a hasty and "unreserved" apology after receiving a letter from Cec Haley, the Conservator of Forests, who was understandably incensed by the falsehoods spread about Forestry. This made Sinclair admit that his father had resigned and was not dismissed. However, he couldn't

---

[11] Sinclair, J. (1973) On the forestry scene. *Moonbi* 16, p. 2

resist taking a parting shot – blaming Forestry for assigning his father demanding fieldwork at the age of 61, which purportedly led to a heart attack.

The reality, however, was far more complicated. After Charlie's service station in Maryborough closed, he and his wife relocated to the close-knit community of Eurong. After working at Orchid Beach Resort for awhile, he got a job with Forestry. Rumours among forestry workers suggested that his performance as a storeman was less than ideal, and his son's combative behaviour likely made things even harder for him at work. It was also widely known that Charlie was not sympathetic to John or his cause, and he was not regarded as his favourite son.

Despite his environmental activism, Sinclair couldn't grasp why the local community largely disliked him. They often labelled him a heartless zealot, lacking compassion for those he sought to put out of work and indifferent to the economic impacts he caused in the region. Sinclair claimed that his wife received threatening phone calls, his children's bike tyres were slashed, and he was booed while leading his scout troop at the Maryborough Show. Given the resentment his actions provoked, it's hardly surprising that hostility ensued.

Instead of reflecting on his behaviour, he blamed the government for deliberately inciting animosity against him. However, he seemed oblivious of the underlying issue: locals resented him for imposing his vision on their community, and showed little regard for how it affected their livelihoods. His crusade jeopardised the jobs of sand miners, and his proposed "solution" of retraining them for work in the tourist industry, such as serving coffees, building walking trails, and supporting his pet project – the light tramline – appeared tone-deaf and insulting. It's no surprise he became a lightning rod for personal attacks.

Many of his wounds were self-inflicted. His refusal to engage constructively with industries, his arrogance in ignoring environmental regulations, and his blatant disregard for the livelihoods of those affected by his campaigns fostered an atmosphere of resentment.

* * * * *

Sinclair's campaigns left a lasting impact on Fraser Island. While he successfully halted sand mining and logging, these achievements had significant consequences. Jobs were lost, and the tourism industry – once viewed as the island's saviour – contributed to environmental degradation. Ultimately, Sinclair's legacy is marked by contradictions: a man who fought to protect the island but whose methods and motivations often undermined his cause.

19

FROM FORESTS TO FOOTSTEPS: MANAGING LAND USE CHANGE ON FRASER ISLAND

Since its early days as a predominantly forestry-based land use, Fraser Island's landscape has undergone significant evolution in response to the growing tourism industry. This transformation not only altered the island's governance but also signalled the gradual decline of forestry as its primary land use.

Until the 1960s, Fraser Island was mainly classified as a state forest managed by Forestry. This dominance was occasionally disrupted by a few exceptions, like the Commonwealth-controlled Sandy Cape Lighthouse reserve and a small lightkeepers' reserve at Hook Point. There were also freehold blocks at Wathumba (160 acres), Moon Point (640 acres), and several smaller blocks at North White Cliffs, originally granted when the quarantine station and telegraph office operated in the late nineteenth century. These early land use patterns laid the foundation for Forestry's operational focus, which remained unchallenged for decades.

Captain Herbert Kent, the last Protector of Aborigines on the island, chose the Wathumba parcel in 1907 for a proposed shark factory at the Wathumba estuary. Isabella Henderson, the wife of Sandy Bay lighthouse keeper, Duncan, was first granted the selection in 1893. After constructing a house and yard, the next owner, Wyn Bagnell, dismantled these structures.[1] The parcel was then sold to Brisbane businessmen led by Benjamin Culpan in 1935 to operate a shark factory, which ran briefly until 1938.[2]

---

[1] Wyn Bagnell transported the buildings to Bridge Creek via bullocks, put them on a barge and brought them to Urangan in 1919. His family rebuilt the house at Dundowran and lived in it for years.

[2] You can read more about the shark factory at https://www.robertonfray.com/2025/06/27/wathumbas-shark-factories-a-forgotten-history-of-fraser-island/

The Moon Point block was chosen by Lars Benson in 1903, located just south of Coongul Creek, to support his nearby grazing lease.[3] It was also an excellent fishing spot with large oyster beds.

The first freehold selection at North White Cliffs was granted to Isabella Henderson in 1893, followed by 50 acres to Mr R. Stokes, 60 acres to Mr G. Wood, and 50 acres to Mr G. Patten.

Tourism beckons: early efforts to regulate

Even during this period of forestry dominance, human activity began to encroach on its territory. Local fishermen spent considerable time on the island and, due to its isolated location, built makeshift shacks in prime spots behind the foredunes along the eastern beach, specifically at Indian Head, Waddy Point, Eli Creek, Poyungan, and Yidney Rocks, creating informal settlements. They occasionally transported visitors on their private boats from Maryborough or Urangan and used vehicles left on the island to access their shacks. At that time, there was no official passenger transport service to the island.

The rise of unplanned and random occupations raised concerns for Forestry, primarily due to increased fire risks. They attempted to control the situation and reduce the number of "squatters", but the restrictive *Forestry Act 1959* offered limited options. They could only issue annual occupation permits, which were inadequate for managing the growing recreational use.

By the early 1960s, the Queensland Government recognised the necessity for more flexible land use regulations. In 1961, a joint report from the Land Commissioner and District Forester Anderson suggested that the best way to manage recreational use was to excise a coastal strip, half a mile wide, from Eurong to Happy Valley, from state forest as vacant crown land. The Lands Department would then administer this land under more suitable provisions in their acts. Although this exchange, carried out in

---

[3] Lars Benson also had a 1,637-acre Agricultural Homestead lease in the same area – see Chapter 5.

1962, did not impact the commercial timber belt, it marked the first significant reduction of Forestry's dominance. This extensive tract of land could accommodate tourism and private developments, and the land acts could better regulate the heavily used camping areas along the eastern beach.

The Lands Department decided to restrict future tourist developments to Eurong, Happy Valley, Andy's Valley, and Poyungan Rocks. At the first two locations, the strip of vacant crown land was increased to one mile in width to support village development, covering approximately 740 acres at each site.

In 1964, two separate private interests submitted unsolicited proposals for tourist developments. One proposed a hotel, a golf course, and an airstrip covering 600 acres within Beauty Spot 80, located between Waddy Point and Indian Head. The other, presented by Sir Reginald Barnewall, suggested a two-stage development on the northern side of Waddy Point. The first stage would involve flying visitors from the mainland to an airstrip constructed north of Waddy Point for a day of surf fishing, while the second stage focused on building accommodation huts and cooking facilities for self-catering groups.

Although Forestry supported extending the strip of land north of Happy Valley to Sandy Cape for conversion to vacant crown land to help with future tourist developments, they opposed any plans to excise the 2,000-acre Beauty Spot 80, effectively cancelling the initial proposal. This area was the only part of the coastal strip that did not convert to vacant crown land and remained as state forest.

In 1965, the Queensland Government invited expressions of interest to develop tourist enterprises on Fraser Island. Two proposals received approval: Barnewall's development and Sid Melksham's vision for a resort at Eurong. The tide was turning as tourism started to gain a foothold that challenged the dominance of forest management.

Section of land on adjoining the eastern beach that was dedicated as Vacant Crown Land. Tinted brown shows the initial excision between Eurong and Happy Valley. The yellow section is the subsequent excision all the way to Sandy Cape. Beauty Spot 80 is shown between Indian Head and Waddy Point. (Queensland State Archives)

The fragmentation of Fraser Island through freehold tenures

In 1966, Forestry and the Lands Department addressed the problem of unregulated shacks and residential occupancy on Fraser Island. A specific concern involved several shacks within Beauty Spot 80, owned by Nick Schulz and Percy Wiedon. The government faced challenges in granting a lease to formalise their occupation. The Land Commissioner recommended that the huts be removed and relocated to a more appropriate site for occupation under a special lease, particularly near the future Orchid Beach resort, which was set to open in 1968.

Percy Wiedon's hut near Waddy Point, late 1970s. (Photo Geoffrey McWilliam)

During the mid-1960s, the demand for residential development on the island increased. While Forestry and the Lands Department preferred to limit land use to tourism and recreation, public demand for residential subdivisions grew significantly. Local government controlled freehold land; however, its legal capacity to manage undesirable development on private land was limited, especially when public interest clashed with the legitimate expectations of property owners.

In 1966, subdivision lots were surveyed at Eurong and Happy Valley, where several fishing shacks already stood. Subsequently, these lots were offered for auction. Other areas previously under Forestry occupation permits at Poyungan Rocks, Poyungan Valley, The Oaks and Yidney Rocks were also converted to freehold.

The contentious rezoning of land at Orchid Beach for a subdivision, originally acquired to expand the resort in the early 1980s, led to the current freehold settlement behind the former resort.

The landscape gradually transformed, making tourism and private ownership the main influences in the island's changing story of land use.

A patchwork of governance

Around the same time that sand mining began, a national park, originally covering 61,306 acres, was established at the island's northern end in late 1971. This area was expanded to 83,126 acres two years later, limited by land availability due to mining tenures. John Sinclair claimed credit for the national park's declaration after advocating for a 100,000-acre reserve in the northern region during a Mining Warden's hearing in May 1971. However, plans to establish a national park had been underway for a long time before that.

The National Parks Association of Queensland applied to the minister in 1965 to create a national park; however, they were not the first to make such a request. In June 1959, Anderson made an innovative proposal. He suggested designating the northern parishes of Carree and Wathumba, comprising approximately 94,900 acres, as a new national park.

After initial investigations, Forestry submitted a proposal to set aside 79,505 acres to the Land Administration Commission and the Department of Mines in March 1966. The latter indicated that mineral exploration and an assessment of mining potential were necessary before they could provide guidance on the proposal.

Forestry's national park forester, Syd Curtis, emphasised the area's recreational, scenic, and biological value, suggesting that all available land south to Lake Bowarrady be designated as a national park, covering 130,000 acres. While this proposal received support from Forestry, it could not be implemented until the results of mineral exploration were finalised. Further delays occurred after the cabinet decision of 31 August 1971, which established an Inter-Departmental Committee to investigate and report on land use in the coastal sands of south-east Queensland.

The overall management of various parts of the island shifted to several government departments, including the Mines, Lands, Forestry, Fishery, and Tourism Departments, along with the Queensland Beach Protection Authority and the Queensland National Parks and Wildlife Service (QNPWS). Additionally, Maryborough City Council in the south and Hervey Bay Town Council in the north were included for freehold parcels. Only Forestry and QNPWS maintained a presence on the island, while other agencies managed their respective areas remotely.

Following the inquiry into sand mining and the cessation of mining activities, funds initially meant to support unemployed workers were redirected to develop recreational facilities on the island. These included adding more toilets and a shower block at Central Station; installing large information signs at Hook Point, Buff Creek and Urang Creek; creating a walking track from Lake Boemingen to Dilli Village; putting up signposts on key roads; transforming the former garage at Central Station into an interpretive centre; and providing toilet facilities at McKenzie, Garawongera, Boemingen, Wabby and Birrabeen Lakes.

Despite these incremental improvements, the island's lack of a cohesive governance framework made it vulnerable to the pressures of increased visitation.

In 1978, the Queensland Government, using funds from the Commonwealth Government, prepared a management plan to determine land use priorities for the newly created vacant crown land strip along the eastern beach, which had the highest concentration of recreational use. Although the plan proposed a user-pay system, the state government chose not to implement it, as it was seen as a politically unpalatable option at the time.

Tourism's tipping point: the rise of vehicular access

The introduction of large vehicular ferries in the 1980s dramatically increased visitor numbers to Fraser Island. However, this influx caused a range of problems, including issues with beach camping, waste management, and general vehicular concerns, such as serious accidents, which overwhelmed the island's fragmented governance structure.

In 1984, the Queensland Cabinet introduced a vehicle access scheme to restore order to Fraser Island's chaotic management. The following year, they passed the *Fraser Island Public Access Act*, which defined the recreational area and established a user-pay system for visitors. The Fraser Island Recreation Authority was created to regulate land use and oversee visitor contributions to the island's upkeep.

Although the government expected to raise up to $2 million from this scheme, community trust eroded as details of the fee structure remained undefined when the act was passed. The legacy of these early missteps continued to influence debates about land use and preservation on Fraser Island in the 1980s. As tourism concerns overshadowed forestry issues, governance on the island increasingly focused on managing recreational visitors, relegating forestry to the sidelines.

As tourism flourished, forest management faced growing criticism. Activists portrayed logging as incompatible with the island's natural beauty and ecological values. This view gained traction alongside the rise of the recreational industry, as the influx of tourists and economic opportunities made forestry appear increasingly outdated and even counterproductive.

Once the backbone of the island's economy, professional forestry management practices were overshadowed by the need to cater to tourism demands. By the late 1980s, efforts to stop logging intensified, largely driven by environmental advocacy.

* * * * *

As I explore in the final chapters, the rise of tourism reshaped Fraser Island's land-use priorities, gradually displacing forestry as the dominant industry. This shift reflected broader societal changes where recreation and preservation became priorities. While the end of logging marked the conclusion of an era, it also highlighted the island's transition to a new identity focused on its unique natural beauty and global appeal as a tourist destination.

20

Tourism reshapes the island

Visitation to the island began centuries ago, when Aboriginal tribes' moieties and others were allowed to harvest tailor from the eastern beach and winter mullet in the waters of Hervey Bay and the Great Sandy Strait. These gatherings were not merely economic exchanges but also cultural events, where mainland tribes brought goods as offerings to access the island's resources. These early exchanges hinted at the island's magnetic allure long before European settlement.

In the late nineteenth century, Fraser Island started attracting the attention of European settlers. North White Cliffs became a popular weekend destination for residents of Maryborough, who sailed over for regattas, picnics, and relaxation. The area's appeal was its easily accessible fresh water and deep, sheltered anchorage. In 1894, about 100 acres were officially excised from the larger quarantine reserve and designated as a recreation reserve, marking the beginning of organised leisure activities on the island.

Fishing soon became a major attraction because of the seasonal migration of mullet and tailor schools as they move north along the coast from mid-May to September. The cool south-westerly winter winds create ideal conditions for pushing the fish from New South Wales rivers to offshore spawning grounds further north.

These annual migrations attracted anglers and astute entrepreneurs who recognised opportunities to attract visitors.

Fishing pioneers and early tourism

The rugged and isolated coastline of Fraser Island presented access challenges. Undeterred, early fishing enthusiasts became trailblazers. They carved paths through the soft sands and navigated around the treacherous coffee rock outcrops on the eastern beach, creating a narrow track around Middle Rocks just wide enough for vehicles to traverse the steep terrain.

They rafted vehicles and trucks to the island to move materials and visitors to their preferred spots. Waddy Point was a popular hub for serious fishermen and their activities, from which they would drive across the island to Wathumba Creek to bring their catch back to Urangan. An official fisherman's reserve existed at Wathumba until the early 1980s.

The early vehicles included various ex-army Chevrolet blitzes, Model T Fords, Morris utes, and tractors, all adept at navigating the soft sandy conditions.

With the beaches all to themselves, these pioneers demonstrated the ingenuity needed to adapt their rugged vehicles to the remote conditions they encountered.

By 1934, fishermen from Maryborough had constructed six shacks at Yidney Rocks. Each shack was comfortably furnished, and a spacious dining room equipped with stoves, lamps, and stretchers served as the main gathering point. Fishing groups could rent the shacks, and guests could bring their own provisions or have meals prepared by their hosts, Ken Miller and his wife Dinah.

Early development

Miller leased a portion of Crown land and, in 1934, with the assistance of Stan Warry, a businessman from Maryborough, set up a resort at Happy Valley, offering a pioneering tourist experience.[1] They built six fully furnished huts and named it the Fraser Island Tourist Resort. Miller was the driver and caretaker, living with Dinah in one of the huts, while Badjala descendant Banjo Owens was the tour guide.

---

[1] According to Geoff McWilliam, Dulcie Cook who worked at the resort, told him the name of the area came from a jar of jam with the brand Happy Valley on it.

Happy Valley Resort c1935. (Courtesy MWBBHS (Image ID_FR018))

Despite plenty of fresh water, the resort lacked bathrooms. All guests washed in a nearby waterfall fed by a stream that cascaded over the coffee rock to the eastern beach, named Governor Falls in honour of a regular visitor and close friend of the Warrys, Queensland Governor Sir Leslie Wilson.

The journey to Happy Valley via Bogimbah Creek, utilising the launches *Juanita* from Urangan and *Jenny K* from Maryborough, enhanced its appeal. Towering kauri trees lined the drive through Yidney Scrub leading to the resort. Warry and Miller also constructed a road from the eastern beach to Lake Wabby for easier access to the renowned lake.

The island's mystique grew in July 1935 when the *Maheno* was beached. Its rusting hull became a permanent tourist attraction, enhancing its maritime history and charm.

Unfortunately, the resort did not last long. The effects of the Great Depression led to its closure in late 1936, and the huts were moved to Scarness. This setback hindered the growth of tourism until the post-war years.

Ad hoc tourism

The 1950s saw the modest emergence of early tourism entrepreneurs on Fraser Island. People like Mel Jensen, Jacob Lack, Percy

Wiedon, Lee Markwell, and Don Adams provided basic tours and accommodations, blending ingenuity with the island's natural beauty.

Jensen took small tour groups to the island in his 1926 Pontiac, known as the "Yidney Rock Hopper", using a single-car barge owned by Col Gardiner. Gardiner removed the truck wheels from the barge when it was launched into the water at Urangan, and Merv Riley's fishing boat, *The Dolphin*, towed it to Moon Point. Jensen built his hut at Yidney Rocks using driftwood and satinay bark slabs that Lack had collected and stacked in the forest to create a flat surface, providing excellent cladding. The hut was also fitted out with items from the *Maheno*.

Jacob Lack hosting tourists on the island in early 1950.
(Courtesy MWBBHS (Image_ID FR289))

Lack conducted tours when he wasn't working in the forest. His boat, the *Orient,* picked up passengers, mostly from outside the

Orient Guesthouse at Scarness and took them to Urang Creek and across the island in his car. He had a couple of huts, one near Indian Head called "Fraser Island Chambers"[2] and another at Eli Creek. They were mainly built from flotsam washed ashore from passing trading ships.

In 1960, Lee Markwell secured a lease from Forestry at Happy Valley, where he constructed a beach shack and a small shed for his use when flying to the island. This was one of six similar places in the front valley section.

Through his company, Island Air, Don Adams flew tourists to an airstrip he built near Woongoolbver Creek on the west coast and supplied a vehicle to take passengers to Lake McKenzie.

Tour operators organise regular tours

The report from the joint inspection by the District Forester and the Land Commissioner in 1961 recommended infrastructure improvements to enhance tourism, including upgraded wharves, better roads, and improved water supplies. They believed that once this kind of infrastructure was put in place:

> Enterprising businessmen will arrange conducted tours to the beauty spots or along the beaches to the various fishing areas.[3]

The environmental campaign against sand mining highlighted the island's unique beauty, inadvertently boosting interest in tourism. Clearly, the proposed infrastructure projects were unnecessary to motivate enterprising businessmen to attract tourists to the island. The construction of two new resorts at Eurong and Orchid Beach initiated regular day tours, transforming Fraser Island from a quiet fishing spot into a destination renowned for its stunning landscapes. The number of day tours surged, and annual visitor numbers tripled.

---

[2] According to Geoff McWilliam, the name came from the local businessmen who stayed at the hut in the 1950s. Their names and humorous descriptions of their occupations were on a sign hung on the wall of the hut.

[3] Gardiner, E. G. (1961) Joint inspection report, 4 July. ITM 282158, QSA.

After purchasing a small block of land at Eurong in the early 1960s, Melksham pioneered day trips to the island. While working full-time as a panel beater in Maryborough, he ran tours on Sundays and during school holidays. He salvaged and refurbished a small sunken boat named the *Rio Marie* and bought a 1928 Model A Ford utility. He fitted it with balloon tyres on the rear wheels and crafted bench seats across the back from driftwood. The tour started at Ungowa Jetty with the honking of the ute's horn, which signalled passengers to board. When the vehicle overheated, it had to stop several times on its journey to and from Lake Birrabeen.

Keith "Slippery" Miles was another who organised day trips. He owned two houses at Yidney Rocks and, along with his son Wes, transported people from Urangan on the *Hiawatha*, taking them to the popular spots on the island.

Jack Reville expanded day trips to cater for larger groups. In 1969, he used his boat, the *Island Queen*, to reach the derelict McKenzie Jetty, where he transported passengers in two old ex-Army blitz trucks fitted with mounted seats and a metal roof canopy to Eurong, Central Station and Lake McKenzie.

Unfortunately, Reville and six passengers lost their lives in July 1970 when his bus careened uncontrollably down a steep slope from Lake McKenzie. He had no brakes, which was common for all trucks on the island at the time, including log trucks, due to the persistent sand that damaged and wore out the brake pads. The tragic accident highlighted the safety risks of unregulated and makeshift tours, prompting government audits, but resulted in minimal change.[4]

By this time, Melksham had shortened his lengthy day trips by widening the rough road to River Heads, making his island crossing quicker. He also purchased and refurbished an old 50-foot launch that rested on the banks of the Burnett River, naming it the *Lady Fraser*. It could carry 58 passengers.

---

[4] You can read more about the accident at https://www.robertonfray.com/2025/07/25/fraser-islands-darkest-day-the-1970-tourist-bus-tragedy/

Melksham also upgraded several old ex-army Chevrolet blitz and Studebaker trucks, which he bought cheaply at an auction in Brisbane. These trucks lacked a roof over the passengers, who sat on wooden planks in the back. Originally red, the trucks were later painted bright orange for better visibility while driving through the forests. One of his trucks was missing a driver's side door and had only half a windscreen.

Sid Melksham's early fleet of converted ex-American Army trucks. (Photo Angela Burger)

Paddy Doran was the first tour operator to run from Rainbow Beach in an old blitz truck he called *Mystery*. He wore his famous yellow forestry helmet while his passengers sat in the back, exposed to the elements. Like Melksham, he was large, had a beard, and went barefoot.

The tour trucks travelled everywhere, even onto the small beach areas at McKenzie, Birrabeen, and Jennings Lakes.

Other tour operators followed, including Wally Toy, who purchased the *Island Queen* from Reville's widow. He ran services between Urangan and Ungowa, or McKenzie's Jetty, and later owned and managed *The Islander*. He had a couple of ex-army blitz trucks waiting on the island. Laurie Bright built and operated *The Crab*, a shallow draft, flat-bottomed vessel that often drifted sideways in a northerly wind. The vessel was aptly named, as it frequently struck every pole while trying to berth at the T-jetty at Urangan.

Rex and Gloria Bacon purchased *The Crab* and ran it for several years, providing leisurely tours of the Great Sandy Strait. When the business encountered difficulties, they turned to Melksham for help in providing tours for their passengers on the island. They persevered until they entered the thriving and profitable whale-watching industry.[5]

John Webster and Barry Murphy operated a flat-bottomed catamaran named MV *Islander*, travelling from Urangan to McKenzies Jetty. Later, Toy introduced a larger and faster launch from Kangaroo Island called the *Philanderer*. He partnered with Melksham; Toy managed the bookings and ferried visitors to the island while Melksham took them to scenic spots. Other tours then started from Noosa, travelling along Teewah Beach past the *Cherry Venture*, including Steve Jensen's 4x4 Safaris.

Melksham was the leading operator, running five canopied trucks that transported an average of 160 passengers daily. In 1983, he purchased a fleet of four-wheel-drive buses to compete with other tour operators, replacing his ageing Studebaker and Chevrolet trucks.

In 1982, Forestry began licensing tour operators to address the numerous disputes between competing interests. To avoid overcrowding at popular sites, they restricted the number of operators, where they could go, and the times they could occupy different locations.

Recreation and timber production initially coexisted well due to the significant spatial separation between these activities. However, this changed dramatically in the 1980s as the island became more accessible to private vehicles and the number of tour groups increased significantly.

---

[5] Unfortunately, Rex had a fatal heart attack and did not survive to see their business flourish. The day after his funeral, *The Crab* went on its first whale watching trip fully booked.

Improved access and booming tourism

Improved access significantly boosted tourism. In 1967, Gordon Elmer's small ferrocement barge, the *Fraser Dawn*, connected the developing settlement at Rainbow Beach to Hook Point at the southern end of the island via a narrow crossing at Inskip Point. This development allowed private vehicle access to the island.

Other similar services emerged from Hervey Bay, although they depended on tide conditions. One such service was former Fisheries patrol officer, Kevin Donnelly, on his small steel barge, the *Waylily*. While his primary business was delivering materials for the Orchid Beach Resort and Forestry, he also ferried visitors using his green Studebaker trucks. Wally Toy operated a small barge as well, although its service was short-lived. Noel Mathison constructed a small ferry, the *Watoomba II*, in his backyard at Howard. In 1975, he began operating between Urangan and Moon Point or Urang Creek.

Noel Mathison and *Watoomba II*. (Photo courtesy Maria Heaven (Mathison))

Elmer eventually organised a larger barge to meet the rising demand. The barge competed with the ex-sand mining barge, *Tom Welsby*, which also carried private vehicles from Inskip Point.

Recognising an opportunity to improve access to Fraser Island's west coast, Melksham commissioned the construction of the *Fraser Venture*, a large barge designed to handle increased traffic efficiently. He aimed to offer a reliable, fast service unaffected by the tide's fluctuations.

He obtained approval to dredge a channel at Woongoolbver Creek, ensuring access even at low tide. In 1984, after undergoing a contentious approval process, he secured parliamentary consent to excise part of the creek mouth from its protected fish habitat. This decision sparked debate but ultimately led to regular crossings according to a timetable.

The *Fraser Venture* was launched on Boxing Day with remarkable success. It gained such popularity that it made up to eight return trips daily during the busy Christmas school holidays, solidifying its role as a key part of island tourism.

Danny Moncur was the first to run day tours exclusively in the island's northern region during the early 1980s. The *Fraser Flyer*, owned by Alan and Rhonda Smith, operated from the T-jetty at Urangan and docked at Urang Creek near the old Hans Bellert hut site. Moncur used former army Bedford trucks to shuttle passengers across the island.

After Moncur lost his tour permit due to an indiscretion, Hervey Bay pharmacist Geoff McWilliam began his popular Top Tours day trips in the north. After struggling to operate with Bacon's *The Crab*, McWilliam purchased the *Tollgate Traveller*, which ran from Urangan, transporting passengers to Moon Point or Coongul Creek. He had a couple of Mercedes Unimogs customised from tractors, not trucks, capable of tackling the island's tough conditions. They featured very high clearance and low crawler gearing.

As his business expanded, McWilliam sold the *Tollgate Traveller* and utilised Don Caswell's larger power catamaran, the *Discovery II*, which could accommodate enough passengers for both his buses. Eventually, because maintaining vehicles left on the island was difficult, McWilliam decided to transfer his water passage to Ken

Fraser Venture on first trip into Buff Creek landing area before dredging of Woongoolbver Creek was completed. (Photo Angela Burger)

Eckert's *Fraser II*, allowing the Unimogs to return to the mainland each day for servicing and fuelling.

After landing, McWilliam crossed the island via the Woralie Track. A typical day included stops at Lake Allom, the *Maheno*, and Eli Creek. Lunch was at Cathedrals, followed by visits to Red

Geoffrey McWilliam's Top Tour Unimog crossing Coongul Creek.
(Photo Geoffrey McWilliam)

Canyon, Champagne Pools, Orchid Beach, Wathumba Creek, and past the palm tree at Bowarrady Creek before heading back to Coongul Creek.

With the success of the *Fraser Venture* operation and how easily visitors could reach his Eurong Resort, Melksham arranged business partnerships with established tour companies for overnight stays at his resort. He also bought an iconic, yet infamous RFW four-wheel-drive truck named the Australian Explorer to begin day tours from the Sunshine Coast in 1987. He also ran Sun Safaris tours from Rainbow Beach using two 14-seat Toyota buses.

The environmental and social impacts of tourism

Although not part of its core operations, Forestry effectively managed the rapid increase in recreational activities on the island. In the state forest, they established camping grounds, built walking tracks, and produced a handbook for tour operators.

However, despite recommendations made years earlier, no infrastructure was provided on the eastern beach to accommodate the increasing numbers of tourists, nor were there any restrictions on the number of vehicles allowed on Fraser Island. Visitors were free to camp wherever they liked. Many cleared vegetated areas for firewood, created new tracks behind the dunes, and exposed the land to erosion. The island's infrastructure – or lack of it – struggled to keep pace with this rapid growth, putting pressure on services. There were no toilets, water, or waste management systems in place. For instance, the management of the rubbish dump south of Eurong was poorly organised, and during westerly winds, rubbish would blow onto the beach, spreading for miles.

In 1983, Forestry staff counted between 1,000 and 1,500 people daily at Central Station, including those on day tours and in private vehicles. When Easter coincided with the Anzac Day holiday the following year, the barge operator at Inskip Point told me that over 3,000 cars were on the island, which I estimated meant about 30,000 people.

Following a tenfold increase in visitor numbers over the previous decade, the government introduced new legislation for a user-pay system to access the island. This included vehicle permits, camping fees and a passenger levy on all tours.

The barge war

Melksham introduced the double-ended *Rainbow Venture* in 1986 to meet the growing demand at Inskip Point. This directly competed with Elmer, who operated the *Eliza Fraser II* and the single-door *Dawn Fraser III*. Melksham believed that Elmer charged high fees and offered an irregular and limited service. This action ignited the notorious "barge war" between the two operators.

It began with exchanges in the media, as both attempted to demonstrate their financial strength, despite privately struggling. Initially, they had a gentleman's agreement to charge the same fee and allow the visitor to choose which barge to take. However, Elmer soon reduced his fee by $5 to $30 for a return trip, while Melksham charged $25, consistent with the fee for the *Fraser Venture*.

There was considerable jockeying among barge captains for favourable positions on the beach to attract vehicles. This included cutting bows crossing the strait to secure prime spots. Such behaviour led to many passenger complaints, raising concerns about potential collisions and safety risks. As a result, designated landing areas were established to ensure straight-line crossings.

Other underhanded tactics included deliberately lengthening mooring ropes to guide vehicles towards a barge, allegations of gunfire directed at barges, claims of assaults on off-duty workers, and malicious complaints made against each other. There were also incidents of break-ins to steal beer and cigarettes.

Each time Elmer lowered his price, Melksham followed suit, claiming he had to utilise the least favoured landing area. Melksham's fares dropped to as low as $5 compared to Elmer's $10. They offered various inducements to potential customers, such as fuel discounts on the island.

Finally, in November 1988, Elmer publicly announced the sale of one of his barges, signalling his intent to retire and sell his business. However, Melksham persisted with his aggressive pricing tactics to end the price war. He offered free passage the following month, knowing that people would stop at his shop in Eurong while also looking for investors for a timeshare in his latest resort development. Rumours even circulated that individuals were paid with cartons of beer to travel to the island! Something had to give.

After suffering substantial losses over eight months, Melksham ultimately chose to purchase Elmer's business, bringing the barge war to an end.

*****

By the late 1980s, tourism on Fraser Island had become a major industry. Millions of dollars were invested in resorts, private campgrounds, and the building of holiday homes. Large ferries carried thousands of vehicles and daily tour groups each year.

Forestry, once the island's dominant industry, became increasingly marginalised. The roads constructed for logging and routine management became congested with tour buses and private vehicles. Meanwhile, popular attractions like Lake McKenzie were overwhelmed with visitors from competing tour operators. The environmental strain highlighted the need for regulation, prompting the Queensland Government to introduce vehicle permits, camping fees, and passenger levies in the mid-1980s.

As tourism continued to grow, Forestry's influence on Fraser Island diminished. Once central to the island's identity, the industry's traditional operations increasingly clashed with its new role as a tourist destination. Environmental activists, emboldened by victories in the North Queensland rainforests and the Conondale Ranges, shifted their focus to the logging practices on Fraser Island.

Forestry faced growing opposition from activists and the public, who now viewed the island as a natural wonder in need of protection. The rise in tourism had transformed Fraser Island's economy and its cultural and environmental narrative, setting the stage for the upcoming conflicts and political manoeuvring.

Part 5

The end of an era

21

WHEN PROTESTS OVERRIDE PROMISES: FRASER ISLAND'S FOREST CONFLICT

> The fact that environmental activists regarded the island as worthy of preservation as a national park after a century of forestry operations and timber extraction is the greatest tribute the Department and industry could receive.[1]

By the 1960s, Australia had seen the emergence of environmental groups, such as the ACF and the Wilderness Society, which began to bring environmental issues to the forefront of politics.

Fraser Island attracted significant attention during the 1970s because of controversies over sand mining. A Federal Government inquiry recommended halting sand mining while commending the island's forestry operations. The Commission reported:

> After inspecting the Island, the Commission has come to the view that, in general, the visual integrity of Fraser Island has not been adversely affected by the carefully controlled logging operations. It seems likely that most visitors to the island ... would be unaware that its timber resources have in fact been exploited for over a hundred years.[2]

However, in late 1973, environmental activists led by John Sinclair depicted logging as a new threat, despite his previous claims of supporting sustainable forestry under certain conditions. Their call to preserve Fraser Island as a national park became a paradoxical tribute to the industry's management practices, despite the long history of forestry operations.

---

[1] Minister Tompkins (1976) Press release, 15 November. ITM 842336, QSA.
[2] The Parliament of the Commonwealth of Australia (1976) *Fraser Island environmental inquiry: Final report of the Commission of Inquiry.* Parliamentary Paper No. 333/1976. Australian Government Publication Service, Canberra, p. 112.

Building momentum against forestry

The 1980s saw a rise in environmental activism, driven by the success of the Wet Tropics rainforest campaign in north Queensland, led by Aila Keto. While forest conservation wasn't initially a primary focus, activists soon began linking it to broader issues of environmental degradation. Symbolic clashes, like the Bloomfield Road controversy in the proposed Cape Tribulation National Park, enabled environmentalists to frame forestry as part of a larger crisis, gaining public support through simplified narratives, despite the more pressing threats posed by real estate development on private land.

Prime Minister Bob Hawke's 1987 nomination of the Wet Tropics for World Heritage Listing on World Environment Day heightened tensions between the federal and state governments, as Queensland opposed federal intervention in land management. The Federal Government used treaty powers to prohibit logging, igniting constitutional debates over state rights versus international obligations.

Ultimately, a change in Queensland's government enabled a smooth resolution, converting state forests in the Wet Tropics into national parks. This resulted in the loss of 500 jobs and 20 million super feet of specialised structural and cabinetry timber supplies.

For Fraser Island's timber industry, however, this set a worrying precedent, similar to the sand mining dispute, where federal intervention ultimately overrode state authority.

Changing political fortunes and their implications

By the late 1980s, a debate emerged about forestry practices in Queensland, particularly concerning the protection of "old growth" forests, especially the satinay–brush box forests on Fraser Island.

The change in government after the 1989 Queensland election marked a shift that threatened the dominance of forestry on the island. The newly elected Labor government began by downgrading the Forestry Department into a division within the Department of Primary Industries.

Labor consistently supported the preservationist position, particularly through John Sinclair's regular critiques of forestry practices. Thus, it was no surprise when they chose to stop logging on Fraser Island, as this had been their policy for several years. In 1986, during a debate over the *Fraser Island Public Access Act 1985*, Labor member Pat Comben responded to the long history of logging on the island, stating, "It is about time they stopped."[3]

Following the election, Comben, the new Minister for Environment and Heritage, reiterated his position and that of his party:

> I remind you that the Labor Party policy is for logging to cease on Fraser Island.[4]

Labor pledged to conduct an inquiry to determine the island's future use, partly to appease the voters and reward activists who supported their campaign. However, this seemed unnecessary since they had already announced that logging would come to an end.

While the government claimed to seek public input on managing Fraser Island, environmental activists called for an immediate halt to logging. This demand arose despite the government's allowance for logging operations to continue during the inquiry, albeit with a reduced quota of one-third.

The drawn-out forest blockade

On 5 June 1990, the Brisbane Rainforest Action Group organised a public meeting to plan protests against logging on Fraser Island during the inquiry out of frustration with the delays in starting the inquiry. Sinclair addressed the gathering about the defence of Fraser Island, emphasising it as Australia's longest-running conservation

---

[3] Pat Comben, Member of Windsor, Motion for disallowance of Regulation on *Fraser Island Public Access Act*, Hansard, 20 February, p. 3693. Accessed 6 December 2024.

[4] Mahoney, K. (1991) Bureau chairman uneasy over Fitzgerald report. *Maryborough Heritage Herald*, 19 June.

battle. However, despite previous claims of not targeting forestry, he justified his change of stance by linking the fear instilled by the industry among its workers to a deliberate smear campaign against him.[5]

The small group decided to disrupt logging operations and pressure the government to uphold its pre-election promise to halt logging. They justified this action by believing that environmentally harmful "panic logging" would occur during the inquiry. Protesters were encouraged to bring chains, locks, ropes, wires, railway lines, welding equipment, axes, and shovels. A police officer who attended the meeting anonymously provided a summary:

> The majority of persons are aged between 20s to 35s – equal spread of male and female. Most appeared hippy/unemployed rent-a crowd ... I think you and your men should be able to pick out the protestors in that I don't think they will be your typical fishermen on the island for a long weekend.[6]

The protest began over the long weekend in June coinciding with the school holidays, and attracted significant media attention, especially as police dismantled tripods and filled trenches to facilitate logging. Many protesters were from overseas and spoke limited English. The primary tactic used by the protesters involved blowing loud whistles as they entered the forests where the timber cutters worked. Since the fallers could not see them, it became too dangerous for them to cut down trees.

Forestry and police officers had to fan out in a wide arc around the tree to be felled to locate and detain the protesters. Once the protesters were cleared from the forest, tree falling could commence. However, other protesters began whistleblowing again, creating a repetitive cycle of removing and detaining protesters, which

---

[5] In typical self-promotion, Sinclair conveniently ignored the much longer conservation battles by Forestry against settlement in the 1930s which threatened large areas of prime commercial forests.

[6] Swanston, J. (1990) *Fraser Island Blockade*. Memo to Sergeant First Class Ken Salmon, Maryborough Police Station, 6 June. ITM 375763, QSA.

significantly distracted the workers and forced them to operate under less-than-ideal safety conditions.

Late on 18 July, shortly after protesters vacated Block 9, timber cutter Bill Nichols was injured by a falling limb after cutting his last tree of the day. A helipad had to be created in the low-lying swampy area to enable his evacuation by helicopter later that evening.

Police established a base on the island, and from the outset, their command issued directives on how officers should conduct themselves:

> If cutting and hauling logs is interfered with, police will not take any action unless justified assistance is requested by the cutters, haulers and millers, and endorsed by Forestry and the government. Police are to act impartially. No arrests are to be made unless there are outstanding circumstances.[7]

Essentially, police were directed to adopt a "softly, softly" approach. They concentrated on maintaining their image, permitting logging to continue while only removing disorderly protesters without making arrests. Protesters who were removed were taken back to their camp and told not to return, although they often ignored this warning without facing any consequences. This caused frustration among the police, who felt their ability to enforce the law was limited, fostering a perception that they were merely protecting lawbreakers.

According to Sargent Ken "Sockeye" Salmon, the police field commander on the island, the protestors had copies of the Confirmation of Directions and the associated regulations before most police officers did. He believed:

> A high-ranking public servant was a member of the protest groups and, therefore, knew of our actions.[8]

---

[7] Regional Commander North Coast Region (1990) *Operation Logging Fraser Island Confirmation of Directions*. Memo to District Officer Maryborough, 16 June. ITM 375763, QSA.

[8] Allan Shillig interview with Ken Salmon in March 2019, from Shillig, A. (2019) *The Last Fraser Island Puntmen: 1965-1992*, Self-published, p. 78.

Salmon expressed concern that the protesters might commit illegal acts without fear of repercussions after senior members of the group in Brisbane told him that many sympathetic environmentalists were within the Labor Party, which would prevent police and Forestry from taking any meaningful action against them.

The situation had become farcical. Unfortunately, the police focused on their performance and the need to uphold the right to protest rather than enforcing the law and safeguarding the workers' legal rights.

Escalation and countermeasures

As the blockade continued, the protesters intensified their tactics by erecting barricades and chaining or gluing themselves to equipment to provoke physical clashes and attract media attention. They were unaware of the irony in their actions. They cut down small regrowth saplings from the very forest they claimed to protect. When challenged, they tried to justify their actions by asserting that it was a minor sacrifice in their larger plan.

In response to the police's passive approach, the timber industry grew increasingly frustrated as it was already facing significant costs from disrupted operations. It was forced to adopt diversionary tactics, such as rerouting trucks and logging in various scattered areas, which only increased its expenses and provided no environmental benefits. The ongoing cat-and-mouse game persisted for months, diverting up to 19 police officers from their regular duties.

The protesters became unhappy with the police's inaction and the media's limited coverage. To draw attention, 43 protesters staged a "peaceful" raid on Postan's camp early on 6 August. They entered the camp by waking Andrew Postan and his wife, Helen, before dawn. The media was tipped off and arrived in helicopters to film activists taking over the site, chaining and gluing themselves to buildings and equipment. They chanted, beat drums, blew trumpets, and flashed strobe lights, behaving rudely and abusively towards the Postans. In a distressed state, Postan went to nearby Poyungan Creek and asked punt operator Larry Shillig to watch over his wife while he flew to the mainland for help.

Logging protesters chained to machinery at Postan's camp. (Photo David Postan)

There were no police on the island that day, and the confrontation continued until they finally arrived. Officers cut chains and used acetone to remove superglued limbs. Some protesters, not even properly glued, screamed in front of the cameras, pretending to be in pain for media attention. The police made no arrests, stating that no offences had taken place, and simply told the protesters to leave.

While the police's relaxed approach may have annoyed the protesters and the waiting media, it also worsened tensions with the timber industry, which felt under siege. Warren Hyne, the managing director of Hyne & Son, expressed the industry's frustrations in a letter to Premier Wayne Goss. He accused the government of failing to protect lawful operations and warned that the industry's patience was running out, risking its support for the inquiry:

You will be aware that the industry has done everything possible to constructively co-operate with the Government and the Fitzgerald Enquiry, including agreeing to a concession on logging during the Enquiry process.

We have been continually harassed and inconvenienced by blockades and other entirely unlawful tactics by so called environmentalists at considerable financial, physical and mental costs to our people. In the interests of not escalating the situation we have accepted that the police and QFS staff have not exercised their powers under the law in our support.

We supported the Fitzgerald Enquiry because we accepted that it was part of a democratic decision making process and we believe we have done everything possible to constructively support its progress. The failure to adequately ensure normal respect for persons and property ... which one would normally expect in a democracy, is causing us to seriously reconsider our position.

Instead of rational and factual debate this issue has been moved by the conservation movement steadily into one of conflict, confrontation and complete disrespect for the law. We believe it is entirely unreasonable for the conservation movement on one hand to be appearing to take part in the rational debate, whilst it is also supporting the protest activities on the Island.

We understand your position is not without difficulty and we also appreciate the personal support you have displayed publicly. However, it does not seem to be being transplanted into action in the field.

We are having difficulty in restraining the attitudes and behaviour of employees in the industry. They are looking to persons like myself for leadership and strong support for their cause. I am finding it increasingly difficult to reconcile that role with continuing co-operation with your government in the absence of a decisive stance and positive action.[9]

---

[9] Hyne, W. (1990) Letter to Hon. Wayne Goss, 8 August. Letter courtesy of Hyne & Son.

Police on the island observed the anger among industry workers that Hyne mentioned. The district officer was concerned about their reputation, especially since they couldn't physically remove or arrest protesters.

Following the Postan's camp raid and Hyne's letter, Forestry and police agreed that willful damage, property destruction, and serious assaults would not be tolerated. However, any enforcement actions had to be carried out under the *Forestry Act 1959*, which effectively limited the police's authority compared to that of forestry workers, unless a serious offence occurred. Forest officers possessed greater powers than the police in a state forest, as stipulated in certain sections of the *Forestry Act*. Once a forestry officer issued clear directions for offenders to leave the forest, and those directions were not complied with, the police made arrests – many of which took place over the next two months.

Meanwhile, John Sinclair accused Forestry and the police of overlooking violations committed by visitors to the island, instead choosing to focus on:

> Reinforcing the rights of the loggers to maintain the environmental vandalism on the island, costing the Queensland taxpayers a small fortune and tying up the resources of an important public service which should be protecting the public interests rather than the interests of loggers.[10]

He wrote to the police commissioner, alleging harassment without providing proof. He accused the police of conducting full body searches in the forest with rubber gloves to intimidate activists, engaging in sexual harassment against female protesters by male officers, illegally impounding protester vehicles and property, handcuffing detained activists to the sides of boats while offering life jackets in case of sinking, tampering with the brakes of an impounded vehicle, and failing to apprehend logging supporters who allegedly assaulted the anti-logging protesters.

---

[10] Sinclair, J. (1990) The Greenie blockade, *Moonbi* 75, p. 7.

However, the Postan family suffered the most stress and consequences from the blockades. In one incident, Andrew Postan faced court charges alleging he had touched a female protester's breasts. Ultimately, he had no case to answer when the circumstances surrounding the unfounded accusation were revealed in court. Postan saw a female protester jump onto a skidder and was about to go under it. He acted swiftly to pull her to safety, saving her life. Instead of expressing gratitude, the protester, through John Sinclair, lodged frivolous charges against him in a calculated attempt to discredit the forestry workers and falsely portray the "peaceful" protesters as innocent victims of bullying and aggressive tactics.

The broader implications

While the government fulfilled its pre-election promise to review the island's future, the activists' decision to blockade logging operations on Fraser Island raised questions about their motivations and the effectiveness of their tactics. The inquiry, meant to be a forum for democratic input, was undermined by protests aimed at pressuring the government. This blatant disregard for the inquiry's process led many to question its legitimacy. The government risked sanctioning the activists' tactics by not suspending the inquiry until they stopped their actions, straining the democratic principles it claimed to uphold.

The logging industry, already facing logistical challenges and disruptions due to protests, confronted the harsh reality of an impending shutdown. For many timber workers, this ongoing situation only compounded their suffering, forcing them to endure months of uncertainty and harassment during what they considered their "dying days."

22

The inquiry and end of logging

The genesis of the inquiry

During the 1989 state election campaign, opposition Labor leader Wayne Goss made several promises regarding Fraser Island. These included expanding the national park estate, protecting environmentally sensitive areas and scientific reserves, and developing a conservation management plan for the island.

However, tensions surfaced with federal colleagues when Labor's Environment Minister, Graham Richardson, unexpectedly announced plans to put Fraser Island forward for World Heritage listing. This provoked a backlash from the timber industry, miners, unions, and even Goss's backbenchers, who objected to federal interference.

Goss feared that yielding to federal pressure would cost him voter support and credibility with the business and resource sectors. The memories of politically damaging compromises related to the Wet Tropics listing, which had affected funding for new national parks, tourism plans, and compensation for displaced industries, loomed large in his decision-making.

To avoid similar pitfalls, if elected, Goss proposed a state-led inquiry, emphasising the need for independence from federal interference in managing state environmental issues, especially since the Resource Assessment Commission inquiry into the logging of native forests in Australia was already underway.

In January 1990, after taking office as premier, Goss announced a public commission of inquiry into the conservation and land management of Fraser Island and the Great Sandy Region. The inquiry, chaired by Tony Fitzgerald, aimed to mediate conflicts between environmentalists and the timber industry while establishing a framework to balance preservation with resource use. The initiative also sought to prevent political and media confrontations from escalating. This attitude was in contrast to the public statements of his environment minister.

Cooperation and conflict

Queensland's major environmental groups united under a joint conservation initiative to work with the inquiry. In contrast, smaller splinter groups resorted to direct actions, including blockades to stop logging on Fraser Island. Aila Keto from the Rainforest Conservation Society leveraged her group's success in scrutinising logging practices during the Wet Tropics fight by presenting strategic submissions that questioned the sustainability of logging on Fraser Island.

The inquiry received 544 submissions, including considerable documentation from Forestry. However, procedural flaws soon emerged. According to Alan Chenoweth, major issues with the inquiry included:

> The basic premise of the Inquiry process was that submissions from interested parties would be received and evaluated as evidence ... An initial discussion paper was prepared by a small staff in the Premier's Department who summarised existing information provided by government departments, facilitated by an inter-Departmental Committee. This paper was immediately criticised for its unquestioning acceptance of disputed Departmental positions, lack of ecological input, biased language and setting an agenda that was too wide and superficial.[1]

It quickly became clear that the inquiry was too ambitious and lacked the technical expertise to assess the submissions beyond merely summarising them.

The arguments presented by environmentalists focused on "old growth" forests. However, of the island's 91,400 acres of tall forests, only 22,000 acres were unlogged or classified as old growth. Of

---

[1] Chenoweth. A. (1992) Fraser Island and the Great Sandy Region: management issues. *Australian Environmental Law News* 77(3):69-78. p. 76.

that amount, just 3,200 acres, or 11 per cent, were available for logging. Many popular tourist areas, such as Pile Valley and Yidney Scrub, consisted of tall forests already preserved as beauty spots. Forestry advocates argued that the debate over old growth forests overlooked the dynamic and resilient nature of forests, which constantly undergo ecological changes.

Arguments also arose regarding the perceived unsustainable environmental impacts of logging, such as changes to forest structure, soil loss, weed invasion, and effects on wildlife. However, Forestry strongly contested that the regrowth blackbutt forests were more ecologically diverse than those they replaced.

On Fraser Island, the patterns of ecology and forest communities displayed resilient, site-specific gradients, even in the face of frequent and occasionally catastrophic natural disturbances such as wildfires and cyclones. The forestry profession claimed that logging simulated these natural disturbances on a much smaller scale, promoting regeneration rather than decline.

Environmentalists asserted that forestry practices caused nutrient depletion and reduced biological productivity. However, these claims were mostly speculative, as no studies had specifically examined Fraser Island. Such criticisms ignored successional processes, which foresters argued demonstrated otherwise. Disturbances like fires and logging were essential for regenerating these processes by stimulating nutrient cycling.

No evidence was presented during the inquiry regarding any "collapse" in the robust tall forests over the 120 years of logging on the island.

Although the inquiry acknowledged that logging created the necessary disturbance for the regeneration and long-term survival of the satinay–brush box forest type, it still recommended halting logging in these forests. This decision put these ecosystems at risk, as their structure had already changed since European settlement. Without regular disturbance, the current conditions favour the emergence of rainforest species once the overstorey trees die, making it difficult for satinay and brush box to regenerate naturally.

Findings and recommendations

On 22 May 1991, Fitzgerald presented his findings. Notably, he endorsed the ongoing harvesting of regrowth blackbutt for a maximum of five years. If this was not viable, logging would cease altogether. The timber industry argued that the government-imposed restrictions rendered blackbutt logging economically unfeasible.

In July 1991, the Queensland Cabinet confirmed that logging would stop by the end of the year, with blackbutt logging extended until 30 June 1992 to allow for a transition period. They also announced a multi-million-dollar financial assistance package for displaced workers, promising full consultation with industry and union representatives. However, industry cynicism was well-founded when it was revealed that $900,000 was allocated for a road already built and that $200,000 to $300,000 was set aside to hire additional public servants for a public relations exercise to "facilitate the flow of information".

The environmentalists neither cared for nor understood the industry. After Hyne & Son opened their new state-of-the-art automated pine sawmill in October 1990, they claimed that the company could replace hardwood timber from Fraser Island with treated pine. While pine was better suited to fill some of the supply gaps caused by the halt to logging in the North Queensland rainforests and could replace $17 million worth of imported timber each year, primarily in housing construction, it could not serve as a substitute for specialised hardwood applications.

For logging contractor Andrew Postan and his family, the decision marked a bitter end to their over 50-year connection with the island. In their final months there, they faced harassment from activists, which further intensified the industry's feeling of betrayal.

Helen Postan asked Premier Goss a direct question at the Hyne & Son mill following his government's decision:

> Alright, what is it that we did wrong?

He replied:

> Helen, you didn't do anything wrong. You're just not the flavour of the month.[2]

Goss summed up the political convenience shaping the government's final decision in just a few words.

In October 1991, Tony Fitzgerald was recognised for his efforts when the Hawke Government appointed him Chairman of the AHC. The AHC had worked for years to include Fraser Island on the World Heritage list.

World Heritage Listing

In his final inquiry report, Fitzgerald noted that Fraser Island met four criteria for inclusion on the World Heritage list. It was therefore not surprising that, in September 1991, just as the ink dried on the Queensland Government's official decision to halt logging on Fraser Island, the Federal Government nominated 2.1 million acres in south-east Queensland for World Heritage listing. This nomination included Fraser Island, the Cooloola Sand Mass, the Wide Bay Military Training Area, and the Great Sandy Strait and its associated tidal shallows.

After an inspection by Dr Jim Thorsell from the International Union for the Conservation of Nature, the nomination was narrowed down to a smaller area of 447,000 acres covering all of Fraser Island.

In December 1992, Fraser Island was granted World Heritage status and recognised for its significant geological and biological features, as well as its natural phenomena.

---

[2] Interview with Helen Postan, 7 October 2024.

John Sinclair, a strong advocate for World Heritage listing, celebrated this achievement, believing it would enhance global recognition and tourism. However, critics cautioned that increased visitation could degrade the island and threaten the very values that secured its listing.

Many visitors had no idea where logging took place, even when driving past areas that had been logged in the past. They didn't realise that nearly all the tall forest areas they observed had been logged at least once. It often surprised them to discover that forestry workers had planted the magnificent hoop and kauri pine plantations around Central Station almost 100 years ago.

The irony went unnoticed by Sinclair, his supporters and the government. Despite claims of environmental damage from 120 years of logging, Fraser Island's forests remained in such splendid condition that they earned World Heritage status. This proved the benefit of over a century of professional management by foresters and the dedicated work of forest workers.

The sad end: from logging to tourism

The last tree was felled in November 1991 by Graham Brady in Compartment 21, McKenzie Logging Area, which is between Northern Road and the old tramline, now part of the Great Walk. The final logs were removed from the island in January 1992, and professional forestry management officially concluded on Sunday, 2 February 1992, marking the end of the island's long history of timber extraction and sustainable forest management.

The decision to end logging on the island replaced one exploitative industry with another: tourism. Forestry's footprint had been relatively small, with commercial forests covering only 28 per cent of the island and less than one per cent logged annually. In comparison, tourism's impact has proven to be far more widespread and relentless, affecting a greater portion of the island every day of the year.

THE INQUIRY AND END OF LOGGING

Graham Brady falling the last tree in November 1991.
(Department of Forestry, courtesy MWBBHS (Image_ID TS135))

Since the chainsaws have fallen silent, tourism has spiralled out of control. Common issues include overflowing rubbish bins, trampled campsites, polluted water supplies, depleted firewood sources, and churned-up roads that have become impassable. The lack of infrastructure to support the growing number of tourists has exacerbated the strain on the island's environment.

This situation conflicts with John Sinclair's vision of a tourism-driven paradise, highlighting the stark contrast with the harsh realities of overuse and neglect. As a result, the island faces arguably more severe challenges than those posed by active forest management.

Reflections on the legacy

The forestry profession takes pride in its stewardship of Fraser Island's forests, which have maintained their ecological integrity even after a century of logging. The flaw in the argument presented by environmental activists was their belief that Fraser Island's ecosystems could only be protected if logging ceased. They overlooked the importance of vegetation patterns, regeneration processes, forest dynamics, and the impacts of disturbances and how ecosystems respond to them.

The decision to halt logging came at a considerable cost: a $2 million inquiry, a $38 million compensation package, and the displacement of 200 workers. While tourism has provided economic gains, its environmental effects raise questions about whether this transition has led to better land management outcomes.

Ultimately, the closure of logging operations symbolised a broader shift in societal values, prioritising global recognition through World Heritage listing over a local, sustainable industry. Whether this shift is a victory for environmentalism or a cautionary tale of political expediency remains open to debate.

23

THE UNCERTAIN FUTURE OF FRASER ISLAND

Environmentalists celebrated the end of forestry operations on Fraser Island in 1992 as a victory; however, subsequent years have shown that halting logging was not an environmental panacea. Shaped by Aboriginal fire management for millennia and recent forestry practices, the island now faces ecological challenges exacerbated by a hands-off preservation approach, which I refer to as benign neglect. The reality is that forests are not static entities. Without major disturbances, they evolve in ways that can affect their long-term health and biodiversity, especially in Australia's eucalypt forests. Along with issues related to tourism, trying to keep Fraser Island as a static museum piece has caused some ecological problems.

The tourism paradox: loving the island to death

John Sinclair, a key figure in the movement to remove industry from Fraser Island, argued that tourism and minimal human interference would best serve the island. Once hailed as the island's economic future, tourism has become a double-edged sword. Fraser Island's status as a World Heritage-listed destination has led to a rapid increase in visitor numbers, reaching approximately 500,000 annually. However, the island risks being loved to death, as the sheer volume of visitors puts immense pressure on its ecosystems.

The island's narrow sandy tracks, once traversed by only a handful of log trucks and work vehicles, were never designed to handle the hundreds of vehicles, large tourist buses, and cars towing camper trailers or oversized caravans that now clog them daily, creating unnecessary hazards and delays. Passing requires one vehicle to pull over, but with limited passing bays, more are carved into the surrounding bush, damaging drainage systems and accelerating erosion. Smaller vehicles are often forced to reverse up steep sections to give way to large tour buses, which worsens the tracks and deepens the ruts. Inexperienced and reckless four-wheel drivers exacerbate the damage, compounding an already difficult situation.

Typical narrow road through the forests on Fraser Island.
(Photo San Van Holsbeeck)

The dunes behind the eastern beach are now marred by off-road vehicle tracks, with minimal enforcement to prevent damage to the vegetation that stabilises the dunes. Rubbish disposal remains a persistent issue, as the island's limited waste management facilities struggle to cope with the growing number of visitors, resulting in litter problems. Indiscriminate firewood cutting further depletes the island's resources, as campers prioritise convenience over preservation.

Overcrowding at key tourist sites like Lake McKenzie and Eli Creek has turned these natural wonders into chaotic, heavily trafficked attractions, far removed from the wilderness experience they once offered. Eli Creek's crystal-clear waters often look more like a public swimming pool rather than a natural wonder, and the cars parked there during busy times resemble a bustling shopping centre.

Instead of maintaining a sustainable balance between preservation and recreation, tourism has become an uncontrollable force that strains the island's ecosystems. Even with preservation policies in place, the immense pressure from mass tourism is transforming the island more profoundly than past logging activities, but with much less control or oversight.

The irony is that in protecting Fraser Island from chainsaws, it is now facing a different kind of impact – caused by excessive foot traffic, vehicle impacts, and poor infrastructure to support responsible tourism. The lack of sustainable visitor management strategies risks damaging the qualities that originally attracted visitors to the island.

The myth of passive preservation

Sinclair's vision has also caused unforeseen ecological consequences. Environmentalists often argue that stopping logging has led to a much better outcome for Fraser Island's forests. However, this perspective overlooks the role of disturbance in forest ecology and the island's remarkable capacity to bounce back from human intervention.

Even areas impacted by sand mining, which caused significant localised disruption to woodland ecosystems, have regenerated so effectively that, to the untrained eye, appear almost identical to their undisturbed surroundings. A prime example is the area shown in the photo below. Forestry initially aimed to improve the productivity of certain low-commercial woodland sites by planting or seeding blackbutt in mined areas. At the far eastern end of Dillingham's Road, one such site in a scribbly gum–bloodwood woodland was recontoured, planted with blackbutt, and fertilised. Today, very few people passing by would realise that the blackbutt is growing outside its typical range.

Rehabilitated sand mining site in scribbly gum–bloodwood woodland planted with blackbutt and fertilised. (Photo taken in July 2023 by the author)

Today's most celebrated forest landscapes, including areas that were once heavily disturbed, challenge the simple idea that "saving" forests from logging is always the best option. The reality is that active management, rather than strict preservation, is often necessary to maintain ecological health and the scenic grandeur that visitors expect when they arrive at Fraser Island.

For example, without active forest management, the blackbutt forests that were previously maintained through silvicultural practices are increasingly being overtaken by more mesic rainforest species, threatening their ability to regenerate and, therefore, sustain themselves.

These forests serve as remnants of past forestry operations, with a notable example in the Poyungan Valley. Without periodic thinning, fire management, or disturbances to promote regeneration, they won't be able to sustain themselves in their current state in the future. Visitors passing through these areas may notice a gradual shift towards rainforest characteristics – thicker undergrowth, less blackbutt regeneration, and altered habitats for native wildlife. While some may see this as natural succession, it results from the abandonment of active management practices that have shaped these landscapes for over a century.

Another example is the Valley of the Giants at the head of Poyungan Creek, an area first logged in the early 20th century without environmental oversight or management controls. Despite its appearance, it is not a remnant old growth area. Loggers selectively removed the most valuable trees leaving the rest without regard for regeneration or future productivity. The largest trees were bypassed during the early logging operations because they were too massive to be felled and handled by the sawmills of that time. Many people interpret this to mean the area was never logged and was "saved". However, there is evidence of past logging in the form of old stumps beyond the road and within the forest. The Great Walking Track at the eastern part of the forest follows the original tramline that accessed the area for logging operations.

While these areas are celebrated as prime examples of the island's magnificent forests, they demonstrate their ability to recover and maintain their splendour despite past disturbances.

This resilience highlights an important point: with careful, science-based management, Fraser Island's forests could have continued to be actively managed while preserving their aesthetic and ecological integrity through a mosaic of forest conditions and diverse ecosystems that maintain their visual appeal. Instead, the forest structure, once supported by silvicultural practices, is fundamentally changing into a more scrubby rainforest. With modern forestry techniques, a better balance between sustainable resource use and preservation could have been achieved.

The consequences of fire mismanagement

The decline of fire management on the island further highlights the dangers of a preservationist approach. Under forestry management, controlled burns were used to reduce fuel loads, protect fire-adapted ecosystems, and minimise catastrophic wildfires. Since forestry operations ceased, fire management has been inconsistent and, at times, largely ineffective.

Firebreaks once maintained for access and wildfire containment have either been closed or repurposed as walking tracks, restricting firefighting crews from conducting backburns or quickly reaching fire-prone areas.

The devastating 2020 wildfire disaster illustrates what happens when preservation ideology prioritises fire exclusion over proactive management. Fuel loads have accumulated unchecked, creating ideal conditions for the uncontrollable blaze that swept across large parts of the island. Despite the evidence, current land managers are still hindered by bureaucratic and ideological resistance to using fire as a landscape management tool, a situation worsened by inflexible staffing arrangements. Alarmingly, there remains a cultural view of fire as a destructive force rather than as an ecological tool, which obstructs the implementation of proactive measures needed to reduce the risk of large, damaging fires.

The anticipated benefits of joint Aboriginal management have not materialised in any meaningful way. Despite official rhetoric about integrating traditional knowledge, modern Aboriginal custodians have had little direct connection to the island since the early 20th century. Consequently, cultural fire regimes have not been reinstated, not that this could be easily achieved, and Aboriginal land management practices have not been significantly revived. Instead, the current approach remains one of benign neglect, further compounding ecological challenges and making it difficult to promote Aboriginal practices. Without active use of fire and other traditional methods, the island's landscapes continue to shift away from their historical structure, leading to increased fuel loads, altered forest compositions, and heightened fire risks.

A manufactured problem: the dingo dilemma

The management of Fraser Island's dingoes further underscores the contradictions in the island's current governance. While they are promoted as a prominent tourist drawcard, dingoes are also seen as a threat to visitors, because they are classified as "wild" animals resulting in strict regulations and occasional culling.

Before 1992, dingoes were primarily self-sufficient predators, but they often supplemented their diet with discarded fish remains from anglers and scavenged whale or turtle carcasses washed ashore. While they largely avoided human interaction, it was well known that they also fed on the waste left by residents. Brumbies, in particular, provided a significant food source, reducing the dingoes' need to approach campsites and tourists. Furthermore, there were few restrictions on handling fish frames and other protein sources.

However, since Fraser Island transitioned to strict preservation status, brumbies have been removed, fish frames must be buried, and rubbish dumps have been fenced off. This removal of vital protein sources has caused dingoes to seek food from tourists, leading to more aggressive encounters and a persistent management dilemma. As a result, dingoes have become more opportunistic scavengers, a direct effect of poor management decisions driven by policy changes that have failed to keep the island in its pre-colonial natural state.

What is most concerning is that dingoes have become less wary of humans. Failure to properly manage dingoes has led to tragic outcomes. In 2001, nine-year-old Clinton Gage was fatally mauled by dingoes, an incident that shocked the nation and prompted a reassessment of dingo management policies. Despite efforts to reduce interactions between dingoes and humans, the problem persists. In the late 1990s, an overseas visitor was cornered in the surf by a dingo for some time before being rescued. More recently, a lone runner on the beach was also herded into the surf by a pack of dingoes, narrowly avoiding serious injury.

These incidents demonstrate the ongoing failure of government authorities to address the root cause of dingo aggression – the disruption of their natural food sources and the hindrance of effective population management. It is always convenient to continually blame visitors every time there is an incident from a bold dingo. The introduction of electric fences, which has involved extensive clearing of forests and heath communities around major settlements and tourist sites, clearly reflects inadequate dingo management.

A new approach to preservation

The challenges facing Fraser Island have not arisen from forestry or resource extraction but originate from a flawed belief – that leaving nature undisturbed is the safest way to protect it. For Australian eucalypt forests, true conservation involves active management rather than exclusionary policies that seek to preserve ecosystems in an idealised, unchanging state. The island's forests, wildlife, and landscapes are dynamic and require thoughtful intervention to sustain their health and character. The current structure of the forests cannot be reimagined as some utopian wonderland untouched by human influence.

The future of Fraser Island's forests and wildlife depends on whether its managers recognise the need for more than just passive preservation. A forest isn't protected just by leaving it alone; it changes over time, sometimes in ways that threaten the very biodiversity it aims to support. The landscapes of Fraser Island we see today were shaped by forestry. Without intervention, they will continue to change, with blackbutt and satinay–brush box forests eventually giving way to dense rainforest. While this transformation may look appealing to some, it puts at risk the species that depend on a more open sclerophyllous structure.

The examples of the Valley of the Giants and Poyungan Valley demonstrate that forests can recover and even thrive after disturbances. Rather than viewing all forms of human intervention as detrimental, preservation efforts should adopt a more pragmatic approach that incorporates management techniques to enhance ecological resilience while keeping the island's visual and natural appeal.

Although tourism benefits the economy, it needs proper management to prevent further degradation. The current open-access model is unsustainable. Imposing restrictions on vehicles, improving waste management, and setting visitor limits in ecologically sensitive areas are essential to avoid irreversible damage.

Similarly, fire must be reintegrated to ensure forest health and minimise the risk of catastrophic wildfires. The reluctance to adopt broadscale aerial prescribed burning at regular intervals stems more from ideology than from science, and unless this changes, Fraser Island will continue to face preventable fire disasters.

Concluding remarks: rethinking Fraser Island's future

John Sinclair's idealistic vision, where the island thrives without resource extraction, has overlooked the need for careful, science-based intervention to safeguard its unique ecosystems.

A hands-off approach to preservation has created problems just as serious as those it sought to prevent. Tourism pressure is compromising the integrity of ecosystems; fire mismanagement has led to devastating wildfires, and the island's iconic dingoes have become problematic due to misguided policies.

If Fraser Island is to remain the natural wonder that many people cherish, its management must move beyond outdated preservationist ideals. Active conservation is rooted in science rather than ideology and is the only way forward. This means recognising that forests require management, fires should be carefully reintroduced, wildlife needs balanced ecosystems, and tourism must be regulated to prevent damaging the landscapes it aims to celebrate.

The challenge for Fraser Island's future is to strike a balance between tourism and effective ecological management. The lesson from Fraser Island is that simply "saving" a forest from logging does not guarantee its long-term health.

Fraser Island's future relies on understanding and applying the principles that have allowed its landscapes to flourish despite past disturbances, rather than leaving it untouched. The island has shown its capacity to recover and thrive. It is now the responsibility of its managers to ensure that this resilience is harnessed rather than jeopardised.

I will conclude with a quote from world-renowned fire historian Stephen Pyne, who captured the essence of the eucalypt in a few impactful words – an ecosystem shaped by disturbance, not by passive neglect:

> *Eucalyptus* is not only the Universal Australian, it is the ideal Australian – versatile, tough, sardonic, contrary, self-mocking, with a deceptive complexity amid the appearance of massive homogeneity; an occupier of disturbed environments; a fire creature.[1]

Modern preservation must remember: what thrives on disturbance dies in its absence.

---

[1] Pyne, S. (1991) *Burning bush: a fire history of Australia.* Henry Holt and Company, New York, p. 25.

BIBLIOGRAPHY

Alexander, M. (1971) *Mrs. Fraser on the fatal shore.* Simon and Schuster, New York.

Anderson, A. (c1960) *Account of forestry activities in the district.* Unpublished address to the Maryborough Historical Society.

Armstrong, S. I. (2010) *The failure of noble sentiments: Bogimbah Mission on Fraser Island.* PhD Thesis, University of New England, Armidale.

Behrendt, L. (2016) *Finding Eliza: power and colonial storytelling.* University of Queensland Press, Brisbane.

Brown, E. (1994) The legend of Eliza Fraser: a survey of the sources. *Journal of the Royal Historical Society of Queensland,* 15(7): 345-60.

Brown, E. (2000) *Cooloola Coast: Noosa to Fraser Island: the Aboriginal and settler histories of a unique environment.* University of Queensland Press, Brisbane.

Brown, E. R. (2004) *William Pettigrew 1825-1906. Sawmiller, surveyor, shipowner and citizen: an immigrant's life in colonial Queensland.* PhD Thesis, School of History, Philosophy, Religion and Classics, University of Queensland, Brisbane.

Brown, E. (2013) Convict Brisbane and the rescue of Eliza Fraser, 1836. *Queensland History Journal,* 21(2):847-54.

Burger, A. (1986) *Fraser Island.* Self published.

Burger, A. (2008) *Last of the barefoot tycoons: the story of Fraser Island's Sid Melksham and the $1,000,000 debacle.* M & B Publishing, Southport.

Burrell, P. J. (1975) Timber tramways on Fraser Island. *Sunshine Express,* 1(4):49-50.

Chenoweth, A. (1992) Fraser Island and the Great Sandy Region: management issues. *Australian Environmental Law News,* 77(3):69-78.

Commission of Inquiry into the conservation, management and use of Fraser Island and the Great Sandy Region (1990) *Final Discussion paper.* Vols I & II, Queensland Government, Chairman G.E. Fitzgerald.

Commission of Inquiry into the conservation, management and use of Fraser Island and the Great Sandy Region (1991) *Final report*, Queensland Government, Chairman G.E. Fitzgerald.

Cook, J. (1968) *Captain Cook's Journal during his First Voyage round the World made in H.M. Bark "Endeavour" 1768-71. A Literal Transcription of the Original MSS. with Notes and Introduction*, edited by Captain W.J.L. Wharton.

Cooke, P. & Huth, J. (2020) A short history of the Maryborough forestry district. *Australian Forest History Society Inc Newsletter*, 81:3-6.

Curtis, J. (1838) *Shipwreck of the Stirling Castle: containing a faithful narrative of the dreadful sufferings of the crew, and the cruel murder of Captain Fraser by the savages: also, the horrible barbarity of the cannibals inflicted upon the captain's widow, whose unparalleled sufferings are stated by herself, and corroborated by the other survivors: to which is added the narrative of the wreck of the Charles Eaton, in the same latitude*. George Virtue, London.

Dalrymple-Hay, R. (1905) *Suitability of New South Wales timbers for railway construction*. Government of New South Wales, Sydney.

Dawson, B. (2014) *In the eye of the beholder: what six nineteenth-century women tell us about indigenous authority and identity*. Australian University Press, Canberra.

Dillon, P. (2022) *Fraser Island: Vrai ou Faux*. Connor Court Publishing, Brisbane.

Drummond, Y. (1992) Progress of Eliza Fraser. *Journal of the Royal Historical Society of Queensland*, 15(1):15-25.

Dwyer, B. & Buchanan, N. (1986) *The rescue of Eliza Fraser*. Cooroora Historical Society, Gympie.

Eckert, V. E. R. (2003) *A history of forestry & timber, Maryborough/Fraser Island*. Self published.

Ellerton, D. et al. (2022) Fraser Island (K'gari) and initiation of the Great Barrier Reef linked by Middle Pleistocene sea-level change. *Nature Geoscience* 15, 1017–1026, doi: 10.1038/s41561-022-01062-6.

Epps, F. C. (1922) *Past, present, and future forestry operations on Fraser Island*. Report of the Proceedings of the Australian Forestry Conference, pp. 68-71, Government Printer, South Africa.

Erbacher, J. & S. (2002) *The Bellerts of Bogimbah.* Self published.

Erbacher, J. & S. (2004) *The story of logging on Fraser Island.* Self published.

Erbacher, J. & S. (2004) *Stories of puntmen.* Self published.

Erbacher, J. & S. (2011) *McKenzie's timber mill: Fraser Island.* Self published.

Erbacher, J. & S. (2012) *Early days on Fraser Island.* Self published.

Evans, R. (1991) *A permanent precedent: dispossession, social control and the Fraser Island reserve and mission, 1897-1904.* University of Queensland. Aboriginal and Torres Strait Islanders Studies Unit No. 5.

Flinders, M. (1814) *A Voyage to Terra Australis* (Volume II). G & W Nicol, London.

Fraser, E. (1837) *Narrative of the capture, sufferings, and miraculous escape of Mrs Eliza Fraser.* Charles S Webb, New York.

Fraser Island Defenders Organisation (1979) Sid Jarvis's Fraser Island 1918-29. *Moonbi,* 40:12-13.

Gibbings, R. (1957) *John Graham convict: an historical narrative.* Barnes, New York.

Hill, W. (1879) *Timber &c. On Frazer's Island.* A Report to the Legislative Assembly, 17 May. Government Printer, Brisbane.

Holzworth, P. (1990) *Sandy's story: some reminiscences of Sandy Luck on Fraser Island's forest history from 1937 onwards.* Unpublished booklet.

Holzworth, P. (1999) Recent forest-use disputes in Queensland: a history of resolution. IN J. Dargavel & Libbis, B. (eds) *Australia's Ever-changing forests IV.* Proceedings of the Fourth National Conference on Australian Forest History. CRES Publications, Canberra, pp. 205-23.

Holzworth, P. (1999) *Monarchs of the woods: the story of the hoop pine in Queensland from settlement to the present.* Queensland Department of Primary Industries, Brisbane.

Holzworth, P. V. (2000) *A history of forestry in Queensland.* Booklet, Forestry Corporate Affairs, QDPI, Brisbane.

Holzworth, P. (2004) *Kauri pine in Queensland: a history of silviculture and harvesting.* Unpublished document.

Huth, J. (2023) *As We Were.* Self-published, Brisbane.

Hyne, J. R. L. (1980) *Hyne-sight: a history of a timber family in Queensland.* Self published.

The Institute of Foresters of Australia (1990) *A submission to the Commission of Inquiry into the conservation, management and use of Fraser Island.*

Kerr, J. (2002) A history of Fraser Island Tramways. *FIDO Backgrounder supplement to Moonbi 103* <https://fido.org.au/light-rail-on-fraser-island/>

Kerr, J. (2009) *Tall timber and tramlines Queensland.* Light Railway Research Society of Australia Inc., Melbourne.

Kitt, J. (2024) *The Big Timberland – my life as a Queensland Forestry Trainee: Part Two.* John Huth Publishing, Little Mountain.

Kowald, M. (1999) *Australia's ever-changing forests IV Fourth National Conference on Australia's Forest History field trip to Fraser Island 22-25* April 1999 – tour notes.

Krishnan, V. *et al* (2019) Without management interventions, endemic wet-sclerophyll forest is transitioning to rainforest in World Heritage listed K'gari (Fraser Island), Australia. *Ecology and Evolution,* 9:1378-93.

Lake, M. (2019) *Australian Forest Woods: Characteristics, uses and identification.* CSIRO Publishing, Canberra.

Lauer, P. K. (ed) (1977) Fraser Island. *Occasional Papers in Anthropology Number 8.* Anthropology Museum, University of Queensland.

Legislative Assembly, Queensland (1875) *Select Committee on forest conservancy; together with the proceedings of the committee and the minutes of evidence.* Government Printer, Brisbane.

Lennon, J. (2012) From K'gari to World Heritage: reading the cultural landscapes of Fraser Island, *Queensland Review,* 19(1):27-38.

Mac Mahon, P. (1905) *The merchantable timbers of Queensland (Australia) with special reference to their uses for railway sleepers, railway carriage and wagon building, and engineering works.* Government Printer, Brisbane.

McNeil, I. (1989) From the archives: McKenzie's Fraser Island (Qld) tramway. *Light Railways,* 104:11-13.

McNiven, I. J., Russell, L. & Schaffer, K. (eds) (1998) *Constructions of colonialism: perspectives on Eliza Fraser's shipwreck*. Leicester University Press, London.

Meston, A. (1905) *Report on Fraser Island*. Report to Legislative Assembly.

Miller, O. (1993) *Fraser Island legends*. Jacaranda Press, Brisbane.

Parsons, R. H. (1994) *The port of Maryborough: a history*. Self published.

Petrie, C. C. (1904) *Tom Petrie's reminiscences of early Queensland, dating from 1837*. Watson, Ferguson & Co., Brisbane.

Petrie, R. (1995) *Early days on Fraser Island 1913-1922*. Go Bush Safaris, Gladesville.

Petrie, W. R. (1921) *A note on "Dundathu" kauri* (Agathis robusta). Forestry Bulletin No 4, Queensland Forest Service, Department of Public Lands, Brisbane.

Podberscek, M. (1993) *Field guide to rainforest trees, shrubs and climbers of Fraser Island using vegetative characters*. Department of Primary Industries, Brisbane.

Powell, J. (1998) *Travel routes, forest towns and settlements*. Queensland CRA/RFA Steering Committee, Queensland Government and Commonwealth of Australia.

Pyne, S. (1991) *Burning bush: a fire history of Australia*. Henry Holt and Company, New York.

Queensland Legislative Assembly (1978) *Fraser Island Management Plan*. Volume 1. Inter-Departmental Committee, Government Printer, Brisbane.

Richards, H. J. (1973) *Duramboi: a story of a white man who lived with Aborigines for fourteen years*. Bardon, Queensland.

Russell, H. S. (1845) Exploring excursions in Australia. *The Journal of the Royal Geographical Society of London*, 15:305-27. < https://www.jstor.org/stable/1797911>

Russell, H. S. (1888) *The genesis of Queensland*. Turner & Henderson, Sydney.

Ryan, L. et al. (2019) *Colonial Frontier Massacres in Australia, 1788 to 1930*. V3.0, University of Newcastle. https://c21ch.newcastle.edu.au/colonialmassacres/map.php

Schaffer, K. (1991) Eliza's trial by media. *Antipodes* 5(2):114-19. <https://www.jstor.org/stable/41958312>

Schaffer, K. (1995) *In the wake of first contact: the Eliza Fraser stories.* Cambridge University Press, Cambridge.

Shillig, A. (2019) *The last Fraser Island puntmen: 1965-1992.* Self published.

Sinclair, J. (1979) *Discovering Fraser Island.* NSW Pacific Maps, Sydney.

Sinclair, J. (1990) *Fraser Island and Cooloola.* Weldon, Sydney.

Sinclair, J. (1994) *Fighting for Fraser Island.* An autobiography with Peter Corris. Kerr Publishing, Sydney.

Stanton, J. P. (1975) *Report on Fraser Island: Natural history, land use, land classification and a proposed framework for its management.* Prepared for the Department of Environment and Conservation.

Swain, E. F. H. (1924) *Notes on the silviculture of hoop pine.* Department of Public Lands, Forest Service, Brisbane.

Tardent, J. L. (1948) Fraser Island. Address to the Royal Geographical Society of Australia, Queensland, 7 May. *Queensland Geographical Journal,* 52:75-98.

Taylor, P. (1994) *Growing up, forestry in Queensland.* Allen & Unwin, Sydney.

The Parliament of the Commonwealth of Australia (1976) *Fraser Island environmental inquiry: Final report of the Commission of Inquiry.* Parliamentary Paper No. 333/1976. Australian Government Publication Service, Canberra.

Thorburn, J. H. (1964) Major lighthouses of Queensland Part 1. *Queensland Heritage,* 1(1):18-29.

Townrow, K. Cao, L. & Langford, J. (1993) *Postan's logging camp Fraser Island: a cultural heritage assessment.* Queensland Department of Environment and Heritage, Maryborough.

Townrow, K. Cao, L. & Langford, J. (1994) *North White Cliffs, Fraser Island: an historic archaeology survey.* Queensland Department of Environment and Heritage, Maryborough.

Vanden Driesen, C. (2009) From "a shrew from the Orkneys" to white indigene: re-inventions of Eliza Fraser. *Coolabah,* 3:35-42.

Walker, K. E. *et al.* (2022) Ecological and cultural understanding as a basis for management of a globally significant island landscape. *Coasts,* 2:152-202. <https://doi.org/10.3390/coasts2030009>

Weisse, A. & Ross, A. (2017) Managing a contested cultural heritage place on K'gari (Fraser Island), Queensland, Australia. *Archaeology in Oceania,* 52:149-60. DOI: 10.1002/arco.5130

Williams, F. (1982) *Written in sand: a history of Fraser Island.* Jacaranda Press, Milton.

Williams, F. R. (2002) *Princess K'gari's Fraser Island: a history of Fraser Island.* Self Published.

Youlden, H. (1853) Shipwreck in Australia. *The Knickerbocker,* 41(4):291-300.

INDEX

A

Aboriginal missions:
    Barambah, 38
    Bogimbah, 35–37
    Durundur, 38
    Yarrabah, 37–38
Aboriginal population, 27, 31
The Aboriginals Protection and Restriction of the Sale of Opium Act, 34
Aborigines, xv, xxvii, 58, 71, 73, 75, 78–79, 129, 251
Acclimatisation Society of Queensland, 84
AC8 Forestry area, xvi
Adams, Don, 264–265
Adamson, John, 96
Aldridge, Harry, 65
Alexander, Michael, 40
alleged massacre, 27–28
Anderson, Andy, 174
Anti-Discrimination Commission Queensland, 30
Armitage, Edward "Ned", x, 81, 101, 103, 106n13, 111, 122, 124, 146–147, 160
Armitage, Norman, 103
Associated Equipment Company (AEC), 217
Australian Conservation Foundation (ACF), xxii, 238–239, 279
Australian Explorer, 272
Australian Heritage Commission (AHC), xxii, 232, 293
Australian National University (ANU), xi, xxii

B

back beach, xv. See also *eastern beach*
Bacon, Rex, 268
bacon wood, xxiv, 13
Badjala Aboriginal, 23, 195
Badjala people, xxxvii, 23
Bagnell, Wyn, 197, 251
Balarrgan, 24. See also *North White Cliffs*
bandicoots, 24
Barbeler, Bob, 203
barge, xiii, xxix–xxx, 75, 152, 211, 213, 246, 251, 264, 269–270, 273–274
barge war, xxx, 273–274
Barker, Col, 214
Barnewall, Reginald, 253
Barry, Jack, 72
Bartholomew, James, 79
Barton, Wally, 150
Baventon, G. M., 233n6
Baxter, John, 40n3, 46
beach oak, xxiii
beach primrose, xxv, 10
beach spinifex, xxvi, 10
Bellert, Hans, 270
Bellert, Johann Heinrich (Harry), 63–64
Bennett, A., 230n5
Bennett Creek area, 210
Bennett, Elliott "Elly", 195–196
Bennett, Roger, 195, 197
Benson, Lars, 67, 252n3
Berthelsen, Albert, 102, 113, 137, 210

Berthelsen brothers, 195, 211
Berthelsen, Thomas Edward, 102, 113, 137, 210
Berthelsen, Tom, 80, 102
Bidwill, John, 27
Bjelke-Petersen, 225, 231, 233, 237, 245
black bean, xxiv
blackbirding, 73
blackbutt, ix, xviii, xx, xxv, 9, 11–13, 85, 92, 94, 205–206, 218, 239, 291–292, 300–301, 304
blackbutt forest, 11–12, 124, 176n2, 179, 181, 183, 189, 291, 300
blackbutt story, 169, 171, 173, 175, 177, 179, 181, 183
Blake, Thom, x
blue gum, xxv, 10
Blue, Jack, 81, 146
blue quandong, xxiii, 163
blueberry ash, xxiii, 10
Board, Leonard, 88, 93, 157
bobtail, xiii, 211, 214
Bogimbah, 24, 35–37, 63–64, 66, 93, 122, 156, 158, 161, 171, 175, 186, 195, 198, 209, 213–214, 263
Bogimbah Aboriginal Reserve, 89, 92
Bogimbah Creek area, 35–36, 66, 79
Bogimbah Mission, 37, 66, 99, 161, 195, 198
Bowen, 140
Bracewell, David, xvii, 27,55
Brady, Graham, 218,294–295
Bribie Island, 48, 57, 224
Bright, Laurie, 267
Brisbane, 25n8, 30n16, 33n22, 36, 58, 64, 71, 127, 129, 135–137, 139, 158n3, 267, 281, 284
Brisbane Botanic Gardens, 64, 88, 129

Brisbane Rainforest Action Group, 281
Brisbane Tanning Company, 36
Bristow, Harry, 75
Brown, Charles, 42, 45, 47
Brumby, Joseph, 66
brush box, 11–12, 80, 96, 103, 108–113, 179, 181, 214, 280, 291–292, 304
Buchanan, Neil, 40
buffalo grass, xxvi, 65
Buffy, Snowy, 205
Bundaberg, 125, 151
bunya bunya country, 56
bunya pine, xxiii, 56–58, 161, 199
Burger, Angela, 51n20, 193n1
Burnett, Gilbert, 88, 91, 134
Byerley, Fred, 84

C

calcium, 18
Caldwell, J. T., 95–97, 108
camphor laurel, xxiv, 163
camps:
    AB Lake, 207
    AC8, 207
    Aqua, 206
    Bill Seelke's, 127
    Bogimba, 209, 213–214
    Coomboo Lakes, 207
    Dundonga, 206
    Figtree, 210
    Garry's, 197, 214
    Gowrie, 188
    McKenzie's, 207
    Michell's, 161
    new Woongoolbver Creek, 199. See also *Central Station*

Old Petrie, xvi, 136, 198
Orange Tree, 144, 198–199. See also *Woongoolbver Creek*
Pierson's, 32
Postan's, x, 211–212, 217, 284–285, 287
Poyungan, 207, 209
Rat's, 127, 206
Red Lagoon, 207
Scrub, xv, 199. See also *Central Station*
Wondunna, 198
Woongoolbver Creek, xv
Yankee Jack, 207, 209
cant hook, xiii, 72
Cape Tribulation National Park, 280
Car ferries:
   Dawn Fraser III, 273
   Eliza Fraser II, 273
   Fraser Dawn, 269
   Fraser Venture, 270–273
   Rainbow Venture, 273
   Watoomba II, 269
Caribbean pine, xxv
Caswell, Don, 270
Cathedrals, 6, 271
Central Station, xv, xviii, xxxi, xxxvii, 21, 77, 97, 122, 125, 129, 133, 144, 163, 186–188, 199–204, 208n5, 209, 212, 214, 219, 257, 266, 273, 294
Champagne Pools, 272
Chenoweth, Alan, 290
Cherbourg, 38
Cherry Venture, 268
coast banksia, xxvi
coastal pig face, xxiii
coastal she-oak, xxiii, 10

Cochran, Ken, 205
coffee rock, 8, 262–263
Comben, Pat, 281
commercial forest, xviii–xix, 11, 120, 181, 183, 191, 282, 294
common hop bush, xxvi, 174
Commonwealth Scientific and Industrial Research Organisation (CSIRO), xxii, 4, 131
Cook, Bob, 214
Cook, James, xxvii, xxxiii, 24, 53
Cooloola Sands, 55, 121, 214, 224
Cooloola sedge frog, 16
Cooper, Curly, 127, 138
Cornwall, Claude, 214
Cornwall, Warwick, 215
Corralis, Joseph, 48
Craig, Jack, 181
creeks:
   Akuna, 66
   Bennett, 110, 126, 149, 195, 210
   Big Aldridge, 188
   Bogimbah, xxviii, 24, 35–36, 63–64, 66, 86, 92, 134, 136, 141, 148, 156, 161, 198, 213, 263
   Bool, 53
   Bowarrady, 19–20, 24, 272
   Bridge, 251
   Buff, 77n7, 257, 271
   Bun Bun, xvi, 99, 110, 206
   Coongul, 24, 252, 270, 272
   Deep, xvi, 122, 147, 191, 195, 210, 213–214, 218
   Dundonga, xvi
   Eli, xxviii, 13, 19–20, 242, 252, 265, 271, 299
   Figtree, 67, 80n14, 141, 188, 209
   First, xvii, 65, 68

Fourth, xvii, 65
Geewan, 58
Panama, 144
Poyungan, 92, 149, 206, 211, 213, 285, 301
Puthoo, 144–145
Second, xvii, 65, 68
Third, xvii
Tumbowah, xvi, 72. See also *Yankee Jack Creek*
Urang, 79, 81, 93, 100–101, 122, 142, 150, 211, 257, 265, 269–270
Waterspout, 77
Wathumba, 21, 67, 197, 262, 272
Woongoolbver, xv–xvi, xviii, 21, 23, 76, 97, 102–103, 105, 109, 122, 125, 144, 198–199, 201, 246, 265, 270–271
Woralie, 141
Yankee Jack, xvi, 66, 72, 78, 86, 89, 137, 141, 157, 195, 207, 209–210, 213
Yidney, 23, 67, 78, 144–145
Crown land, 27, 85, 88–89, 252–254, 257, 262
Crown Lands Act, 89
Crown Lands Alienation Act of 1868, 85
crows ash, xxvi, 163
Culpan, Benjamin, 251
Cunningham, John, 78–79
Cunningham, Thomas Errol "Joe", ix, 148, 209, 213–214, 216–218
Cunningham, Tom, ix
Curtis, John, 41
Curtis, Syd, 256
cypress pine, 10, 14, 71, 150, 161, 163, 188, 209

D

Darge, Robert, 40
Davison, George, 218
Davis, James, 55
Dempster, George, 75
Dicken, George, 64
Dilli Village, xvii, 64, 68, 192, 257
Dillingham, 300. See also *Dilli Village*
Dillon, Paul, 30
dingo, 14, 303–304
dilemma, 303
Donnelly, Kevin, 269
Doran, Paddy, 267
Doyle, Michael, 48
Duck Island, 59
Duke, Bill, 205
Dundathu, xxvii, 71–72, 75, 77, 122, 141, 195
dusky coral pea, xxiv
Dwyer, Barry, 40, 49

E

eastern beach, xv, xxix, 4, 6, 8, 10, 15, 19, 29, 45, 48, 77, 189, 223, 252–254, 258, 261–263, 272, 299
Eckert, Dick, xv, 133, 198
Eckert, Ken, 270–271
Edwardson, William, xxvii, 54
Elliot, William, 48
Elmer, Gordon, xxix–xxx, 269
Empire Wharf, 138
Epps, Fred, 161, 198
eucalyptus, xxiv–xxv, 160, 162, 306
Eurong, 64–66, 68, 120, 125, 248, 252–254, 256, 265–266, 272–274

INDEX

Eurong Bush Fire Brigade, 193
Europeans, 25–27, 31–34, 44, 53, 198
experiments, 9n1, 109, 162, 167, 169, 177–178, 180

F

Fahy, John, 55
Fairlie & Sons, 79
Falmouth Dock, 138–140
Fayaway, 73, 73n4, 74
Figtree Logging Area, 191
fire-exclusion policy, 188
fire mismanagement, 302, 305
fire occurrences, 9
firebreaks, 186–187, 189–192, 302
Fish, Roy, 214
Fitzgerald, Tony, 289, 293
Fletcher, Toby, 203
Flinders, Matthew, xxvii, 26, 53
foambark, xxvi
Forestry Act, xv, 89, 252, 287
Forestry Branch of the Queensland Department of Public Lands, xv
Forestry camps, 63, 206
Forestry settlements, 198
Forestry transport, 150
Forestry vessels:
  Adventure, 150
  Heather, 150
  Korawinga, 150–152, 203
  Korawinga II, 151, 205
  Relief, 150
  Satinay, 150, 218
Fraser, Eliza, 26–27, 39, 39n1, 40n2, 41n12, 42–51
Fraser Island Defenders Organisation (FIDO), 226–227, 229, 233–235, 237n1, 240, 241n8, 243, 246–247
Fraser Island Public Access Act, xxx, 258, 281
Fraser Island Recreation Authority, 258
Fraser Island Run, xvii, 64
Fraser Island Tourist Resort, 262
Fraser Island turpentine, xxv, 80, 129, 131, 134. See also *satinay*
Fraser, James, xxvii, xxxviii, 41-47, 51
Fraser, John, 42
freehold land, xviii, 255
Freeman, Bill, 214
French Guiana cabinet, 137
Fuller, Reverend Edward, xxvii, 32
Fyans, Foster, 40, 49

G

Gardiner, E. G., 265n3
Gardiner, Jack, 203, 208
Gatton Agricultural College, 235
Gebbett, Evelyn, 123, 132
Geoghan, Buck, 161
Gilchrist, Jack, 203
Glendon, Jackie, 127
goat's foot vine, xxiii, 10
Gordon, Doug, 205
Goss, Wayne, 285, 289, 293
Gossner, George, 152
Government Gazette, 57
Graham, John, 40n7, 49, 55
grass tree, xxvi, 14
Great Barrier Reef, 4, 7, 42–43
Great Depression, 118, 127, 263
Great Sandy Peninsula, xxvii, 53–54

Great Sandy Strait, 6, 15, 23, 48, 54, 57–61, 144, 206, 209, 213, 261, 268, 293
Great Walk, 206, 294
Grenning, Victor, 163
grey ironbark, xxv, 10, 133, 243
Gribble, Ernest, 37, 198
Groom, Ray, 238
Gympie, xxiv, 40, 59–60, 66, 75, 163, 219
    goldfields, 60
    messmate, xxiv, 163

H

Haley, Cec, 247
Hanley, Philadelphia, 94
Hansen, Hans, 146
Hansen, John, 211
Hansen, Johnny, 150
Hansen, Percy, 133
Happy Valley, 191, 197, 243, 252–254, 256, 262–263, 265
Harbour Master, 75
Harrold, Arthur, 236
Hart, Robert, 79, 130
Hay, Richard Dalrymple, 131, 131n6
Heath, George, 61
Henderson, Duncan, 67, 251
Henderson, Isabella, 67, 251–252
Hervey Bay, 15, 53, 58–59, 64, 246, 257, 261, 269–270
Hervey Bay Town Council, 242, 246, 257
Hill, Walter, 64, 85, 129, 155
Hodge, Robert, 40
Holmes, George, 198

Hook Point, 7, 23, 47, 50, 63, 203, 251, 257, 269
hoop pine, 13, 78, 80, 83, 201–202, 207
Hooper, E. D. M., 157n2
Hope, Vic, x, 210
Hopewell, Gary, ix, 133n12
Hume, Walter C., 88
Huth, John, ix, 208n4
Hyne & Son, 92–105, 122, 125, 128, 134, 213–215, 239, 285–286, 292–293
Hyne, Harry, 95
Hyne, Lambert, 209
Hyne, Warren, 285–286

I

Indian Head, 3–4, 6–7, 24, 30, 53, 65, 68, 252–254, 265
Indian Head Run, 65, 68
Island Queen, 266–267

J

Jarvis, Alf, 123
Jarvis, Bert, 127
Jarvis, Bill, 199
Jarvis, Walter, 113
Jennings, Stan, 195, 210
Jensen, Mel, 263–264
Jensen, Steve "Bronco", x, 268
jinker, xiii, 77, 107, 113, 215
John Callan Park Hospital, 97
Joliffe, William, 58
Jolly, Norman, 135–136, 161
Jones, Ruth, x, 112–116, 138
Jones, Syd "Danny", 218
Josefski, Fred, 152

INDEX

K

Kangaroo Island, 268
kauri pine, 13, 32, 35, 59, 71, 78, 80, 155–159, 161, 201, 294
kauri reforestation, challenges of, 155
Kent, Herbert, 251
Keto, Aila, 280, 290
Kilkivan, 215
king fern, xxv
Kitt, John, 208
Kopp, Eddie, 214, 216
Kopp, Max, 214
Krogh, Jack, 214

L

Lack, Jacob, 211, 263–264
Lade, Frederick, 88
Lake, Morris, 131n8
lakes:
    AB, 207. See also *Allom*
    Allom, 207, 271
    Basin, 18
    Birrabeen, 68, 120, 125, 189, 212, 214, 266
    Boemingen, xvi, 17, 64, 68, 203, 257
    Bowarrady, 18, 80, 89n8, 203, 257
    Coomboo, 207
    Garawongera, 18
    Jennings, 214, 267
    McKenzie, 17–18, 175, 186, 189, 203, 219, 265–266, 275, 299
    Wabby, 6, 19, 23–24, 127, 197, 263
landing sites, 44, 53, 58, 271, 274. See also *log dumps*

Lauer, Peter, 29
lemon-scented spotted gum, xxiv, 163
Lewis, Codford "Taffy", 214–215
Little Strug, 127
loblolly pine, xxv, 161, 202
log barge:
    Culgoa, 81, 145
    Dagmar, 81, 146
    Essex, 144
    Geraldine, 81, 146
    Geraldine II, 146
    Goori, 148
    Hopewell, 147–149
    K'Gari, 148–149
    Kundu, 148
    Lass O'Gowrie, 146, 148
    Muriel, 144, 150
    Otter, 148
    Palmer, 147
    Pelican, 148
    Slave, 81, 145
    Watoomba, 147
    Wave, 146
log dumps, xi, 81, 121–122, 141–145, 152, 180. See also *landing sites*
longleaf pine, xxv, 161
Luck, Allan, 200–201
Luck, Bill, 218
Luck, Ivan, 203
Luck, Lawrence "Sandy", 200–201, 203, 218
Luke, George, ix, 208

M

Mac Mahon, Philip, 88, 98–99, 101, 134n16, 135, 160, 186

macrozamia, xxvi, 13, 24
macrozamia nuts, 24
Maheno, xxviii, 144, 263–264, 271
Mahoney, K., 281
mangrove species, xxvi
maritime pine, xxv, 163
Markwell, Lee, 264–265
Mary and Wide Bay region, 23
Maryborough, 3, 11, 27–28, 31–36, 54, 59–65, 192, 211–214, 218, 257, 261–263, 266, 281–283
Maryborough Field Naturalist Club, 236
Maryborough Wide Bay and Burnett Historical Society (MWBBHS), 111–116, 125, 138, 142, 185, 210, 263–264, 295
Mathison, Charlie, 142, 147
Mathison, Christie, 81, 145, 147
Mathison, Matthias, 81, 145
Mathison, Noel, 269
mauve-flowered forest boronia, xxvi, 13
McDowall, Archibald, 35, 66, 86, 93, 155–156
McKenzie, Charles, x, 112–116, 138
McKenzie, Hepburn, x, 107, 125, 138
McKenzie's operation, x, xxviii, 111, 116, 119, 136, 187
McLean, Tom, 136
McLiver, George, 102, 197
McLiver, John, 80, 102
McPherson, John Robert, 5
McWilliam, Geoffrey, x, 73n4, 242n9, 262n1, 265n2, 270
Melksham, Sid, xxx, 208, 245–246, 253, 266–268, 270, 272–274
Meston, Archibald, xv, xxviii, 33-35, 37, 96–97
midyim berry, xxiv, 10

Miles, Keith "Slippery", 266
Miller, Ken, 262
Miller, Olga, 23, 244
Mitchell, George, 55
Mitchell, Ronald, 35, 66, 81, 156
Mitchell, William, 96
Mocatta, A. W., 162
Moncur, Danny, 270
Monterey pine, xxv, 161
Moon Point, 14, 66, 67n15, 93, 190, 251–252, 264, 269–270
Moreton Bay ash, xxiv, 10
Moreton Bay lighthouse, 61n12
Moreton Bay Penal Settlement, 40, 49, 57
Morgan, Edward, 66, 93
Morgan, Jim, 203
Muriel Bell, 76
Murphy, Barry, 268

N

national park, 89, 99, 105, 183, 225, 241, 256–257, 279–280, 289
Ngulungbara, 24
Nichols, Bill, 283
Nielson, Cec "Sandbank Cec", 151–152, 203
Norfolk Island pine, xxv, 161
North White Cliffs, 23–24, 33–35, 144, 146, 198, 251–252, 261
North White Cliffs School, xxviii
northern silky oak, xxvi, 163

O

Old Station, xv, 199. See also *Central Station*
opium, 27, 33–34, 37

INDEX

Orchid Beach, 16, 66, 68, 248, 255–256, 265, 269, 272

Orchid Beach Resort, xxix, 248, 255, 269

Orchid Beach township, 66

Orient Guesthouse, 265

original guardians, 23, 25, 27, 29, 31, 33, 35, 37

Otter, Charles, 40, 40n8, 48–49, 49n18

Owens, Garry, 197

Owens, Henry "Banjo", 196

Owens, Isaac "Ike", 196

P

Pacific Islanders, 60

Panama, 72, 74

pandanus palm, xxv, 10

parbuckle system, xiii, 141

pea flowers, xxiv, 14

Pearce, Singer, 127

peat swamps, 14

Pegg, Dick, ix, 191, 201n2, 218

Petrie, Andrew, xxvii–xxviii, 25, 55–59, 161

Petrie expedition, 55

Petrie, Rollo, 199

Petrie, Tom, xxvii, 71

Petrie, Walter, xxviii, 77, 144, 161–162, 172, 198

Pettigrew, William, 71–72, 75, 79, 121, 133, 145

Pialba, 36. See also *Hervey Bay*

picabeen palm, xxiii, 13

Pidgeon, Eddie "Wonga", 204

pig face, xxiii

Pigott, John "Yankee Jack", xvii, xxvii, 72

Pile Valley, xxviii, 129, 131, 151, 163, 206, 291

pink bindweed, xxiii, 10

pink bloodwood, xxiv

The Pinnacles, 8, 17

Pinus species:
    Caribbean pine, xxv
    loblolly pine, xxv, 161, 202
    longleaf pine, xxv, 161
    maritime pine, xxv, 163
    Norfolk Island pine, xxv, 161
    Roxburgh pine, xxv, 161
    slash pine, xxv, 164
    weeping Mexican pine, xxv

Pizzey, Jack, 235

plantations, 155–160, 163, 165, 167, 187, 207, 294

podzolisation, xiii, 9

Police Magistrate, 75

possums, 24, 36

Postan, Andrew, 213, 216, 218, 284, 288, 292

Postan, Andy, xvii, xxviii, 192, 210–216

Postan, Helen, ix, 293

Postans, Laurie, xvii, 209, 211, 213, 215, 217–218

potassium, 18

Poyungan Rocks, 8, 252–253, 256

Pyne, S., 306n1

Q

Queensland, 234–238, 241, 246, 252–253, 256–258, 263, 275, 280, 287, 290, 292–293

Queensland Beach Protection Authority, 67, 257

Queensland colony, 61

Queensland Forest Service, xv, 77

Queensland Legislative Assembly, 131
Queensland maple, xxvi, 161
Queensland National Parks and Wildlife Service (QNPWS), xxii, 257
Queensland State Archives (QSA), 34, 36, 54, 90–91, 95, 97, 233, 239, 254, 265, 279, 282–283

R
Rainbow Gorge, 8
red ash, xxvi
red bloodwood, xxiv
Red Canyon, 8, 272
red cedar, xxiv, 78, 107, 161
red flowering gum, xxiv
Red Lagoon, 207
red stringybark, xxv, 11, 110, 135, 167, 214
Reeves, Ethel, 198
regeneration burning, 174, 176, 180
    challenges of, 174
    season of, 176
reptiles, 15
Reville, Jack, xxix, 266
Richardson, Graham, 289
Rivers:
    Brisbane River, 58, 76
    Burnett River, 30, 266
    Condamine River, 58
    Hunter River, 59
    Maroochy River, 57–58
    Mary River, xxvii, 32, 54–55, 58–60, 63, 71–73, 132
    Morouchidor River, 57. See also *Maroochy River*
    Susan River, 71

Rooney Point, 62, 73
rose gum, xxiv, 201, 206
Ross, Freddy, 196–197
Roxburgh pine, xxv, 161
Roy Rufus artificial reef, 148
Rudder, John, 201
Ryan, Lyndall, 28

S
Saint, Harold, 203
Salmon, Sargent Ken "Sockeye", 283–284
saltwater couch, xxvi, 10, 197
sand blow, xiv, 5–6, 19
sand dune, xiii, 5, 14, 16, 58, 190
sand mining, 223–245, 249, 256–257, 265, 269, 279–280, 300
Sandy Cape, 7, 24–26, 53–54, 61–67, 79, 94, 197, 251, 253–254
Sandy Cape Lighthouse, xxvii–xxviii, 61–63, 67, 79, 94, 251
Sandy soil, 11, 14, 16, 167, 206
satinay, 11–13, 32, 78, 80, 85, 92, 214, 218, 243, 264, 280, 291–292, 304
    utilisation of, 137
satine, xxiv, 137
Schofield, Jacob, 42
Schulz, Nick, 255
scribbly gum, xxv, 10, 13, 300
scrub:
    Bogimbah, 171, 186, 198
    Bowarrady, 18–20, 78, 159, 190, 203, 257, 272
    carrol, xxiv, 13, 161
    Dundonga, xvi, 215
    Poyungan, 8, 79, 92, 122, 149, 252–253, 256, 285, 301, 305
    Quandong, 100, 104, 124–125

INDEX

rainforest, xviii, 201, 275, 280–281, 290, 292, 300–302, 305

Woongoolbver, 77

Yidney, 78, 263, 291

Searey, Patrick, xvii, 63, 75

sedge, xiv, xxiii, 14, 16

Seelke, Bill, xvii, 32n21, 80, 111, 120, 127, 142

Sengstock, Edmond "Ezzy", 210

Seventy-Five Mile Beach, xv, 7. See also *eastern beach*

Sharman, Elten, 198

she-oak, xxiii–xxv, 10–11

Sheridan, Richard, 59

Shillig, Allan, 148, 283

Shillig, Des, 148

Shillig, Larry, 285

Short, Bill, 213

silviculture, ix, xiv, 35, 105, 136, 155, 170–171, 178

Simpson, Neil, 148

Sinclair, John, 133, 226, 227n4, 234–235, 237n1, 239n4, 239n5, 241n7, 241n8, 243n10, 247n11, 281, 287n10, 288, 294–295, 297, 305

slash pine, xxv, 164

Smart, J., 78

Smith, Alan, 270

Smith, Arthur, 133

Smith, Neville, 210–211

snigging, xiii–xiv, 210, 214–215

sodium, 18

Sorrensen, Peter, 80, 99, 123

South White Cliffs, 32, 150. See also *Ungowa*

spotted gum, xxiv, 163–164

State forest, 85, 88–90, 99, 105, 159, 272, 280, 287

State Forests and National Parks Act 1906, 89, 99, 105

Stirling Castle shipwreck survivors, xxvii

Stone, Edward, 42

strangler fig, xxiv, 13

Stuart, Henry Russell, xxvii, xxxvii, 57

Suez Canal, 131–132

Sullivan, Clarrie, 214

sundew, xxiii, 14

Sundstrupt, Bertle, 146

sustained yield, xix, 180–181

Swain, Edward Harold Fulcher, 136n19, 163, 170

Swain's vision, 170, 183

swamp:

    banksia, xxvi, 14

    mahogany, xxv, 110, 134

    paperbark, xxv, 10, 17

Swanson, John, 214, 218

Swanston, J., 282

Sydney, 26–27, 30, 40–42, 51, 54–55, 73–74, 97, 127, 131, 138, 140, 161, 199

T

tallowwood, 9, 11, 13, 78–79, 81, 85, 92, 94, 98–99, 171, 177, 212, 214

Tanner, Herbie, 203

Tardent, Jules, 58, 158, 159n4, 163n9

tea tree, xxv, 10, 13, 192

telegraph line, 63–64

Thames Docks, 133

Thomas, A. H., 84

Thorburn, J. H., 61

Thorpe, Arthur, 126

Thorsell, Jim, 293

timber getters, 71, 75, 91, 99, 130
timber utilisation, 11, 75, 85, 89, 108
Tin Can Bay, 55, 71, 121, 224–225
Titanium Alloy Manufacturing Company, 223
Tom Welsby, 269
Top Tours, 270
tour boats:
- *The Crab*, 267–268, 270
- *Discovery II*, 270
- *The Dolphin*, 264
- *Fraser Flyer*, 270
- *Fraser II*, 271
- *Hiawatha*, 266
- *The Islander*, 267
- *Jenny K*, 263
- *Juanita*, 263
- *Lady Fraser*, 266
- *MV Islander*, 268
- *Orient*, 265
- *Philanderer*, 268
- *Rio Marie*, 266
- *Tollgate Traveller*, 270
- *Waylily*, 269

tourism, 131, 191, 233–234, 240–242, 249, 289, 294–297, 299, 305–306
Townsville, 123, 140
Toy, Wally, 267, 269
tramlines, xi, 66, 120–123, 125, 127. See also *tramway*
tramway, 62, 94, 100–101, 105, 107, 114, 118, 121–128, 144, 161, 163, 210
Tumbowah Creek, xvi, 72. See also *Yankee Jack Creek*
turpentine, 9, 80, 85, 92, 129, 131–135, 138. See also *satinay*
2020 wildfire disaster, 302

U

Ungowa, 32, 77, 120, 150, 188, 204–209, 214, 219, 241, 266–267

V

vine forest (rainforest), xviii

W

Waddy Point, 3–4, 6–7, 26, 44, 68, 252–254, 262
Walker, Frederick, 28
Walker, John, 121
wallabies, 24
wallum banksia, xxvi
wallum country, 5, 185, 191–192
wallum froglet, 16
wallum rocket frog, 16
wallum sedge frog, 16
Ward, Ernest, 219
Warry, Stan, 262
Wathumba, 14, 21, 67, 197, 251, 256, 262, 272
wattle, xxiv, 10, 174, 177, 206
Weaver, Tom, 150
Webber, Frank "Bendy", 139, 146
Webster, John, 268
wedding bush, xxiv, 13
weeping Mexican pine, xxv
Wells, Owen, 123
Wendt, Fred, 123
Wex, George "Choker", 203
Whale, Ron, 80
white beech, xxiv, 13, 72, 78, 81, 132, 151
white cedar, xxiv, 163
white cypress pine, xxiii, 10
White, George, 219
white teak, xxiv, 163

INDEX

Wide Bay boronia, xxvi, 13
widow-maker, xiv, 218
Wiedon, Percy, 255, 264
Williams, Fred, 33, 133n12, 148n1, 162n7, 219n8
Wilschefski, August, 80, 102, 137, 195, 210
Wilschefski brothers, 102, 137, 210
Wilschefski, Henry, 80, 102, 137, 195, 210
Wilson, Alice, 32n21
Wilson, Andrew, 32, 79
Wilson, Colin, ix
Wilson, George, 213, 218
Wilson, Hart, 79, 84, 91–105, 110, 122, 125, 146, 148, 161, 181–182, 211–215, 239
Wilson, Jim, 213
Wilson, John, 213, 215
Wilson, Leslie, 263
Wilson, Mel "Sleepy", 214–215
Wilson, Peter, ix
Wondunna, Fred, 197–198

wooden yoke, xiv, 77
Woody Island, 63–64, 147–148
Woongoolbver skipway, 122. See also *tramway*
Woralie track, 271
World Heritage Area, xxx, 183
World Heritage Listing, 238, 280, 289, 293–294, 296
World Heritage status, 237–238, 293–294
World War I, 133, 135
World War II, 64, 140, 173, 216

Y

Yankee Jack, 210
Yankee Jack Creek, xvi, 66, 72, 78, 86, 141, 195, 207, 209–210, 213
Yidney Rock Hopper, 264
Yidney Rocks, 8, 46, 252, 256, 262, 264, 266
Youlden, Harry, 40n4, 48n17

Z

zeta curve, xiv, 7

www.ingramcontent.com/pod-product-compliance
Lightning Source LLC
Chambersburg PA
CBHW071358300426
44114CB00016B/2109